Women Entrepreneurs

D0141316

Women Entrepreneurs offers a collection of almost two dozen cases that explore the process by which women become entrepreneurs, as well as the opportunities and challenges they face in growing their businesses.

With a particular focus on the intersection between entrepreneurship and economic development, the cases are drawn from across a range of industries and countries. They offer insights into a number of issues women entrepreneurs face, such as launching a business, diversification, and internationalization, as well as covering a number of business functions, including finance, marketing, and human resource management. Each case is presented with a summary highlighting the themes it covers, and ends with a set of questions to guide classroom discussion. The book also includes a summary of existing literature on entrepreneurship to help contextualize the cases.

This casebook would be the ideal companion in an entrepreneurship class, particularly for students with an interest in female entrepreneurship or economic development.

Mauro F. Guillén is the Director of the Joseph H. Lauder Institute, a management and international studies program at the University of Pennsylvania, USA. He is also Dr. Felix Zandman Endowed Professor in International Management at the Wharton School.

With data from a Goldman Sachs/Lauder Institute study.

Women Entrepreneurs

Inspiring Stories from
Emerging Economies and
Developing Countries

Edited with
an introduction
by Mauro F. Guillén

*The Joseph H. Lauder Institute for Management and
International Studies, The Wharton School*
guillen@wharton.upenn.edu

From Left to Right: Victoria Kisyombe (Center) with Professor Klaus Schwab
(Founder and Executive Chairman, World Economic Forum) and President Jakaya
Mrisho Kikwete (President of the Republic of Tanzania); Angélica Moreno;
Pianporn Deetes; Maha al Ghunaim; Azza Fahmy; Maria Helena Monteiro

Routledge
Taylor & Francis Group

NEW YORK AND LONDON

First published 2014
by Routledge
711 Third Avenue, New York, NY 10017

Simultaneously published in the UK
by Routledge
2 Park Square, Milton Park, Abingdon, Oxon OX14 4RN

Routledge is an imprint of the Taylor & Francis Group, an informa business

© 2014 Taylor & Francis

Library of Congress Cataloging in Publication Data
Women entrepreneurs: inspiring stories from emerging economies
and developing countries/edited by Mauro Guillén.
   p. cm.
   Includes bibliographical references and index.
   1. Businesswomen—Developing countries.   2. Self-employed
women—Developing countries.   3. Women-owned business
enterprises—Developing countries.   4. Entrepreneurship—
Developing countries.   I. Guillén, Mauro F.
   HD6072.6.D44W66 2013
   338′.0409252091724—dc23
   2012031610

ISBN: 978-0-415-52347-9 (hbk)
ISBN: 978-0-415-52348-6 (pbk)
ISBN: 978-0-203-12098-9 (ebk)

Typeset in Garamond 3 by
Florence Production Ltd, Stoodleigh, Devon, UK
Printed and bound in Great Britain by
TJ International Ltd, Padstow, Cornwall

Contents

Illustrations

Tables

Figures

1 The World of Women Entrepreneurs

Mauro F. Guillén

"This has been an amazing experience," observed Victoria Kisyombe, a brave entrepreneur who founded a leasing company in Tanzania to help other entrepreneurs gain access to the coolers and freezers, baking ovens, sewing machines, gravel-making machines, or tractors and trucks they needed to pursue their dreams. "It is a business that allows me to give to others, but has simultaneously contributed so much to my own personal development." Victoria's experience is both unique and commonplace throughout the developing world. Myriad women entrepreneurs have launched a business, some in response to a perceived opportunity, many out of necessity given a lack of viable employment alternatives. This book places the inspirational stories of women like Victoria in the wider context of how it feels and what it means to be an entrepreneur in developing countries and emerging economies, in which starting any kind of business can be a daunting challenge, especially for women.

Women entrepreneurs in the developing world are so important because they can truly make a difference. In spite of decades of massive efforts to promote economic development and eradicate poverty, human societies differ vastly in terms of the quantity and quality of economic and social wellbeing that individuals can hope to enjoy during their lifetimes. These fundamental differences manifest themselves at all levels, namely across continents, countries, rural and urban areas, social classes, and communities. Governments and nonprofits have attempted to create markets, launched development programs, built physical infrastructure, and created new institutions; and yet, poverty and lack of opportunity continue to be rampant realities in much of the developing world.

This book offers a fresh look at development efforts through the lens of women entrepreneurs. Economic development is much more than mere economic growth; it entails a social as well as an economic transformation, some measure of innovation, and attention to sustainability and environmental issues. The role of entrepreneurship by women in the process of economic development is complex, and it requires paying attention to education, culture, gender dynamics, and family structures and traditions, to name but a few important factors.

When one thinks about women entrepreneurs in developing countries and emerging economies, a number of tantalizing questions come to mind: Can entrepreneurship by women make a difference in economic development? Or does entrepreneurship by women contribute to perpetuating traditional economic practices and activities? Do women who are already economically and socially advantaged benefit the most from entrepreneurship? Do men and women face fundamentally different opportunities, obstacles, and challenges when it comes to entrepreneurship? Do women use resources and manage their ventures differently from men?

Previous case-study research on women entrepreneurs has provided some answers to these questions (e.g. Snyder 2000; Browne 2001; Bruni 2005; Harley 2007; World Bank 2009). In this book we also approach the study of women entrepreneurs through the case method. Case studies are used in research for the purposes of empirical description and classification, theory building and testing, clinical diagnosis, professional preparation, and program evaluation (Hamel 1993; Yin 2003; Flyvbjerg, 2006). They have become increasingly popular in the field of management and entrepreneurship research (Eisenhardt 1989). While in this book we do not develop or test theory based on case studies of women entrepreneurs, in the concluding chapter we seek to organize the evidence and to point out some intriguing commonalities across the cases.

Each case presents a set of unique yearnings, circumstances, accomplishments, and limitations. The intent is not to produce generalizations about what needs to be done in order to alleviate poverty and encourage development, but to document the diverse experiences of women entrepreneurs in the hope that scholars, policymakers, and aspiring women entrepreneurs may find inspiration in them. Before embarking on that journey around the developing world, however, we must reflect on the successes and failures of economic development efforts over the last decades, since they have set the stage for the activities of women entrepreneurs.

Peddling Development

The vast shifts in global economic and geopolitical affairs brought about by the Great Depression and World War II created a context conducive to experimentation with new ways of promoting economic growth and development, both in the technologically advanced countries and in the developing world, which underwent a rapid process of political emancipation and change as the colonial era came to an abrupt end. Governments and policymakers experimented with different theories, models and recipes to induce economic transformations with the goal of accelerating growth. While some of their efforts were met by astounding successes, most failed to create the kind of self-sustaining economic dynamism that could raise a majority of the population out of poverty.

Entrepreneurship—the complex array of activities involved in imagining, launching, and managing a venture, whether for profit or not—did not receive enough attention from economic theorists, advisors, and government officials, who preferred to think about development in terms of macroeconomic policymaking, cultural obstacles, and the lack of physical infrastructure. Governments thought that the best way to accelerate economic growth so as to improve the living standards of the population was to lay the foundations for a large-scale transformation that should include the abandonment of traditional values in favor of modern ones, the development of cities, and investments in new types of industrial activities, typically capital-intensive ones.

By the 1970s, however, it had become readily apparent that in most parts of the developing world standards of living were not improving as fast as would have been desirable. Given the lack of success at eradicating poverty, and the recurrent crises that afflicted many developing economies, economists and policymakers searched for new ways to address the fundamental challenges of economic growth and development. Starting in the 1980s, in the wake of some of the worst economic and financial crises in the developing world, a new approach focusing on the institutional underpinnings of economic dynamism emerged. The key proposal was to ensure that developing countries would have the economic, financial and social institutions in place necessary for small businesses to grow, create jobs, and hence contribute to development. Policymakers had finally realized that small businesses accounted for the bulk of employment in developing countries, even more so than in developed ones.

Enter Gender

Development scholars and policymakers did not pay systematic attention to women as economic actors, entrepreneurs and business owners until quite recently. The United Nations Decade for Women (1975–1985) laid the foundations for a new wave of programs focused on promoting women's role in the economy as a way to accelerate economic development. Thus, this approach was not only to advance gender equality as a goal in its own right, but also to explore ways in which women's economic activities could contribute to economic growth and to economic development, in the sense of a transformation of the economy through innovation.

By the beginning of the 1990s entrepreneurship by women had become a cornerstone of economic development. Policymakers had realized that without vibrant women entrepreneurs countries would be wasting or under-utilizing half of the talent pool. As Helen Clark, the administrator of the United Nations Development Programme, has recently put it,

by unlocking the tremendous potential of women entrepreneurs and addressing the obstacles they face, such as access to credit and finance, and their inability to inherit or hold land titles or benefit from government budgetary allocations, we can reduce inequality and stimulate economic growth.[1]

These thoughts are echoed by Sibongile Sambo, founder of an airline company:

> Historically, women in South Africa, particularly black women, have not been afforded the opportunities of starting and running their own enterprises and making a full contribution to our economy. At SRS Aviation we are taking advantage of the new political freedom to create economic freedom. It is an opportunity that my mother and aunt did not have. But I do, and intend to grab it.[2]

Entrepreneurship, however, has always been a difficult career path for women. A recent World Bank report covering 128 developed and developing economies found a considerable degree of legal discrimination against women in areas that thwart entrepreneurship. For instance, as of 2009, in forty-five countries women did not have the same legal capacity to act or engage in economic transactions as men, in forty-nine countries women were prevented from working in certain industries, and in thirty-two countries they did not have equal inheritance rights. Equal legal rights were found to result in a greater percentage of businesses owned or managed by women.[3]

Studies have documented that entrepreneurs, whether men or women, tend to initiate activities related to their previous job experience. Given that women tend to be active in a few specific occupations, sectors or industries, the effect of previous experience on entrepreneurial activity generated a segregated pattern of entrepreneurship by gender, with women overwhelmingly launching new ventures in the service sector in general, and in retail and personal services in particular, where capital requirements tend to be lower and their household and self-employment experience more relevant. They are also more likely to launch a venture in traditional industries as opposed to technologically advanced ones.

For women, entrepreneurship can be liberating and conducive to economic well-being, but it can also become a frustrating experience due to the many barriers they face along the way, many of which are unique to female as opposed to male entrepreneurs. As Azza Fahmy, founder of a famous jewelry firm with 165 employees, observed, "my new experience was out of the ordinary for any conventional, young Egyptian woman in a traditional environment, but I was determined to go on." Or consider the example of Wu Huanshu, whose company manufactures clothing accessories and is widely considered to be the first female entrepreneur in China to have incorporated her own firm.

I still remember an official from the Dongcheng district office [. . .] said I should get a permit for my business to make it legal. I was a bit reluctant because I thought the permit might be used later to brand me as a capitalist roader.[4]

When it comes to entrepreneurship, perhaps the two most important gender-related differences are that women tend to go into fields of activity related to their most frequent previous experiences (e.g. personal services, retail, the creative crafts, and traditional industries), and that ventures founded, owned and/or managed by women tend to grow less over time, mostly as a result of structural constraints of various sorts. One of them is lack of knowledge of, and experience in, business. As Aissa Dionne, a Senegalese interior designer, remarked, "at the beginning I didn't even know how to do an invoice. I was asking friends for advice."[5]

Discrimination against women when it comes to funding represents in many countries a hindrance to economic growth. "I started working in Santiago, in a textile company," says Isabel Roa, a Chilean entrepreneur. "I then began to knit myself and to sell from door to door. The biggest problem I had was that when I started I did not have capital. I solved this by saving and getting loans."[6]

Perhaps one important reason why women experience many obstacles along the road to launching and growing their venture is that they are more likely than men to become entrepreneurs out of necessity. "I realized the limited choice available and also the fact that since the time when I myself went to school, the number of schools and seats had not increased," explains Nasreen Kasuri, who founded a school in Pakistan.

I also realized that my children would not be fortunate enough to benefit from the quality of instruction that I had benefited from. The only way I could meet such a challenge was to set up a school which could provide quality education to my children and others.[7]

In fact, the *Global Entrepreneurship Monitor*, an annual survey of entrepreneurial activity around the world, documents that in most countries women tend to become entrepreneurs for lack of other alternatives.

Entrepreneurship by women is surrounded by many controversies. One of them refers to networking. Women entrepreneurs often complain that they do not have access to the necessary resources for launching and growing their venture because their network connections are insufficient. Those resources include not only material ones but also advice, mentorship, and role models. Most studies show that women entrepreneurs in developed countries have fewer network ties in general. Both men and women entrepreneurs tend to have same-gendered ties, which makes it more difficult for women to find mentors and role models in fields in which there are few of them. These differences are largely attributable to prior employment history and job experience. In fact, regardless of gender, salaried men and women tend to have more network contacts than the self-employed. Another problematic aspect of networking has to do with the feeling of being in the minority. "I have grown beyond that sensitivity of reacting to the term 'woman entrepreneur,'" explains Indian biotech entrepreneur Kiram Mazumdar-Shaw. "I now think it will be a matter of pride to be called so as there are now a number of flourishing female entrepreneurs in our country, and let's face it, women in business get noticed much more than men!"[8]

Another hotly debated issue concerns work/family balance. Women's role in the family is frequently seen as both constraining and enabling entrepreneurship. On the one hand, research has shown that the family obligations shouldered by women can detract energy and time from other activities and make it harder for them to build the experience, reputation, and networks necessary for success. On the other, research also indicates that entrepreneurship can help women make more flexible arrangements to balance work and family than the typical 9-to-5 job, and that family life can be an inspiration for certain entrepreneurial activities. Still, many women are constrained by issues of work/family balance, sometimes in unexpected ways. Martha Debayle, a Nicaraguan-born Mexican media entrepreneur, comments: "I remember my Mom saying, 'but whose mind could possibly conceive this business that does not turn out a cent and look how exhausted you are, how irresponsible! You're everything your two daughters have in this world.'"

A no less important debate has emerged over whether women entrepreneurs have distinct preferences for imagining, organizing and managing a venture, and may define success in terms of goal achievement, a better work/family balance or community benefits as opposed to growth, profits and fame. In this vein, Rwandan handicrafts entrepreneur Janet Kkubana observed:

> I have survivors, I have widows, I have women whose husbands are in prison. To see them sitting under one roof weaving and doing business together is a huge achievement. This women are now together, earning an income. It is amazing.[9]

Or Annette Zamora, the Rapanui social entrepreneur focused on preserving and popularizing the ancient culture of her magical island, reflected:

> I don't know if I have been successful. I have received recognition but I don't know that I have a clear concept of what successful means. The Foundation—I see it as yet another thing that I should have done; I see it as an accomplishment only in that I achieved something I have hoped to do.

The chapters that follow present cases of women who imagined, launched, and managed an entrepreneurial venture somewhere in the developing world, to varying degrees of success, confronting various types of barriers, and finding different kinds of fulfillment. These inspiring stories offer insights into the ingenuity and persistence of entrepreneurs, their needs and desires, and the striking ways in which they assess their own experiences.

We begin our journey around the world by examining how women use the local resources at their disposal to launch a venture: a Mexican educational toy company, a Tanzanian leasing company, an Indian genomics outsourcing firm, a Turkish apparel maker, and a Brazilian coffee grower. Next we assess the various strategies for business growth available to women in developing countries in the cases of a South African airline, a Brazilian restaurant, an Argentine travel agency, a Mexican magazine publishing company, and a Chinese consumer electronics firm. We continue with how women entrepreneurs deal with the challenges of organizing and leading effectively, illustrated by the travails of an Egyptian jeweler, a Mexican pottery maker, a Kuwaiti investment banker, and a Mexican caterer. Entrepreneurship by women frequently has a social bent, as the cases of a cultural entrepreneur from the Pacific island of Rapa Nui, knitwear in China, Peruvian fashion, and environmental awareness in Thailand illustrate. Finally, we will hear from women who operate across national boundaries, including a Japanese-Brazilian entrepreneur who founded a hotel chain, an Algerian woman who opened a beauty salon in Paris, and a Korean-Chinese woman who designs and makes traditional Korean clothing.

We chose these cases from a variety of countries and industries to illustrate the range of experiences of women entrepreneurs in developing and emerging economies (Gerring 2007). After identifying the woman entrepreneur and securing her collaboration, which occurred in every instance, we used field interviews and secondary sources to document the background and career of the entrepreneur, the national and local context in which the venture was founded, the characteristics of the business activity and the industry, and other relevant information. The chapters that follow describe the opportunities and the challenges faced by these women, and exemplify their contributions to the well-being of their communities and to economic development.

Notes

1   UNIFEM (2010: 3).
2   World Bank (2009).
3   World Bank (2010).
4   *BusinessWomen* October 14, 2008.
5   World Bank (2009).

6   *El Mercurio Online* June 19, 2008.
7   *Pakistan Economics* November 6–12, 2000.
8   *The Hindu* March 22, 2004.
9   World Bank (2009).

References

Browne, Katherine E. 2001. "Female Entrepreneurship in the Caribbean: A Multisite, Pilot Investigation of Gender and Work." *Human Organization* 60(4): 326–342.

Bruni, Attila. 2005. *Gender and Entrepreneurship: An Ethnographic Approach.* New York: Routledge.

Eisenhardt, Kathleen M. 1989. "Building Theories from Case Study Research." *Academy of Management Review* 14: 532–550.

Flyvbjerg, Bent. 2006. "Five Misunderstandings about Case-Study Research." *Qualitative Inquiry* 12: 219–245.

Gerring, John. 2007. *Case Study Research.* New York: Cambridge University Press.

Hamel, Jacques. 1993. *Case Study Methods.* Newbury Park, CA: Sage.

Harley, Sharon. 2007. *Women's Labor in the Global Economy: Speaking in Multiple Voices.* New Brunswick, NJ: Rutgers University Press.

Snyder, Margaret. 2000. *Women in African Economies: From Burning Sun to Boardroom.* Kampala, Uganda: Fountain Publishers.

UNIFEM. 2010. *Annual Report 2009–2010.* New York: United Nations Development Fund for Women.

World Bank. 2009. *Doing Business: Women in Africa.* Washington, DC: World Bank.

—— 2010. *Women, Business, and the Law.* Washington, DC: World Bank.

Yin, Robert K. 2003. *Case Study Research: Design and Methods.* Third edition. Thousand Oaks, CA: Sage.

Part I

Launching the Venture

Women pursue entrepreneurial opportunities for a variety of reasons. Research indicates that they tend to be driven by necessity rather than by opportunity to a greater extent than male entrepreneurs are, especially in developing countries. Both men and women tend to launch ventures related to their areas of expertise, mostly the result of previous employment or household work. They experience a large number of cultural, economic, and social obstacles (see Chapter 23 for a summary of the research findings). In this section we learn about the often-serendipitous process by which women entrepreneurs decide to launch their businesses and take the first steps. We hear from a group of Mexican women who focused on educational toys, a Tanzanian entrepreneur who saw an opportunity in offering credit to other aspiring entrepreneurs, an Indian biotechnology entrepreneur, a Turkish designer and fabricator of organic apparel, and a Brazilian woman who became passionate about coffee.

2 Jugaré

Educational Toys from Mexico

*Claudia González Brambila, Virginia Kalis,
Humberto Valencia-Herrera, Eduardo Zelaya,
and Pablo Galindo Herrera*

*Four friends with complementary skills launched a toy company that makes and
sells educational toys. Their early success surprised them. Their greatest challenges
were to find a way to become profitable and to avoid letting their venture interfere
with their family lives.*

Figure 2.1 Jugaré's Logo

On a rainy summer afternoon in July 2009, Marcela Huet, Ibó Angulo,
Hilda Díaz, and Laura Cortés were enjoying lattes at Café Punta del Cielo
in Mexico City. The four were happy to be together again and chatting
about how to expand their business in the short and long run. They had
been working together for several years, but their ideas about how to expand
their business differed. Laura, the production manager, thought it was time
to prepare and document a business model for franchising. Ibó had been
talking with the purchasing manager of a client, Casa Palacio, about selling
Jugaré toys in the home furnishings store. Hilda felt it was better to start
selling the toys at a museum store and had spoken with the manager at
Museo Universitario de Arte Contemporáneo (MAC) at the Universidad
Nacional Autónoma, who seemed interested in Jugaré products. And
Marcela thought the current model was fine and, if they were able to establish an adequate fund-raising strategy, Jugaré's growth would be guaran-
teed. The conversation was intense, and the four friends were a bit
uncertain about the strategies needed to expand their business.

The Birth of an Idea

The four friends-turned-entrepreneurs had different skill sets and professional backgrounds. Marcela received her B.A. in communication and had spent 11 years in marketing at a record company. In 2004, she stepped out as a freelance public relations agent for several companies and then established her own agency. She has two young children and loves movies, theater, traveling, and being with her family. Laura has been her friend since 1987. Marcela met Hilda and Ibó at EMI Music in 1995 and introduced them to Laura.

Hilda received her B.A. in graphic design and began working at a design agency during her second semester. She is passionate about reading, art books, and photography. She loves painting and sports. She married in 1994 and has two daughters. Her dream is to visit the most important museums in the world.

Laura obtained her B.A. in business administration. A serial entrepreneur, she began working in the financial sector during her third semester. While in college she started Lorela, a business that rents appliances for parties and catering. In 1996 she launched Velaroma, a business dedicated to the production and sale of candles. She also earned a B.A. in professional high cuisine at the Centro Culinario Ambrosia. She is married with two daughters.

A designer at heart, Ibó has been a founding member of Zappata Diseñadores since 1994. She has received awards in the design field, including "Merit Winner" *HOW Magazine* (1994); Award for Publication Excellence (1997); Premio al Diseño (2001); and Premio Quorum (2002). She has also been mentioned in several publications, such as *The Best of Brochure Design*, *1,000 Greetings*, and, more recently, *Growing Graphics Design for Kids*. She is passionate about design, photography, her family, her daughter, her dog, and the simple aspects of life.

On February 28, 2004, these four women were celebrating Marcela's baby shower. Marcela had just resigned from her job, had received her severance pay, and wanted to start a new venture with her closest friends —Ibó, Hilda, and Laura. All of them were excited about the idea of becoming entrepreneurs.

The four friends met regularly to discuss what type of business they could start. They were all in their late twenties and had infants and toddlers. They realized that the available toys on the market did not encourage children's creativity. For instance, Hilda's daughter received twenty Barbie dolls at her birthday party. The four friends saw this as an opportunity. No one was designing toys that fostered imaginations. The friends decided to focus on interesting children in participating in daily home activities in fun and imaginative ways. In addition, Ibó's mother had a store in the La Condesa neighborhood that had been vacant for some time. Located near downtown Mexico City, La Condesa is one of the most fashionable areas, with many high-end shops, bars, and restaurants.

Ibó and Hilda, the designers in the group, developed several prototypes for the first kits. Laura, the business administrator, initiated a production plan to manufacture the toys. Marcela, the marketing specialist, was in charge of remodeling the store.

The adventure began, with an initial investment of US$20,000 ($5,000 from each entrepreneur). The friends' living rooms became the workshops for manufacturing a dozen of each of the twelve different kits. By December 8, 2005, the first Jugaré store opened its doors as a new "Place to grow playing."

The friends thought of Jugaré as "a fresh and innovative learning concept, 100 percent Mexican, concerned with children's development, imagination, and creativity through play, encouraging in this way a bond between parents and kids," according to an early marketing brochure. "We believe toys are a great source of learning for our children, and what a nice way to learn!" The company's slogan was "Toys that foster intelligent play."

The Toy Industry in Mexico

Children aged 12 and younger are the primary consumers in the toy and game market, estimated to be 30 million people in Mexico. Although this country has a shrinking population in this segment, the growing purchasing power of working adults is expected to increase demand a bit in the coming years.

Large firms offer a wide variety of toys and have economy-of-scale advantages in purchasing, manufacturing, distributing, selling, and marketing. This explains why the toy and game market in Mexico is dominated by large firms such as Mattel and Hasbro. The small firms are able to compete by specializing in specific product markets, such as educational or traditional toys.

Toy manufacturers face increasing competition from electronic entertainment for children, including the Internet, video games, television, and other consumer electronics. In Mexico, about 75 percent of videogames offered at very cheap prices are thought to be counterfeit or pirated.

The toy and game industry in Mexico is highly seasonal, with the strongest sales occurring during the Christmas season—including Three Wise Men's Day (January 6)—and for Children's Day (April 30).

Toys sold in Mexico are manufactured primarily by large multinational firms such as Mattel and Hasbro. The industry is highly concentrated, with the main manufacturers amassing most of the sales. These two large firms support sales efforts through publicity and advertising, and both have strong infrastructures devoted to new product innovation and development.

A major concern for Mexican toy manufacturers is the toys imported illegally from East Asian countries, mainly China. In Mexico, Chinese toy manufacturers face stiff tariffs, some up to 1,000 percent. There is also an illegal market in counterfeit toys, offered primarily through the informal sector. It is possible that these tariffs will be reduced in the future, given that China has been a member of the World Trade Organization since 2001.

The strong competition from the main international and East Asian toy manufacturers has forced Mexican toy firms to concentrate on niche markets. The 2004 Economic Mexican Census registered 281 toy distributors in Mexico, employing on average fourteen persons, with annual sales of US$15.3 million each and assets of US$0.5 million.[1] In the educational market, the strongest manufacturing and distribution firm is Algara, which offers children many science-oriented toys and games, such as chemistry games, marine biology activities, and microscopes. Many of the local manufacturers have outdated manufacturing plants, which puts them at a disadvantage when they compete with Chinese manufacturers.

Other educational toy firms offering products in Mexico include Alex Toys, Juguetes Nip, and Imaginarium. Alex Toys is a well-known manufacturer in the U.S. and sells its products in Mexican department stores and at the Gandhi bookstores in Mexico City. Juguetes Nip specializes in painting and decorative toys imported from the U.S., with three stores in Mexico City. Imaginarium, with eleven stores at large shopping malls in major Mexican cities, distributes toys and children's furniture. Its prices are 35–45 percent higher than Jugaré's, and it has strong brand recognition.

The traditional toys-and-games market is a niche dominated by small family firms. Because they often lack distribution channels, they can offer their toys only in their local communities. Some of these toys are distributed through public and movable street markets on wheels (*mercados sobre ruedas*)[2] in the main urban areas. These products usually lack attractive packaging, but they are offered at relatively cheap prices and are sold tax-free.

This market has shown strong growth in recent years. It increased by nearly 15 percent in 2007 and by 18 percent in 2008, reaching US$23 billion in sales.[3] The 2009 slowdown in growth resulted mainly from the country's economic downturn, driven by increased oil prices and decreasing remittances from the U.S. due to the financial crisis.

Most retail toy sales take place at supermarkets, such as Walmart (more than 700 stores), Soriana (160 hypermarts and 260 stores), and Comercial Mexicana (27 hypermarts, 175 stores), which are the main chain stores in Mexico. In addition, there are specialized toy stores, which are primarily micro-firms with one or two employees (54 percent of the sales). Many of them operate in public and/or movable street markets. Other retail channels include department stores, gift shops, and drugstores. These main retail firms are using "just-in-time" processes to a greater extent, forcing local producers to bear the burden of inventories and accounts receivable.

Many toy and game companies outsource toy parts to multiple third-party manufacturers and then assemble and package the final products. Most companies produce toys through third-party contract manufacturers in the Far East, primarily China, due to its low production and labor costs. However, some companies prefer to use Mexican manufacturing locations to avoid the lengthy transportation time. To minimize this problem, most companies in the Far East must produce toys well in advance of when customers take delivery; and some large retailers place positional orders over a year in advance for toys manufactured abroad. Given that actual sales may often vary from projections, there are frequent inventory excesses and shortages. In Mexico, the major raw materials used to manufacture toys and games are rubber (31 percent of the total cost), plastic (24 percent), paper (18 percent), and cloth (18 percent).[4]

The First Steps

The entrepreneurs expected to sell US$1,200 in merchandise in the first month—December 2005. By the end of the first week, they had sold US$800 of their inventory, and the store looked almost empty. Customers bought everything in sight, and the owners were already worried about not being able to meet market demand—a nice problem to have. Table 2.1 shows the quarterly income of each store (for all of 2008 and the first quarter of 2009).

That month was one of the most hectic Decembers at Jugaré. The four friends needed to produce more toys faster. In addition, because it was Christmas time, their houses could not look like factories because of the season's family events. Thus, they moved production to a little room located next to the store. This room was outfitted with two tables, and the four friends assembled the toys themselves as fast as they could. By January they were exhausted, so they decided to hire one woman to be in charge of store sales and two other women to be production assistants.

The overwhelming market acceptance of the Jugaré products was very exciting and gave the friends the confidence to start expanding their catalogue, offering up to eighty different toy kits by the end of their first 18 months of operation. Jugaré products are designed for well-do-do children between ages 3 and 12 whose mothers are concerned about the overuse of electronic games and are seeking alternatives for play and learning. Moreover, because the friends' own toys were not suitable for children under 3, they introduced new products from other brands for this particular group. (About 80 percent of the displayed products in the Jugaré stores are the company's own products, and the rest are made up of other brands.)

The idea that was born at Marcela's baby shower turned out to be so successful that investors were now interested in franchising the business model. The four founders knew that Jugaré needed to expand. However, they wanted to keep the brand for themselves, as well as the toy production.

Table 2.1 Jugaré's Quarterly Income Statement by Store (in US$)

Store	2008 1st quarter	2nd quarter	3rd quarter	4th quarter	2009 1st quarter
Santa Teresa					
Revenue	387,627	466,254	305,227	451,120	341,830
Cost of goods sold	167,379	207,122	133,619	173,802	130,637
Packaging	7,510	3,365	12,790	—	21,396
Gross profit	212,738	255,767	158,818	277,318	189,797
Fixed expenses	176,688	171,288	193,184	193,011	152,477
Variable expenses	4,864	4,242	3,095	4,411	6,499
Financing expenses	11,996	14,170	7,929	13,512	9,600
Total expenses	193,548	189,700	204,208	210,934	168,576
Profit before taxes	19,190	66,067	−45,390	66,384	21,221
Zentrika					
Revenue	201,432	212,417	132,573	199,380	169,231
Cost of goods sold	88,865	96,835	58,980	83,076	67,704
Packaging	—	10,970	5,040	—	9,720
Gross profit	112,567	104,612	68,552	116,304	91,806
Fixed expenses	116,899	116,784	125,547	126,600	97,269
Variable expenses	2,496	740	770	925	2,129
Financing expenses	6,238	6,654	3,860	6,262	4,847
Total expenses	125,633	124,179	130,177	133,788	104,246
Profit before taxes	−13,066	−19,567	−61,625	−17,484	−12,439
Metepec					
Revenue	—	—	—	—	46,715
Cost of goods sold	—	—	—	—	18,415
Packaging	—	—	—	—	4,917
Gross profit	—	—	—	—	23,383
Fixed expenses	—	—	—	—	64,661
Variable expenses	—	—	—	—	60
Financing expenses	—	—	—	—	863
Total expenses	—	—	—	—	65,584
Profit before taxes	—	—	—	—	−42,200
Condensa					
Revenue	198,807	214,735	160,552	246,572	133,948
Cost of goods sold	85,650	97,633	71,476	100,857	52,468
Packaging	—	—	11,850	—	8,906
Gross profit	113,157	117,102	77,226	145,714	72,574
Fixed expenses	82,732	83,966	79,511	81,246	49,735
Variable expenses	1,682	1,597	1,558	657	899
Financing expenses	4,765	5,312	3,534	5,995	3,005
Total expenses	89,178	90,875	84,603	87,898	53,638
Profit before taxes	23,979	26,228	−7,377	57,817	18,936

Source: Jugaré.

On the other hand, they did not have money to open a new store on their own. So they decided to create three different legal entities: one for the workshop, a second for the La Condesa store and the registered brand of Jugaré, and a third to handle opening new stores with new capital investors.

The Design and Production Process

The four friends knew that product innovation was Jugaré's core competitive advantage. Thus, all of them participated in the brainstorming process (phase 1). They constantly looked at daily activities from a child's point of view to identify interests that could be turned into educational adventures. The golden rule for enhancing creativity among the team had always been that all ideas could and should be discussed. Once the group had a good idea, Hilda and Ibó, the two designers, developed a prototype (phase 2). Then they would all get a steady stream of feedback, not only from adults, but especially from children. During phase 3, each prototype was evaluated and refined. Then implementation began.

At this point, Laura, the production manager, made a list of the raw materials needed to produce each new kit. Then the four friends searched for the best supplier in terms of quality and cost. This process could be problematic. Sometimes the best supplier, in terms of quality, was unable to produce the required quantity. Other times, the supplier charged a high unit price because the order was not large enough to be considered wholesale. Table 2.2 details the company's cost structure for different kinds of products (see also Figure 2.2).

Laura programmed an Excel macro spreadsheet that linked the name of each kit with the quantity and unit price of the raw materials needed to produce it. This way, all the owners knew the cost of each kit. The first production batch was 100 kits. Assembly was undertaken on large tables and organized in a production line.

The decorative box is a crucial aspect of Jugaré's products. Each box is designed creatively with many colorful details. The founders are convinced that the best publicity for their brand is their showy boxes on the gift tables at birthday parties. Each kit is packaged carefully and then distributed to the stores. The flashy boxes have been so successful that, in a recent international competition on design for kids ("Growing Graphics"), Jugaré was selected as one of the finalists and is to be featured in the publication.

The stores send a weekly sales report to Marcela, who is in charge of the sales projections. She then sends the requirements to Laura, who schedules the production of kits. Each production batch is a minimum of 100 kits.

Given that most of the kits have up to fifty different raw materials, a more efficient system of inventory management became imperative—not

Table 2.2 Jugaré's Cost Structure by Product (in US$)

	US$
Mi Cochino Favorito	
Sales price to stores	109.70
Cost of sales:	
Raw materials	81.40
Labor	5.00
Fixed costs	5.00
Osito de Tela	
Sales price to stores	113.50
Cost of sales:	
Raw materials	86.96
Labor	2.50
Fixed costs	5.00
Limpio Mi Casita	
Sales price to stores	67.60
Cost of sales:	
Raw materials	48.83
Labor	2.50
Fixed costs	5.00
Pizza Mia	
Sales price to stores	126.50
Cost of sales:	
Raw materials	102.01
Labor	5.00
Fixed costs	5.00
Mi Mejor Amigo Guajer	
Sales price to stores	74.30
Cost of sales:	
Raw materials	54.33
Labor	2.50
Fixed costs	5.00

Source: Jugaré.

only for physical inventory but also for a system that allows for enterprise resource planning (ERP). The main obstacle for this purchase is the lack of capital. Another limitation is that, despite the company's enormous growth, it is still small, so all purchases are handled in cash and only one supplier gives them credit.

The partners' own skills have not been sufficient to manage the growth of production. Marshaling their talents and energies, they decided to hire a consultant to help them organize the production, inventory management, material purchases, manufacturing, logistics, and so on.

Figure 2.2 Various Jugaré Products

Source: Jugaré.

Devising a Strategy for Growth

This is the decision breakpoint for Jugaré. As a result of their initial success, the entrepreneurs must determine the best growth strategy for the future of their company. One option they are considering is franchising. Some of the pros they must consider are whether this could represent a fast expansion all over the country, without any additional equity, and whether any risk associated with the growth would be shared with the franchisees. Among the cons are that the friends have not yet assembled all the documentation they need to franchise—e.g., business plans, training schedules, operation manuals, and management procedures to maintain the same quality of the current stores.

Another option they are considering is selling the merchandise at different retail stores. The products could be commercialized at specialty stores such as Casa Palacio, MUAC, Gandhi bookstores, and Museo del Niño, among others. The products could also be sold directly to wholesale vendors such as Walmart and Comercial Mexicana. Marcela posits that this would be good because many of the kits could be sold in a short period of time, the market share would rise rapidly, and a larger group of customers would become aware of the Jugaré brand. Laura, however, feels the main disadvantage is that, at the moment, the workshop lacks sufficient production capacity to satisfy the great demand these stores would require. She is also concerned about the production and distribution costs associated with a significant expansion.

The entrepreneurs are also considering the importance of forming strategic alliances with outside clients—e.g., Piccolo Mondo, Gymboree, private or public elementary schools, or children's entertainment companies. Whatever strategy they choose, they will also have to take into account the advertising and marketing strategies, the control and production planning, and the management and control costs.

QUESTIONS

The four friends finished their lattes and left to pick up their daughters from ballet school, all the while asking themselves:

1   Which strategy is best for growing Jugaré? How are we going to get the necessary capital to finance that growth?
2   How are we going to turn this enthusiasm into profitability?
3   How are we going to balance all of this growth with our family lives?

Notes

1   INEGI (2006), *Industria Manufacturera, Censos Económicos 2004*, Aguascalientes, Mexico: Instituto Nacional de Geografía, Estadística e Informática, ISBN: 970–13–4700–5, p. 42.

2   The *mercados sobre ruedas* are street merchants who change their location daily. They have small shops, each one specializing in different products—e.g., fruits, vegetables, clothes, small appliances, and toys.

3   Euromonitor International Inc. (2009), *Toys and Games in México*, Country Report, London, http://www.euromonitor.com/Toys_And_Games, consulted on August 8, 2009.

4   INEGI (2006), *Industria Manufacturera, Censos Económicos 2004*, Aguascalientes, Mexico: Instituto Nacional de Geografía, Estadística e Informática, ISBN: 970–13–4700–5, table 4.

3 Victoria Kisyombe and SELFINA

Building a Leasing Business in Tanzania

Maya Perl-Kot

Women in Tanzania needed all manner of equipment to pursue their entrepreneurial dreams: coolers and freezers, sewing machines, baking ovens, gravel-making machines, tractors and trucks. But they lacked the funds. With the support of her family, Victoria Kisyombe, a veterinarian by training, organized what eventually became Tanzania's largest leasing company focusing on extending micro-credit to women.

Figure 3.1 SELFINA Logo
Source: Reproduced with permission from SELFINA, October 29, 2012.

SELFINA, a micro-leasing business that Victoria Kisyombe envisioned from a personal family challenge, grew into a unique company that had an impact on tens of thousands of lives. The company provided invaluable equipment leasing opportunities to women entrepreneurs on a financial basis, which allowed clients to pay toward ultimate ownership. It accepted women who were often turned away by traditional financial institutions, and offered business training as well as other services critical to clients' success.

A woman of humble origins from the inland part of Tanzania, Victoria saw her exceptional vision mature into a thriving company that had issued over 22,000 lease contracts. Her business idea—spurred by personal necessity, an entrepreneurial spirit, and the social needs she witnessed around her—was an innovative one for Tanzania: SELFINA was one of only a handful of organizations that provided leasing on a micro-credit basis, and the largest one that focused exclusively on women. Under Victoria's extraordinary leadership, SELFINA drew both domestic and international attention, which, in turn, resulted in increased financing sources for the firm, enabling it to continue to expand its client base. "This has been an amazing experience," she recalled. "It is a business that allows me to give to others, but has simultaneously contributed so much to my own personal development."

The Origin of an Idea

Victoria was the daughter of farmers from Mbeya, a city of over 2 million residents in the southwestern highlands of Tanzania. After studying for her bachelor's degree in a nearby city and completing her master's degree in tropical veterinary medicine at the University of Edinburgh in the United Kingdom, fully funded by a British Council scholarship, she worked for the local government, treating animals in her town and in the surrounding villages.

She had not intended to end up in the financing business. But when she saw a need she could not ignore—Tanzanian women's need to provide for themselves and their families—innovation came naturally. The urgency of the situation was clear: Women were expected to help support their families but, particularly in rural areas, had virtually no employment opportunities. Small enterprises—selling produce, groceries, or other items—were often the only alternative. But women lacked access to productivity-enhancing technology to improve, or even basic assets necessary to start, these businesses. They were either unaware of where and how to seek them out or, upon trying, were turned away by local financial institutions. Despite national laws that declared and mandated equal rights for men and women, many customary and cultural laws still impeded women's financial freedom.

The specific problems are diverse: women are oftentimes the breadwinners for large, extended families, playing an integral role in the rural economy, but they cannot obtain the equipment to maximize their income. In Tanzania, to get assets, one needs collateral which, for the majority of Tanzanians, could only consist of land. Women are largely uneducated about the need to obtain official deeds for land that may have been passed down between generations. Thus, when the time comes to use the land as collateral, women seldom have a way to prove ownership. Moreover, even when official ownership does become a salient issue, property is seldom registered in the woman's name. Although the law equates the two genders, the reality of things is different. Obtaining a deed can be a cumbersome and complicated task. The consequence of these various elements is clear: women lack collateral and, as a result, lack the ability to get the assets they need.

The injustice of the situation did not elude Victoria. While thinking about possible ways to address it, she was able to conceptualize another dimension: an opportunity to make a profit by offering the services that women lacked. SELFINA (Sero Lease and Finance Ltd.), the company Victoria started, offered a credit window exclusively for women and focused on two products: (1) leasing equipment on a financial, rather than an operational, basis (where the lessee had the right to ultimately own the assets); and (2) buying women's equipment when they needed liquidity and then allowing them to keep the equipment on lease.

Women and Tanzania's Social Fabric

SELFINA's operating environment was a challenging one. Incomes in Tanzania were low and left little room for investment or savings. The country ranked 157th in income per capita according to the World Bank's 2008 *World Development Indicators Report*,[1] with average individual annual earnings of less than US$1,200. Even for existing small enterprises, paying back loans (or leases) could take a significant toll on a family's disposable income—not to mention the added difficulty of completing a convoluted registration and start-up process that new businesses faced. Many women shied away from entrepreneurial endeavors for fear of financing ventures that would not succeed, or of becoming indebted without the ability to repay commitments.

In addition, the HIV/AIDS epidemic created a further burden for Tanzanian women. Although Tanzania fared well relative to some neighboring countries, more than 6 percent of the population carried the virus in 2007. The disease often altered traditional family structures and left young women, with few skills and little education, in charge of providing for extended families. From a business perspective, offering leases to such women required both an in-depth understanding of their intricate family situations and, at times, the ability to refuse contracts despite the hardships the clients faced.

Finally, the lending and leasing industry in Tanzania was extremely underdeveloped and underfunded. Despite national guidelines and legislation meant to facilitate microfinance lending, actually starting an organization remained an extremely challenging task. The Microfinance Companies and Microcredit Activities Regulations, and the 2006 Banking and Financial Institutions Act, gave the Bank of Tanzania authority to oversee all micro-lending activities,[2] and mandated a minimum capital requirement of 800 million Tanzania shillings (TZS), about US$600,000, from multi-branch microfinance institutions (MFIs).[3] Because of the relatively high benchmark, only nine microfinance organizations were operating in Tanzania in 2007, with US$67 million in total portfolio value[4] and a range of products generally limited to savings and credit;[5] SELFINA was one of only three MFIs that provided leasing services.[6] The government offered little institutional support, and the financial sector lacked the transparency and communication capabilities needed to nurture successful firms.

Despite these multiple external challenges, Victoria's combination of ambition, resourcefulness, and innovation enabled SELFINA to overcome barriers and transcend industry scope. But the road was never easy.

Unusual Beginnings

SELFINA began out of a personal tragedy. In 1991 Victoria's husband passed away, leaving her to care for three young children on her own. Victoria's salary as a veterinarian was not enough to sustain the household—let alone save any money to guarantee future security. Her husband's only bequest was a cow named Sero, the word for "leader" in Maasai, the tribe to which he belonged. Sero produced enough milk for the family to consume in addition to a sizeable surplus that Victoria was able to sell in the local market. Combining this revenue stream with her wages allowed Victoria to send her children to school, purchase necessary goods, and even accumulate some savings. Sero's value as a productive asset became clear immediately:

> I could see how instrumental a resource like Sero was to my family and the opportunity she awarded me to reach beyond basic subsistence. I could also see that other women lack similar income-generating assets. Unless they inherit them, like I did, women have hardly any avenues for attaining one. I would have never had enough disposable income to purchase a cow by myself. And without collateral back-up, the local bank would have not given a loan to a woman in my situation in order to buy one. It's a vicious cycle: without assets we cannot get money, and without money we cannot get assets.

It was then that Victoria became inspired to start a company to address the situation. Although she had no formal education or training in business and economics, she understood the principles of leasing: Purchase equipment that clients need and rent it at a reasonable, fair rate that still generates a profit. A leasing company would satisfy both women's need for productive assets and Victoria's own desire for personal and professional growth. By observing the business environment around her, Victoria understood the types of equipment that would be most useful. Refrigerators and freezers for small convenience stores, sewing machines for making clothing, and productivity-enhancing farm tools (whether livestock or machines) were at the top of her list. As Victoria knew, anything that could either improve the profitability of existing enterprises or allow women to start new ones would be in high demand.

Victoria took her idea seriously. She began circulating it among family, friends and colleagues, who were all supportive. Not only were the products of a leasing company in high demand, they said, but the leadership of a woman personally familiar with the circumstances and difficulties clients faced could really set the company apart from competitors.

Encouraged by the positive feedback she received, and impelled by a desire to seek the advice of decision makers, in 1993 Victoria left her veterinarian job in Mbeya and moved with her three children to Dar es Salaam, Tanzania's largest city. She wanted to establish herself and the seeds of her business in the country's financial, social, and professional hub.

While laying the foundations for SELFINA, as she was familiarizing herself with Dar es Salaam's micro-lending industry, Victoria embarked on another, related endeavor. She started SEBA (Sero Businesswomen Association), a nonprofit organization whose aim was to empower and create a vibrant community for women entrepreneurs. SEBA offered training and lessons in practical business issues such as accounting, people management, and negotiation—allowing women to supplement monetary support with professional coaching. "SEBA was an idea intrinsically linked to my goals in coming to Dar es Salaam," Victoria observed.

> I wanted to build my business and certainly had financial goals in mind but, at the same time, I wanted to create something holistic and robust; a place where women could get not only the equipment they want, but also the information and contacts they need in order to succeed in a sustainable way.

As secretary-general of SEBA, Victoria was able to earn an income and, at the same time, capitalize on the connections she had been making in Dar es Salaam's industry circles. Aided by money she had saved and received from various sources, Victoria devised a pilot study program to test her leasing business idea. She selected forty women who, based on personal acquaintance or in-depth research, she believed would achieve relatively quick paybacks, and made their lease terms short in order to complete the pilot within a certain time frame. She bought several pieces of equipment—primarily sewing machines, secretarial equipment, freezers and refrigerators—and leased these to the women.

The equipment had the predicted impact on the businesses and, with the help of increased earnings, the women met their payments. At the time, more important than making a small profit was the fact that Victoria had proven the feasibility of her idea to banks and potential investors. The repayment rate was virtually perfect, and Victoria had firmly established the precedent that would help in going forward with her business plan. Moreover, the response she received from the women was extremely positive. They all appreciated the opportunity she had afforded them and were enthusiastic about additional lines of credit to help grow their businesses. "The responses from the women in the pilot were incredibly gratifying," Victoria said. "These women would have been turned away by the local bank and were forced to fend for themselves. I came along as an intermediary who was willing to give them a chance."

Victoria was confident, but knew that real success required a larger scope. She needed more clients. However, she faced a serious business strategy challenge in this area: in the absence of an organized credit-assessment mechanism (customary in the West) and without requesting sizeable collateral from clients, judging women's ability to repay proved to be difficult. Although according to the contracts, Victoria effectively owned the equipment until it was paid in full (thus making it de facto collateral), the repossession mechanism was costly, time-consuming and, therefore, unreliable. So, while validating the market demand for her product, the pilot study also reinforced the need to choose clients effectively. Victoria deduced these key takeaways and decided to take the next big step.

Founding Sero Lease and Finance Ltd.

In April 2002, after working arduously to raise capital and navigate through bureaucratic channels, Victoria finally registered Sero Lease and Finance Ltd., dubbed SELFINA in short. Much like her future clients, she too faced a collateral problem when trying to borrow from the bank. Her own father came to her rescue by transferring the deed of the family's land into her name. "He was a great man and a constructive figure in my life. Despite a lot of traditional conventions that mostly disenfranchise women, my father was an encouraging man who supported my ambition," she noted admiringly,

> He knew that without property to my name I could never get my business going—and he made the ultimate sacrifice by putting the family residence on the line. That requires almost blind trust, and I'll always be grateful for the opportunity I received.

With US$110,000 of investment capital and US$20,000 in bank loans, Victoria's venture was a huge risk—especially with her parents' home at stake—but she knew there was no other way. "If I didn't take a chance, I knew my mobility and freedom would always be limited. Beyond that, I sensed a calling in what I was pursuing. It meant something to me, and it would mean something to a lot of other women."

Thanks to the lessons Victoria applied from the pilot, at its inception SELFINA was already beyond its teething stage, and she knew not to overstretch its operations. As Managing Director of the company, she hired experts in women advocacy, law, accounting, and finance as her staff.

Together, they developed a rigorous framework with specific metrics to assess applicants, estimate the monthly payments they would be able to meet and, thus, determine the maximal size of each contract.

The selection methodology included several stages.[7] First, potential clients came to SELFINA offices to learn about the company, the general leasing process, and the specific requirements to obtain a lease. These requirements included an established, operational business or an advanced business plan in place; a guarantor to co-sign any contract; and the ability to participate with a down-payment of up to 15 percent of the value of the desired equipment. The latter was meant to give the client an initial sense of ownership and a personal stake in the lease, as well as to spread the company's risk exposure.

Clients then filed a lease application form, where they gave details about themselves and their business. The staff reviewed applications during weekly selection meetings and, upon approval of the application, a SELFINA loan officer visited the woman to conduct an investigation. The officer examined the applicant's residence as well as the location of the business, and scrutinized the earning potential of the lease equipment. The officer then returned to company with a full assessment report, and the staff made a final decision regarding the application.[8]

Ultimately, the criteria Victoria developed proved to be reliable predictors and the women SELFINA chose were successful borrowers, gradually becoming owners of the equipment they leased. The interest she generally charged—at 2.8 percent monthly and 30 percent annually still high by Western standards—was lower than what banks charged the same women, and the attractiveness of her product was clear.

Victoria entered a wide variety of industries, including cooling, machinery, transportation, and livestock. The new SELFINA bought and leased freezers and refrigerators for drinks or produce; sewing, gravel-making, and baking machines; tractors, cars, and trucks (see Figure 3.2), and a variety of farm animals. Her advantages as a large, consolidated business entity were clear: She could negotiate better prices for equipment when SELFINA purchased large quantities, and she had enough collateral to receive increasingly lower interest rates from the bank which she then passed on to her clients.

Marketing, Expansion, and Business Structure

The business model worked, and SELFINA became a huge success. More-over, that success had a multiplying effect: With more women repaying their leases, institutions were more willing to provide money for SELFINA—and the more money SELFINA had, the more it was able to lend. From just a few dozen clients in 2002, SELFINA was financing over 200 in 2004. As clients accomplished a 98 percent repayment rate, confidence in the company grew and demand for its products skyrocketed.

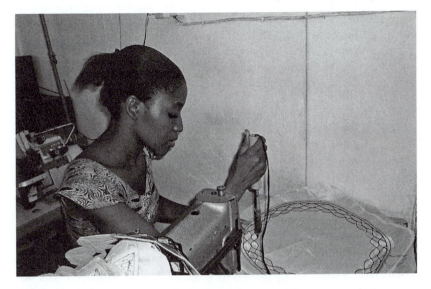

Figure 3.2 Sewing Equipment Leased Through SELFINA
Source: Reproduced with permission from SELFINA, October 29, 2012.

Then the real wave occurred: In less than 5 years, between 2004 and 2009, SELFINA expanded its client base from approximately 200 contracts to more than 16,000. Portfolio volume also grew exponentially, by over 600 percent, and by the end of 2008 stood at TZS 7,000 million, about US$5 million. All of this growth was without advertising; by word-of-mouth alone, SELFINA received more requests than it could fund. "The foundations we established initially were critical in guaranteeing the company's future," Victoria noted. "It was a highly professional approach that focused on the mutual business benefits, both for SELFINA and the lease holder."

Horizontal growth, which constituted new "low-cost" women leasing amounts of US$3,000 to US$4,000, grew by about 80 percent annually. Vertically, "active women"—graduated lessees seeking second, third, or fourth terms—requested increasingly larger contracts. Such leases reached anywhere from US$7,000 to US$25,000. The Global Bridge Fund (GBF), an affiliate of the World Bank and the International Finance Corporation and a part of ACCION, an American nonprofit that specializes in micro-finance, helped SELFINA create the "Next Stage Fund," an initiative to provide one-on-one training for these "active women."

At the same time, SELFINA pursued geographical expansion, opening nine additional branches across Tanzania. After identifying regions or provinces where services seemed lucrative, Victoria utilized local activists or community leaders to identify each locality's true potential. She then traveled to personally establish the foundations of the branch. Employees were selected based on competence and fit, and underwent comprehensive training from SELFINA staff in all of the company's regulations and codes. Finally, Victoria officially appointed the managers and closely monitored each new branch during the first months of activity, participating in all leasing activity decisions and traveling frequently to the location to assess progress.

SELFINA grew in size, and by 2009 had more than 100 employees. While the company maintained a flat operating structure, it had clear roles and responsibility assignments to ensure that each function was fulfilled. Every branch had distinct business units and positions: accountants reported on local portfolios once a week and, on a daily basis, sent an email report of any irregularities; the operations team visited lessees and sent an updated report of client files once a week; and headquarters was in charge of final authorization of any new clients based on the company-wide rules.

The refusal rate generally remained at 1 percent. Women who were not approved as clients were advised to seek credit from smaller micro-lending organizations until they established their credentials with SELFINA and could lease in larger sums:

> Saying no and refusing a loan is incredibly difficult, especially since I knew how badly each woman needs the equipment. But I also knew that if we do not keep to our limits, we will be failing the company. I couldn't afford to let that happen. Making tough decisions is a business necessity you cannot avoid.

With over 22,000 leases in total and 15,000 active contracts, SELFINA had US$1.1 million in equity by the middle of 2009. Together with additional funding totaling US$3 million it had received but not yet leased out, the company had more than US$10 million in operating capital in the middle of 2009.

National and International Recognition

The rapid growth SELFINA experienced drew continued domestic and international attention. Because there was no similar Tanzanian for-profit business with a comparable business model and customer base, Victoria became a national figure in women's advocacy circles and an expert on property rights and micro-leasing. She appeared on television frequently and was deeply involved in the country's overhaul of property-leasing laws, which resulted in the Financial Leasing Act that dramatically increased women's rights and promoted leasing as a tool for economic progress.[9] When, in April 2008, Parliament passed the bill, she received a personal mention from the president of the United Republic of Tanzania, the Honorable Jakaya Mrisho Kikwete, who spoke about the jobs SELFINA had created and the number of women it had assisted.

Victoria was also identified by international organizations and agencies as a role model for business entrepreneurs. She was one of seven women profiled in the World Bank's 2008 report *Doing Business: Women in Africa*.[10] In 2007 she traveled to Washington, D.C., to speak before the president of the World Bank and six foreign ministers as part of a conference on gender and development. "It was really emotional and rewarding to hear the leader of the nation acknowledging everything that we do," she recalled. "And the opportunity to go abroad and speak to such important international figures—well, that is something I could have never even dreamed of before. I was extremely excited to have been selected."

The spotlight furnished more than intangible exposure for Victoria. It was also an unparalleled source of publicity that built SELFINA's reputation. It created borrowing potential for the company, through which its recognition and prestige constantly increased: Exim Bank, a local Tanzanian institution, lent SELFINA TZS1 billion, about US$1 million, and Deutsche Bank extended US$100,000. PriceWaterhouseCooper implemented a two-month pro bono engagement to improve operational strategy, and, in addition to the Next Stage Fund, the GBF also supplied technology and communication assistance. The company incorporated various software applications, such as Loan Performer, to automate receipt making, and drastically improved the accuracy of and control over bookkeeping and portfolio management.

Beyond Business: Self Fulfillment

Throughout SELFINA's rapid expansion, Victoria never neglected SEBA or the social cause behind her enterprise:

> It feels great that my initiative has developed so much. I am constantly thinking of additional ways to grow the vision—and myself. Getting funding is important, but getting the proper training for our staff and clients is also vital. Whether in large companies or small enterprises, women often lack not domain knowledge but business know-how. They may be experts at understanding the local supply and demand, but not know the basics of record-keeping, let alone managing other people. Women are not *expected* to be managers most of the time. That is why initiatives such as the GBF Next Stage Fund are so important. They supplement the financial products we provide with additional, invaluable skills. I hope that, despite the current global economic crisis, we can sustain the same levels of growth and keep adding new clients at similar rates.

SELFINA's growth as a business had a profound impact on Victoria's personal development, and she admitted readily to the incredible sense of achievement she received from the company.

The challenges along the way were significant. Until SELFINA became self-sufficient, there were many instances when I had little or no income. Any revenue we generated I ploughed back into the firm, and oftentimes I had to rely on my parents for assistance. I am proud that SELFINA is now profitable, and that I am independent.

Victoria mentioned the immediate feedback from clients as one of the most rewarding aspects of her industry: Results were concrete and measurable. The impact the equipment had on clients was visible from the moment they received it, and they would return to SELFINA praising the company for its services. "It's amazing that we were able to achieve such rapid growth," she observed. "Even more amazing is that we help shape the future of thousands of women—and that I am in control of my own future at the same time."

Victoria's family was extremely proud of her accomplishments. Her parents were uniquely supportive of her idea, even in its infancy—a luxury Victoria knew not all women enjoyed. Her three children all attained prosperous careers of their own. Her oldest daughter even worked for a year in the accounting and finance arm of the company. Although she eventually left to pursue studies in the United States, she supported her mother's business from afar and hoped to return in some capacity in the future. "In Tanzania women are expected to work, yes, but not to take initiative. My family is amazing in this respect, having not only allowed me to pursue my dream but actually helping me realize it."

All of Victoria's children acknowledged the unparalleled benefits that SELFINA and their mother's entrepreneurial spirit provided for the family, in terms of flexibility, independent time-setting, and financial security. Had she had a regular job, Victoria would never have been able to relocate to Dar es Salaam and send the children to Tanzania's best university or abroad for schooling. Despite the long hours and hard work that SELFINA demanded, Victoria knew how much better it was compared to the alternative scenario:

> Leaving Mbeya was initially a sacrifice; we abandoned a close-knit support mechanism to move to a large, foreign city. But, ultimately, it was well worth it. I was lucky to have friends and distant relatives who took care of the children when they were little while I was in the office. Without this assistance I would not have been able to devote the time required to start my own business. In such a poor country, there are very few opportunities for financial or social mobility. My family helped me capitalize on one such opportunity, and I hope that I have been able to repay them for that help.

Challenges and Hopes for the Future

With near-perfect repayment rates and growing attention around SELFINA, Victoria's success was apparent. Still, she believed there were additional avenues for expansion and wanted to set the bar even higher. Entering foreign markets was one particularly appealing idea. "We have to leverage and utilize our publicity in order to grow the company, as well as export the concept and enlarge it."

At the same time, SELFINA faced many challenges. Even with strong institutional financial performance, getting credit for the company often required a guarantor. Despite the good track-record and positive exposure, local banks were sometimes reluctant to lend large sums without one. The company lacked this type of stable support, which led to expenditures for procurement, bureaucratic, and administrative tasks every time a guarantor was needed. One of Victoria's top priorities was to secure a permanent guarantor that would allow the company to be more agile in its responses to market demands and borrow more quickly. Another priority was to incorporate more technology and connectivity into the company, in the form of more computers, better software, and additional training. "Innovation continues to be a strong driver of our performance. Technology is critical in making businesses, including SELFINA, more efficient. We want to fully utilize technological advances in order to maximize our impact."

Overall, Victoria hoped to open two SELFINA branches each year over a four-year period, including some in Tanzania's more disenfranchised regions where she believed demand for leasing products would be especially high. With at least five employees to open each branch, she intended to increase her staff by about 50 percent and the number of women served by 5,000 over the same period. Since each woman provided for additional family members, the number of lives that SELFINA had influenced surpassed 185,000 and, when in 2009 she received the International Alliance for Women (TIAW) World of Difference Award from the GBF, Victoria announced a target of impacting a total of 440,000 lives by 2014.[11]

> I want to find a way to really optimize synergies between SELFINA, SEBA, internal projects and some of the resources offered by international organizations. There are so many opportunities and so much knowledge out there and I would like to aggregate all of it in our business model. This company, which commemorates Sero, just one cow I happened to receive years ago, is a way to earn a profit—but also a chance to do something good. I want to keep it growing, and keep setting and achieving new goals.

QUESTIONS

1 What types of economic, financial and social resources did Victoria use to launch her leasing business?
2 In what ways did Victoria's business add value to the customer?
3 In what ways is Victoria's experience an example to emulate?

Notes

1 The World Bank, *World Development Indicators* (accessed October 1, 2009).
2 The Parliament of the United Republic of Tanzania, "The Banking and Financial Institutions Act," 2006, Part III, section 14, www.bot-tz.org/BankingSupervision/BAFIA2006.pdf (accessed January 21, 2010).
3 The Parliament of the United Republic of Tanzania, "Microfinance Companies and Microcredit Activities Regulation," 2004, www.microfinanceregulationcenter.org/files/26961_file_MICROFINANCE_COMPANIES_AND_MICROCREDIT_ACTIVITIES_REGULATIONS_2004.pdf (accessed January 20, 2010).
4 MixMarket Microfinance Information eXchange, "Microfinance in Tanzania," 2007, www.mixmarket.org/mfi/country/Tanzania (accessed January 21, 2010).
5 The Economist Intelligence Unit, "Global Microscope on the Microfinance Business Environment," 2009, http://idbdocs.iadb.org/wsdocs/getdocument.aspx?docnum=2189221, pp. 39–40 (accessed November 12, 2010).
6 MixMarket Microfinance Information eXchange, "Microfinance in Tanzania."
7 Caroline Pinder, "SELFINA (Sero Lease and Finance Company)—Tanzania," The Enterprise Development Impact Assessment Information Service (EDIAIS), 2001, www.sed.manchester.ac.uk/research/iarc/ediais/word-files/SELFINA.doc (accessed January 20, 2010).
8 Ibid.
9 The Parliament of the United Republic of Tanzania, "The Financial Leasing Act," 2008, www.parliament.go.tz/Polis/PAMS/Docs/5–2008.pdf (accessed January 20, 2010).
10 The World Bank, International Finance Corporation, World Bank Group Gender Action Plan and Vital Voices Global Partnership, *Doing Business: Women in Africa*, www.doingbusiness.org/documents/Women_in_Africa.pdf, p. 41 (accessed January 18, 2010).
11 The Grassroots Business Fund, "Dr. Victoria Wins 2009 TIAW World of Difference Award," November 2009, www.gbfund.org/?q=Dr_Victoria_Wins_TIAW_Award (accessed December 2, 2009).

4 Ocimum Biosolutions

Genomics Outsourcing in India

Amanda Knauer

Instead of capitalizing on her graduate education in the U.S. by working for an established multinational company, Anu Ancharya decided to return to her native India to launch a genomics outsourcing company. After just 10 years and three acquisitions in Europe and the U.S., her company is one of the leading players in the global biomedical outsourcing industry.

Figure 4.1 Ocimum Logo

Anu Ancharya was destined for a career in science. The daughter of a physics professor, she grew up in Bengal, India, doing science experiments with her three siblings under the supervision of her father. "My dad recorded an interview with us every year, asking us why we wanted to do what we wanted to do," she recalls:

> From the beginning, I said that I wanted to study physics, from the fourth or fifth grade, all the way until I went to college. When I started, my first year I was a little disillusioned, and I realized that wasn't my calling. I wanted to excel in something, and realized that if I couldn't excel in it, it probably was not worth pursuing as a career. I decided to analyze my strengths, and very quickly, I realized I wanted to get into business.

Lacking money for studying an MBA at an American university, she decided to apply for a physics Ph.D. program, and was admitted at the University of Illinois. After a year, she persuaded the head of the Management of Information Systems (MIS) department to accept her in its master's program. The head of the program, who was Indian, took Anu aside and asked why she was abandoning her doctorate. "At the time I told him that I wanted to really start a business of my own and to do that I needed to study MIS; that in five years I would start a business, and I first wanted to work for a startup. It was more to convince him, but it turned out to be what happened," she says with a laugh.

Five years later, in 2001, Anu Ancharya founded Ocimum Biosolutions, a global leader in genomics outsourcing.

Forming a Company

Knowing that she wanted to start a company, Anu and her husband Subash Lungareddy began exploring and pursuing a range of ideas, including a unified voice, fax, messaging service and a bandwidth trading site. "We realized it wasn't about the idea. If you get three people in a room, you get an idea. The real value is in the execution." They were looking for a business that would allow them to leverage the low costs of operating in India, mostly afforded by an inexpensive, educated workforce. In 1997, Anu's friend Dr. P. Sujatha, a molecular geneticist working with a rice company at the time, wanted to develop software to examine a rice genome. Two years later, the three revisited the concept, and determined that it met their criteria. "It seemed like a field that was rapidly emerging . . . The trends were very positive." Once they had decided that it was a solid business idea to pursue, they returned to Hyderabad, India, and founded Ocimum with about US$300,000 of their own startup capital.

Anu's warm and outgoing personality positioned her well for the role of CEO. Of her husband Subash, on the other hand, Anu says that "he's a very quiet sort of person. He's detail oriented, but he wouldn't like to go meet strangers at conferences. When he goes to a conference, he comes back with 20 business cards. When I go, I come back with 250." Subash took the position of CFO.

A classified ad proved both India's wealth of human resources and lack of biotechnology specialists: in 3 days, they received 2,000 résumés and made four initial hires, including HR and IT managers, and two developers. Despite the number of eager candidates, few were trained in both biological sciences and IT. "Very soon, we realized that getting the right people to build the product was going to be a nightmare," said Anu. The challenge presented an opportunity: with a 1-year development timeline and a need for cash flow, they created a training institute to cross-train students in life science and IT. "So the revenue challenges were met through training."[1] Furthermore, the institute created a healthy pipeline of individuals trained to fit Ocimum's hiring needs, and about 10 percent of its top students were offered jobs with the company.

With this human infrastructure in place, they built Biotracker, a resource planning product which handles samples and research processes for scientists in academic labs, allowing them to manage workflows and data. "The first product I sold to a customer before it was completely ready, like everyone else does," Anu says with a laugh. Delivered on time, the product sold for US$30,000 to an academic lab in India.

Over the next 2 years, the company created a gene expression product as well as an innovative RNA software product, iRNA Check, to aid researchers in the silencing of certain genes, the first product of its type on the market. By that time, Ocimum had grown to about twenty-five employees in India. "At that point, we wanted to build scale," says Anu. With about $1 million in revenue at the time,

> we had proven that it was a model that there was some money to be made in the space . . . We didn't have the deep pockets to go and spend a few million on marketing these products, so it was decided that we would look at a few different ways to enhance our scale and revenue.

Growth through Acquisitions

Reflecting on the founding and growth of Ocimum, Anu observes that "there is a very small border between taking a lot of risk and being stupid." Back in the early days of her venture, she had to figure out exactly where that dividing line lay.

In 2004, Ocimum acquired the microarray division of a client, MWG, a genomics products and services company based in Germany. Microarrays are a series of microscopic DNA spots attached to a solid surface, which is later used to analyze the genes. MWG was the leading genomics company in Europe at the time, and the acquisition made Ocimum an international player. "Everyone was wondering who was this little company out of India intent on buying a large European company. We received publicity worth around US$1 million," said Anu. With little planning, Ocimum acquired MWG's microarray division in an asset buyout. The microarray technology had cost MWG some 8 years and more than US$15 million to develop (though the value depreciates quickly with time). Ocimum purchased the asset for $220,000, without any outside financing. With a physical presence now in Germany, Japan, and the U.S., Ocimum opened a lab in India, where it transferred much of the technology from MWG. The acquisition opened up the entire European market to the still-small Ocimum. In addition, the company, formerly selling predominantly through Anu at trade shows, acquired MWG's professional sales team.

Armed with the microarray technology, Ocimum now planned to become a leading company in India in the field of oligonucleotides or lab genetic consumables. With an equity and debt deal from the International Finance Corporation (IFC), the private equity branch of the World Bank, Ocimum purchased the Biomolecules Division of Netherlands-based

Isogen Life Sciences in 2006. The company was too small to achieve scale, however, and was ultimately unsustainable. Anu said, "I didn't feel excited enough to spend too much time there."

Still focused on the plant sciences at the time, in 2007, Ocimum wanted to enter the pharmaceutical market and looked for a third acquisition that would give them access to this profitable field. U.S.-based Gene Logic, which Anu described as "one of the darlings of the genomic era," had a market cap of $2 billion, a 15-year working relationship with most of the big pharmaceutical companies in the U.S., and gene databases unique to the industry.

Gene Logic's gene databases were created about 10 years ago, from blood and tissue samples from ninety-one different medical centers around the U.S. Aggregating gene expression studies, Gene Logic created a database of these samples that cost the company nearly $150 million. At the time, many pharmaceutical companies used the data for early drug discovery; today, a lot of customers use it for clinical trials for discovery validation or biomarkers. (Markers are used to determine if an individual suffers from a specific disease.)

"It was a company that seemed a little out of reach, at least at the beginning years of Ocimum," said Anu. Eager to acquire its databases and leverage its U.S. client list to expand into the services sector, Ocimum purchased the genomic assets division of Gene Logic for $10 million.

Anu describes some difficulties with the acquisition, driven largely by the fact of a young Indian upstart acquiring an established American company. "It was one of the harder transitions for the employees there." To help with the transition, Subash and Anu spent about half of their time at the Gene Logic offices in Maryland, with the sixty-five new Ocimum employees. First among the challenges was to get the Gene Logic employees to reduce their spending and adapt a startup spirit; those who could not adapt were let go. "You don't know how cheap I am," Anu says with a laugh. For example, using Priceline to book hotels, Ocimum spends US$50 for rooms at the Hilton, compared to US$160 that they would spend if they booked through traditional means at corporate rates. "Those are the kind of changes we needed to bring in."

An Expanding Line of Products and Services

"Some of our products are multi-hundred-thousand-dollar products, some are hundred-dollar products," says Sowmya Vel, assistant vice president of marketing, branding and outreach. "The people you sell to are different, too, sometimes scientists, sometimes technicians." In a matter of just a few years Ocimum has built a bewildering array of products and services.

One of Ocimum's first products, Biotracker, is a software program that allows research labs to track samples, workflows, and information output. The product is licensed mostly to academic life sciences labs for between

US$200,000 and US$300,000 per year, and requires customization for each client. The purchasing decision is usually left to the head of the IT department of the lab or institution.

> Once a sale is closed, we travel to the client's site to understand clients' requirements. We sit with the scientist or lab manager, and try to understand their requirements, try to understand whatever they are doing manually that we can automate. We agree with the customer on the scope, which becomes the basis of the execution

explains Kolanu Reddy, an assistant vice president. "Then the team comes back to India [and] we translate those requirements to technical specifications that are understood by programmers." The process takes anywhere between 3 and 12 months. Ocimum charges the client about US$40 per person per hour worked, and the occasional large pharmaceutical contract can cost about US$1.2 million.

The company has also ventured into databases. With DNA from 22,000 patient tissue and blood samples, Ocimum's gene expression databases and interfaces, branded BioExpress, are used by academic and industry labs for early stage drug discovery in large disease areas: oncology, inflammatory diseases, cardiovascular, and central nervous system. Full access to the database can cost up to US$5 million for a perpetual license, with sixteen of the top twenty pharmaceutical companies and half of the top twenty biotech companies using the product. For smaller labs with limited needs, the annual license to limited database access plus maintenance costs US$5,000. Pricing is not fixed as solutions are typically customized for each client.

Ocimum's database, purchased in the Gene Logic acquisition, is considered the largest and most comprehensive in the industry. There are a number of public databases available that lack the ease of use and reliability of information of BioExpress. Competitor databases have public data, of which 90 percent is not trustworthy. Vel explains that "public databases require a lot of cleaning before a dataset is considered accurate enough to use." Without any additional investment, the database will be useful to Ocimum for just another 2 years.

Ocimum has also entered the lab consumables (oligonucleotides) business. First level techniques used in most biological labs, oligonucleotides are PCR reactions, or amplifications of a single piece of DNA to create small primers needed for experimentation. These small DNA fragments have a variety of uses in a lab, including bacterial cloning. High-levels of PCR reactions need to be outsourced. Most labs are too small to justify the expense of the machines required to make oligonucleotides, which cost a few hundred thousand dollars, so they typically outsource this part of the research process. Oligonucleotides being a volume business, Ocimum charges between a few cents and a dollar per base. Oligonucleotide customers tend to be mostly academic labs. Ocimum is one of the biggest suppliers to academic labs in India.

After experiencing a few years of exponential growth, the markets crashed in 2008, curbing Ocimum's expansion plans. Having spent the previous 4 months strategizing to acquire its biggest competitor, Ocimum suddenly could not raise the capital to fund the acquisition, forcing the company to throw in the towel. Furthermore, the new economic conditions left the company cash constrained. Anu took this significant barrier to Ocimum's growth-by-acquisition model in her stride: "We always have to figure out a way to adjust." The founders successfully convinced board members to increase their investment and keep the company afloat.

Branding and Sales

Branding your business after growing via acquisitions requires a great deal of care. After the Gene Logic acquisition, the "Gene Logic" brand name was maintained to "capitalize on the genomics goodwill which was associated with the brand."[2] Today, both the Ocimum and Gene Logic brand names are displayed on corporate materials. Vel explains that branding is important even in an industry often driven by commodities:

> With something like the database product, some services that we offer, a brand name really helps, because people are worried about the quality of the data. Based on the information in the database, they might invest US$1 billion for drug discovery. Data quality is not the same in every database.

Ocimum has separate direct sales teams for services, IT, and lab information products. These teams are comprised of Ph.D.s with deep understanding of the company's products and services. All direct sales teams in the U.S. are supported by a parallel team in India that handles account work, including searching for and identifying potential customers and contacts. Each member of the sales team has sales targets and individual incentives for performance. The company enforces strict consequences if sales targets are unmet.

Ocimum exploits the Gene Logic brand name to increase sales in the U.S. To sell to a new client, a service team sales executive will first introduce the company as Gene Logic and give an overview of its services. The client usually responds by auditing Ocimum, examining its processes and implementation of certain projects. If satisfied, the client will grant Ocimum a pilot project. After that, "once you get a customer interested, you go to their friends," said Anu.

The acquisition of Gene Logic was instrumental in giving Ocimum access to the large pharmaceutical companies, and now drives its business growth. "You have a pre-existing relationship with a lot of pharma companies; we look at the top 50 companies and make sure that they are all customers," says Anu. "When something new is happening, you want to be there very early." Ocimum is also eliminating customers that generate less revenue. "We want to be more focused."

Ocimum's Corporate Culture

The Ocimum offices in Hyderabad are accessible by dark elevator in a rundown building. A friendly young receptionist warmly greets visitors and invites them to wait on a worn love seat, which appears to have been acquired second-hand when the company was founded 10 years ago. A shelving unit featuring a number of plaques of recognition for the speedy growth of the company is the only hint of Ocimum's success.

The office itself is dark, predominantly brown, and lacking any kind of intentional decor other than a few sketches of Parisian scenery acquired and hung by Anu. A young-looking workforce sits before rows of computers, focused intently on the screens in front of them.

Ten years after founding the company, Anu continues to run Ocimum like a startup, bootstrapping and maintaining an entrepreneurial culture as she manages 200 people in two offices in Hyderabad. In July 2011 the company moved to a brand new, 5-acre campus ten times the size of its current office (Figure 4.2).

The founders have tried to create a culture of fun and openness at their Hyderabad HQ. "What made me stick here for so long was the culture," explains Kolanu Reddy.

> We kept it open, there aren't too many of levels of bureaucracy. At any time, people can reach anyone; there is no hint of trying to suppress someone. We always have the opportunity or space to do what you think is best.

Initially, the founders tried to limit the flow of information, but they soon realized it was better for the employees to be more open, communicating the bad news along with the good. "Sometimes people don't like it, they always want to hear good things, but it is important that they know," said Anu.

The independently elected Sunshine Committee is responsible for organizing monthly employee events, including participation in 10-kilometer races, community service, poetry readings or dance events. "Typically, we work pretty hard, but we also have fun," says Anu. Twice a year, the Sunshine Committee hosts an all-day event for all employees, like a cricket match or a day at a resort, followed by a fun-filled awards ceremony; these biannual events last until 4 a.m.

The culture in the company's India offices has been more difficult to export to acquired offices, which have older employees. "In the beginning,

Figure 4.2 The New Ocimum Campus in Hyderabad, India
Source: Ocimum Biosolutions.

when we tried to do that in Gene Logic, we found the late night partying did not work there," Anu said with a laugh.

Anu is especially sensitive to the difficulties of being a woman in a male-dominated workplace. About 30 percent of Ocimum's Indian employees are women, and many of them are much quieter than their male counterparts. Anu aims to get them to be more assertive. Every Women's Day, she takes the women in the office out for a party. The all-female peer group emboldens the women: "Typically we find the behavior of the women to be very different when they are in this group."

Finally, Ocimum offers its employees generous marriage and maternity leave policies, with 3 months of paid maternity leave. "It's a very good place to work, especially for ladies. We have flexible office timings," says Jaishree Ravi, assistant vice president of quality systems and one of Ocimum's first employees. "If we have a PTA meeting to attend, I can go out and come back; all I have to do is log in nine hours of work."

The Fuzzy Divide between the Personal and Professional

"I know I have someone who is always there. I am getting all the support not just from a husband but also from a friend and partner," Anu intimated.

> Since he is my friend first, running the company together has been simpler. Whether it is personal or professional we know we have each other's support all the time. We don't have defined roles and we interchange always when required. That has always been the advantage for me. [3]

While the ambiguity in the definition of their roles might benefit Anu and Subash, employees mentioned that lack of clear job division creates the occasional difficulty in working for the husband-and-wife team. The swapping of responsibilities creates confusion about to whom employees should be reporting, and one half-joked, "I don't know who my boss is."

Help at home makes the entrepreneur's busy lifestyle manageable. A mother of two small girls, Neha and Akhila (aged 8 and 2), Anu says that they are used to her hectic travel schedule. "My kids now are pretty much used to the fact that I am not available half of the time." The family lives with Anu's in-laws, who help raise the girls.

"I sleep very little. In the last ten years, I haven't slept much," says Anu. "I like to do a lot of things. Sleep gets sacrificed. I sleep for four hours a night. I can go without sleep for a few days and be fine."

Looking Forward

In 2011, pharmaceutical companies in the U.S. faced the expiry of patents on ten blockbuster drugs that generated a total of US$50 billion in combined annual revenue. With a narrow R&D pipeline of potential replacements, the industry was undergoing massive layoffs (a total of over 100,000 jobs lost in 2009 and 2010), and drug companies have been forced to redesign their innovation streams.[4] According to Anu, this is obliging almost every pharmaceutical company to shift the way they do their trials and discovery, from using chemistry and more traditional means of looking for a protein for a blockbuster drug, to drug discovery for smaller portions of the population, or "personalized medicines."[5] Most pharmaceutical companies now run between 30 and 40 percent of current trials in that form, and are increasingly looking for partners in the R&D process. These developments may bring new opportunities to Ocimum. "Pharma companies need someone who can take them through the entire process," predicts Anu.

Over the past decade, Ocimum built its business on four very different products and services that serve different customers, with a variety of competitors, across the globe. Today, the company is readying itself to leverage that product diversity as the drug industry looks for more complete outsourcing solutions. With its unique array of products and services, Ocimum wants to position itself as a one-stop shop for bioresearch services, "a next-door lab that could provide services across the spectrum at the right time and a friendly price."[6] The intention of the RaaS strategy is to take the databases, samples, and IT that Ocimum currently offers individually, and package these as a complete solution. According to Anu, the move is timely as the industry shifts away from outsourcing pieces of drug discovery and development to outsourcing larger chunks of the process to an "outsourcing partner," and will allow pharmaceutical companies to reduce costs.

Anu lists the various advantages of such a partnership, including a reduction in drug development time and ultimately reducing time-to-market, lower costs from outsourcing to companies in India or China, and a reduction in risk by allowing pharmaceutical companies to extend their R&D pipelines.[7] In theory, Research as a Service (RaaS) would also ease the development process and facilitate project management by integrating multiple software platforms into a single interface for the user. "Researchers have to interact with many different vendors; it is a logistical and managerial nightmare," asserts Vinay Kumar, Ocimum's vice president. "The RaaS scenario is to have a researcher enter in requirements for the kind of study he wants to do, what he wants the final study to look like, and everything else is taken care of by Ocimum."

Anu plans to continue on the path of growth through acquisition. She aims to grow Ocimum to US$100 million a year in revenue over the next 5 years. Despite the tremendous growth of her company, Anu says she still hasn't reached the point where she feels successful, in spite of a series of awards and distinctions she has won over the years. In 2006 she was elected by *Red Herring Magazine* to the list of "25 Tech Titans under 35." In 2008 she was named by *Biospectrum* "Entrepreneur of the Year," and given the Astia Life Science Innovators Award; and in 2011 the World Economic Forum selected her as one of "190 Young Global Leaders."

QUESTIONS

1   Should Ocimum focus its growth in just one or two areas, or continue spreading its resources across four of them?

2   What are the advantages and disadvantages of a growth-by-acquisition strategy?

3   Should Anu surrender day-to-day decision making to a professional manager and focus her energies on strategy-making and on her young daughters?

Notes

1   *Biospectrum* magazine, December 2008, Biospectrumindia.com
2   *Biospectrum* magazine, December 2008, Biospectrumindia.com, p. 6.
3   *Biospectrum* magazine, December 2008, p. 54. "Drug Firms Face Billions in Losses in '11 as Patents End." *New York Times*, March 6, 2011.
4   Ibid.
5   Ibid.
6   Acharya, Anu. 2011. "Research as a Service (RaaS): Creating a New Trend." In *Pharmaceutical Outsourcing: Discovery and Preclinical Services*, ed. Marguerita Lim-Wilby and William C. Stevens, Jr. San Diego, CA: PharmaMedia, p. 4.
7   Ibid. p. 7.

5 Nej

Organic Apparel from Turkey

Alison Jonas

Her vision was to found a company that would design, make and market organic apparel free from pesticides or synthetic chemicals. Using the resources available in Turkey, the world's largest producer of organic cotton, Nejla Güvenç launched a business that does well while doing good. One of the most significant challenges she faced was to obtain funding. She came up with a creative way of securing it.

Figure 5.1 Nej Logo

Nestled in an unassuming walk-up in the fashionable district of Nişantaşi, Istanbul, Nej headquarters' demure exterior speaks to its soft-handed and philosophical approach to the otherwise cut-throat fashion business. Still, its roots in some of the most coveted real estate in the city—its neighbors include Topshop, Starbucks and a string of Fifth Avenue-caliber retail outlets—is a testament to the company's presence in the Turkish fashion market.

The Nej atelier boasts a spa-like ambiance, whisking one off of the boisterous streets and into an incense-infused oasis in a single breath. "I designed it myself," Nejla Güvenç—the company's founder and namesake —commented humbly, referring to the modern yet elegantly furnished office space and studio. Organic garments carefully placed by season, style and fabric line the wood-paneled walls. "Fashion design pervades all aspects of life—including interior design," Güvenç explained. Indeed, her simplistic yet artistic style is reflected in both the garments themselves and their surroundings.

Modest Beginnings: Foray into Fashion

Born in 1969 in Istanbul, Nejla was a gifted child artist and first learned of the design profession after seeing it in a movie in her youth. Though her parents envisioned a career in teaching for their daughter—she has an undeniable youthful exuberance—she had her sights set on fashion design at an early age. When it came time to pursue higher education, Nejla lived in Istanbul with her aunt while studying industrial design at the Anatolian Business Institute; at the time, the fashion design major did not yet exist. She later transferred to the Tasarı Fashion Design Institute to study fashion design at a location closer to her family.

After school, Nejla worked as a designer at Derishow from 1993 to 2000, then moved on to another prominent fashion house, Beymen, where she designed collections from 2000 to 2001. Still, despite her success at Beymen, Nejla craved more creative freedom. "I wanted to craft my own identity and audience," she recalled. She left her post in 2000 to become a freelance designer.

Birth of a Brand

Shortly after her departure from Beymen, Nejla began to satisfy her passion for all things pure by exploring the wave of organic fabrics that slowly appeared on the manufacturing scene. As the organic movement gained momentum, she was an early supporter and avid consumer of its products, citing the closeness with nature and the products' positive effects on the mind and soul.

Nejla defied the economic challenges most others in the retail sector faced given the economic crisis in the early 2000s; while reduced consumer spending plagued fashion behemoths across the globe, Nejla forged ahead with her dream of growing her own fashion empire. Years of building trust with manufacturers began to pay off, as many of the sourcing agents with whom she had worked at Derishow and Beymen began to reach out to Nejla with the hopes of collaborating on the establishment of her very own brand. Nejla finally settled on one manufacturing partner to launch her company with. The venture was aptly named Nej.

In 2002, after just one year of working exclusively with its manufacturing partner, the Nej company had sufficient funds to go out on its own and was officially established. Now the sole owner of the Nej company and no longer constrained by the manufacturer's production pressures, Nejla began marketing her clothes under the Nej brand, simultaneously forging partnerships with several other manufacturers. The creation of the brand itself grew out of consumer demand and requests for a Nej-inspired label— a promising indication of the brand's future growth potential.

The Nej brand is defined by its fashionable, high-quality organic designs (see Figure 5.2). The inspiration for this approach—admittedly more costly

Figure 5.2 Sample Pieces from the Nej Collection 2011
Source: Photos provided by Alison Jonas.

to produce and appealing to a smaller customer base—is rooted in Nejla's optimism about the future and the potential of the Turkish people, paired with an intrinsic appreciation for the arts.

"We would like to do something good for the next generation," Nejla said of her brand, referring to the eco-friendly organic fabrics used in all Nej apparel. Moreover, she cited the personal benefits one derives from organic apparel: "All the negative energy leaves when you wear organic." She further noted the antibacterial and ultraviolet-resistent nature of organic fabrics that lend themselves to indirect cancer prevention.

The Nej brand also stands for a series of paradoxes on a more abstract level. Nejla, a spiritual individual by nature, emphasized the broader implications for a brand which has grown out of Istanbul, located at the intersection of Europe and Asia, with deep roots as a center of ancient civilizations. "Our designs are taking inspiration from the past and inspiring the future . . . we think in opposites," she noted, referring to the juxtaposition of past/future and Europe/Asia. She continued to describe her designs "as a place where her philosophy and identity meets the old and the new, art and industry, simplicity and extravagance, fun and originality."

Ever the optimist with a seemingly unending arsenal of ambition, Nejla detailed her global ambitions for the Nej brand—ambitions which have been greatly influenced by her patriotism. "We are trying to establish a new Turkish image," she said, referring to the widespread political and economic perceptions of Turkey as a developing nation (a term which Nejla dislikes). "By erasing boundaries, we hope to discover the new Nej woman across the globe." Indeed, the brand seeks to defy historical prejudices against Turkish people and their capabilities, and to redefine the vast potential of this growing nation.

The Nej Woman

With this brand identity in mind, Nejla described the target customer as a chic global woman who expresses herself through her clothing and who can identify with cultures across the world. As a result, designs are not inspired in region or ethnicity, but rather geared towards a nomadic, global customer. "People—and Turkish people, especially—are nomadic; it is stamped on our souls," Nejla reflected. While most of her customers are currently from northern Europe—particularly Sweden and Switzerland —Nejla hoped to dramatically broaden the brand's reach over time. Indeed, she was confident about the brand's "stickiness" with consumers. "Once you wear organic, you never turn back," she said confidently, emphasizing the importance of forging a relationship with the consumer. The Nej customer seeks timeless designs that integrate harmonious color schemes, allowing the brand to find its niche in a neither high nor low fashion segment.

Organic Fabrics

According to the Organic Trade Association,

> cotton is considered the world's "dirtiest" crop due to its heavy use of insecticides, the most hazardous pesticides to human and animal health. Cotton covers 2.5 percent of the world's cultivated land yet uses 16 percent of the world's insecticides, more than any other single major crop.[1]

By contrast, organic fibers are those that are produced without the use of pesticides or synthetic chemicals, with organic cotton being the most common organic fiber. Organic advocates cite benefits of the reduced environmental impact and elimination of the harmful effects of pesticides on communities that organic production brings. In its 2010 *Global Report*, the Pesticide Action Network (PAN) cited the staggering statistics with regard to the impact of pesticides on human life:

> [C]hemicals, in particular pesticides, continue to have severe negative and unacceptable effects on the health of communities and the environ-ment, especially in developing countries. According to the World Health Organisation acute pesticide poisoning will affect three million people and account for 20,000 unintentional deaths each year.[2]

The Green Directory, Australia's authority on sustainability, echoed the grim statistics:

> It is estimated that less than 10 percent of the chemicals used on cotton actually serve the purpose of eliminating pests; the rest are absorbed into the plant, air, soil and water. Pesticides don't only harm the earth; statistics report that 60 percent of field workers in the cotton industry show symptoms of permanent poisoning.[3]

In light of the risks of conventional production methods, organic cotton production has experienced significant growth over the past decade, driven by increased consumer demand and brand commitment to "going green." According to the Organic Exchange, a non-profit that seeks to promote organic practices in the textile value chain, from 2001 to 2009 the organic cotton market experienced an average annual growth rate of 40 percent.[4] In 2007, 2008 and 2009, the market for organic cotton grew from $1.9 billion to $3.2 billion to $4.3 billion, respectively, with production in over twenty countries.[5]

The organization's 2009 *Farm and Fiber Report* further notes that, despite the global economic crisis, global organic cotton production grew 20 percent to 175,113 metric tons and 253,000 hectares in 2008–2009.[6] Turkey is the largest organic producer globally, according to the Organic Trade Association, followed by India and the U.S.[7]

In establishing a 100 percent organic business, finding affordable organic partners was a challenge for Nej. As a growing business, Nej initially could not afford the raw materials for its premium brand, and thus sought out three prominent organic fabric producers with whom the company could craft a mutually beneficial arrangement: Yesim Tekstil, Soktas and Bossa would provide complimentary fabrics for all of Nej's fashions, and in return Nej would distribute the producers' research studies (indeed, brochures are scattered throughout the Nej studio), promote the manufacturers at trade fairs and prominently display their labels on the finished goods. This arrangement has proved to be an extremely valuable component of Nej's operations and has lasted to this day. A fourth organic manufacturer, Mertipek, works with the brand as well, though Nej pays for the materials it uses, unlike its relationships with other producers.

Securing Funding

In Nej's infancy, an early source of funding that the company exploited to support its design business came through the consulting services that the company offered. In a major breakthrough for the brand, Nej was selected in 2002 to provide consulting services for Turquality, a government-sponsored development program. The program seeks to strengthen Turkish brands and "create a positive image of Turkish products"[8] by recommending "advisors" (i.e., consultants) to each selected brand. The campaign's slogan—"10 Brands in 10 Years"—is suggestive of its goal to promote ten local Turkish brands over the course of a decade.

After a thorough and highly competitive 1.5-year application process, Nej was selected for this consultant role. Nej benefits from its involvement in this initiative both financially and from a public relations perspective; brands receiving consulting services compensate Nej and in return are reimbursed by the government for the fee paid to Nej and other advisors. The funds that Nej has raised through this process have been critical in supporting the company's core design business, especially in its early years.

Between 2002 and 2004, Nej produced primarily for local Turkish boutiques in order to strengthen its brand name. Still, with long-term goals to broaden the brand's geographic reach, the Nej team needed additional funding to participate in the international trade fairs which are critical to securing orders and establishing relationships with distribution partners.

Securing government support was one of the most difficult aspects of growing the business in its infancy. Nejla recalled the impact of the Turkish economic landscape on the company's quest for funding.

> In Turkey, unlike in the U.S. and many other countries, support from banks or the government goes mostly to businesses at either end of the spectrum—those that are already well established, or industries that are very underdeveloped. There is no middle ground. So it's difficult to find funding if you are somewhere in between.

Despite this challenge, in 2003 Nej applied for government funding.

The year-long application process proved worthwhile, as Nej was just one of ten brands approved for funding by the General Secretariat of the Istanbul Textile and Apparel Exporters' Union (ITKIB) in 2004. Through ITKIB, approved brands such as Nej are able to gain funding to attend the trade shows which are so crucial to the growth and continuity of the business. ITKIB pays for half of the designers' costs of attending the fair, while the Foreign Commerce Undersecretariat of Turkey pays for the balance.

Through the support of ITKIB, Nej has secured enough financial backing to attend the costly international trade fairs that are invaluable opportunities to secure orders and establish distribution partnerships. While early orders were relatively small, Güvenç and her team were not discouraged, even accepting orders at a loss in order to forge relationships with customers. By virtue of the relatively small population of organic apparel consumers, the manufacturers that Nej could work with were limited to those that could accommodate smaller order quantities than the mass merchants required. Still, over time, order quantities increased significantly enough to yield a profit; Nej currently secures an average of fifteen orders per trade fair and institutes price and quantity minimums.

The company is able to avoid inventory carrying costs by operating on a make to order basis.

Marketing the Brand

Nej's marketing strategy, while somewhat unconventional, has served to bolster the brand's core customer base and solidify its stature as a premium label. Rather than choosing the direct advertising route, Nej markets its fashions primarily through interviews and participation in or sponsorship of public events. As Nejla noted, "Customers should feel the need to know us, rather than us finding them."

Güvenç has promoted the brand indirectly through appearances on television (she guest-judged the Turkish version of *Project Runway*), radio (she recently launched her very own talk show), digital media and parties. Moreover, appearances at trade fairs in Paris, Tokyo and Berlin as well as Istanbul are utilized to educate potential future customers about the virtues of organic apparel.

Nej has also been quick to leverage digital media, building up a robust Facebook page with frequent updates on the brand. The company's own website was still under development in 2011, though Nejla does not foresee e-commerce becoming a main pillar of the company's business model, as the company's make to order model does not allow for carrying inventory.

Organic fabrics are generally known to be priced at a premium relative to conventional fabrics due to their more costly production process, but supporters of organic cite the long-term environmental and personal benefits of organic fibers in justifying their higher price.[9] Nej is no exception to this practice; its fashions are premium-priced, partially by virtue of their higher production costs compared to non-organic apparel, and partially to maintain an exclusivity around the brand.

Nej currently enjoys a strong position in the Turkish organic apparel market; no other fashion house produces 100 percent organic, and Güvenç estimated that her closest competitors produce only 5 percent organic. The brand's strong point of differentiation and its unique philosophy render it well positioned to compete in a market which will likely see more saturation in the next several decades. Still, Nejla acknowledged the virtues of competition in growing the figurative pie: "Rivals are good because it will make us better known—there may be strength in numbers. We are just one color of the rainbow."

Nejla and her brand have gradually built a growing international following with a particularly strong presence in northern Europe and Japan, due in large part to the brand's growing presence at trade shows, festivals and fashion weeks across the globe. Her collections have been successfully launched in Turkey, France, England, Sweden, Portugal, Denmark, Greece, Benelux, Israel and Korea. Nejla's popularity as a designer has grown so much that she is known in celebrity circles and has clothed the likes of Madonna. She is an administrative board member of the Turkey Fashion and Ready-to-Wear Federation and an administrative member of the Fashion Designer's Association of Turkey.

The Nej consulting practice has also grown considerably, providing trend reports to customers, brand consulting and collection consulting for clients such as Zara (Spain), Zapa (Paris), Ecru (Paris), Rogan (New York), Chrisjansenes (Brussels), Iro (Paris), Gloria Estelles (Spain), Pierre Cardin (Paris), Hugo Boss (Germany), Gap (USA), Nike (USA), Banana Republic (USA), Massimo Dutti (Spain), and Nergis Holding (Yesim Tekstil San.Tic. A.S.) (Turkey).

The Future of Nej

Well aware of the intense scrutiny with which consumers now evaluate their purchases, Nejla attributed her fashions' high quality and timeless style to their continued success at a time when customers are cutting back on retail expenditures. Nej's strong relationships with its customers and the philosophical influence in its designs, she explained, have helped the brand weather the storm.

While nearly all businesses have been hit by the recent global economic crisis, Nejla remained confident about her company's resilience. "Opportunities are born out of crises," she noted, reflecting the trials of her own career and the criticism she endured upon leaving Beymen. "There's a French saying that artists' lives are difficult because being creative happens in times of crisis." Indeed, Nej's success demonstrates that past trials have only served to spur the growth that the company has experienced over the past decade.

While Nejla is passionate about the virtues of organic materials, she acknowledged that it would not be realistic for organic materials to penetrate all consumer product categories. Nevertheless, she hopes to expand her fashions to include organic sleepwear, lingerie, swimwear, and possibly fragrances. "It balances your energy while you're sleeping," she explained of organic sleepwear.

"The brand is like your baby," Nejla reflected with an infectious smile, as she sipped a Turkish coffee. "The workplace is like a marriage—for better or worse, you stick with it." Indeed, this determination to prevail explains much of her success in growing Nej over the past decade. Nejla cited her relationships with family, friends and her trusted employees as the main pillars of her success and the drivers behind her ability to compete in the cut-throat fashion business. Unsurprisingly, she also considered interpersonal difficulties—and not necessarily competition or other external market factors—the biggest challenge in growing a business. Still, she cringed at the thought of her business as an "accomplishment," explaining that to say something is an accomplishment is to imply it is finished—

and she is always trying to do more. Her greatest fear is that life will not be long enough to realize her dream of growing the brand to compete with the likes of Chanel, LVMH and other world-renowned fashion houses.

"At the end of each day," Nejla reflected,

> I think about what I did for the brand and for myself today. My personal life is inseparable from the brand. If I can't find something good that I did, I get sad—but in a positive way. I know I can do bigger and better things.

For now, those bigger and better things mean focusing on key near-term goals for the Nej brand, such as establishing a stronger presence in the Japanese and northern European markets, expanding into new organic product categories, and reconciling the make-to-order business model to an increasingly e-commerce-oriented marketplace.

QUESTIONS

1   Would you recommend Nejla's funding strategy to other entrepreneurs?
2   Do you think Nej should continue to be a small niche market player or target the broader mass market?
3   Should Nej launch other apparel lines to complement its existing offerings?

Notes

1   Organic Trade Association (www.ota.com/organic/environment/cotton_environment. html).
2   Pesticide Action Network, *2010 Global Report* (www.pan-international.org/ panint/files/PAN-Global-Report.pdf).
3   The Green Directory (www.thegreendirectory.com.au/clothing/organic-cotton-clothing/organic-cotton-clothing.html).
4   Organic Exchange, *Annual Report 2009* (http://organicexchange.org/oecms/images/ stories/publications/OE_Annual_Report_2009.pdf).
5   Organic Exchange, 2008 and 2009 annual reports (http://organicexchange.org/ oecms/images/stories/publications/OE_Annual_Report_2009.pdf).
6   Organic Exchange, *2009 Farm and Fiber Report* (http://organicexchange.org/oecms/ images/stories/publications/OE_Annual_Report_2009.pdf).
7   Organic Trade Association website (www.ota.com/organic/mt/organic_cotton. html).
8   Republic of Turkey, "Turquality," www.turquality.com
9   Harmony Art, "Why Harmony Art Organic Cotton?," www.harmonyart.com/ organic-textiles/OrganicVSConventional.html

6 Café Helena

Not Your Average Cup of Coffee

María Fernanda Trigo

Coffee was Maria Helena Monteiro's passion. Although she lacked the expertise to run a plantation and market the product, she risked her family's savings and lived far from her husband and daughters to pursue her dream. She learned the growing and roasting techniques, the best ways to organize and lead her employees, and how to differentiate the product. She is one of a handful of female Brazilian coffee entrepreneurs.

In 1999 Maria Helena Monteiro decided to follow her dream and become an entrepreneur, even though this meant living 4 hours away by car from her husband and daughters. She was committed to cultivating her dream in a traditionally male-dominated industry, coffee growing. Her native Brazil is the world's largest producer, with a long and proud history of coffee growing, roasting, and exporting.

The coffee business was not new to Maria Helena. She grew up on her grandfather's country estate during the military dictatorship of the 1960s and early 1970s. She studied at the College of Social Sciences at the State University of São Paulo (UNESP) in the city of Araraquara, where she met her future husband. They moved to São Paulo in 1974, and she embarked on her career as a professor. A year later she joined a multinational human resources firm, where she had a stellar career, starting as a recruiter and working her way up to partner. Her tenure included a 9-year-long assignment in Rio de Janeiro. She left the firm in 1998.

Maria Helena remembers wanting to own Monte Alto, her grandfather's estate, from an early age because of her emotional attachment to the land. Monte Alto had produced coffee until the early 1950s. Growing up there, Maria Helena saw her grandfather become a prominent coffee exporter. In time, Monte Alto stopped producing coffee and switched to growing cotton and other crops. Later, Maria Helena's grandfather divided the land among his children and grandchildren.

Maria Helena began by buying her father's share. He gladly sold it to her because he no longer had the financial resources needed to work the land, which had been degraded by continuous cultivation. She then purchased the rest of the land from family members with the savings she and her husband had accumulated during their careers. Today the estate encompasses 242 hectares, most of which are devoted to cultivating coffee, while a small part still functions as a farm.

After acquiring the land, Maria Helena was ready to pursue her dream, "to revive the old and forgotten coffee tradition in the region."[1] While she grew up surrounded by coffee leaves, she was not well versed in agribusiness. She encountered a general lack of support among the coffee experts she contacted and was derided by those in the industry for being a novice. As she recalls, "Criticism filled the streets of the town with the general belief being that I was wasting my family resources in an industry that formed part of the past of the region, not the future."[2]

Monte Alto is in the municipality of Dourado, located in the state of São Paulo, 270 kilometers from the capital, between the cities of São Carlos, Jaú, Araraquara, and Brotas.[3] The town was founded around 1880 and became known as the Heart City because of its heightened import-ance in the coffee industry during the 1890s. By the time it had attained political independence in 1897, electricity, paved roads, potable water, and the railroad had all come to the town.[4] When coffee prices plummeted in the wake of the 1929 crash, all the plantations in the region switched from growing coffee to planting more profitable crops such as cotton and corn.[5]

Early Challenges

Despite her lack of agricultural experience, Maria Helena enthusiastically embraced the tasks of managing the planting, farming, collecting, process-ing, distribution, and commercialization of coffee. She had few reference points to follow in the region, as it no longer produced this product. She hired technical advisors and struggled to find an administrator who could run the entire operation for her. However, her first lesson, she says, was to recognize that things worked better when she was present. Thus, she decided, with her family's support, to leave the city and move 4 hours away to administer the business on the estate before her money ran out and her dream vanished. She dismissed the administrator and the agron-omist she had hired and spent the next 4 months immersed in reading about coffee and learning when and how to plant and collect and how to grade and sort the beans. She recalls,

> With total dedication I began conquering my space and learning more each day. . . . I grew accustomed to being out in the sun, in the rough style of the rural people, to live without my family, my daughters, who many times phoned because they needed something. . . . I would finish the conversation with my heart in my hands.

Ultimately, her venture would not have succeeded without her being on site and involved with everything. She advises, "Be always present, participating in every activity, overseeing everything that has been established. . . . It is necessary to be dedicated, persistent, and committed to your objectives." She adds that "a key factor is to ensure the buy-in of the professionals and employees involved in the business."[6]

Maria Helena's next challenge was to gain the respect and commitment of the workers. Because the region's agriculture was focused on other crops, it was difficult for her to hire experienced workers to plant, grow, and collect the coffee grains. The few she could find were startled to see a woman running the business, especially one with little knowledge about growing coffee. Suppliers were also hard to come by because most doubted the sustainability of her coffee plantation. Maria Helena explains that most rural people preferred to work on orange farms, the new predominant crop in the region.

To overcome these challenges and to become more attuned to her laborers' needs, Maria Helena sought help from the rural workers' union. Then she personally trained the workers on how to collect the coffee grains as a way of motivating them and gaining their commitment. She remembers using a great deal of dialogue, attention, and care. Over time her efforts paid off, as new workers began showing up on their own. She admits it took at least 3 years before she finally felt more secure and knowledgeable about the coffee industry.

Growing Pains

A turning point for Maria Helena's aspirations came with her first harvest. Coffee prices had fallen on the world market, causing her to rethink her strategy and seek an alternative way to add value to her product if she were to recover her steep investment in the land. She took her inspiration from the fact that, while Brazil is both the largest coffee producer and one of the largest consumer markets, the majority of Brazilians do not drink high-quality coffee. In fact, the consultancy Euromonitor International found that most coffee drinkers in Brazil consume standard and economy brands because of a widely held belief that all coffee types are essentially the same, a perception that resulted from the popularization of the product.[7]

According to a report by the U.S. Department of Agriculture, Brazil sometimes accounts for about a third of the world's coffee output.[8] The majority of Brazilian exports are green beans, which are a commodity. Therefore, their large volume generates little value. As Maria Helena explains, green coffee grains are usually sold to international roasting companies, which then process and mix them with other grains and market the final product under their own brands at higher prices. For instance, while traditional green grains sold in 2005 for US$50 for a 60-kilogram sack, gourmet coffee sold for up to US$245 a sack.[9]

In 1999 the Brazilian Specialty Coffee Association (BSCA), with the support of the Ministry of Agriculture, began to promote the production of high-quality coffee through contests and other types of programs.[10] Recently, the Brazilian Coffee Industry Association (ABIC) launched two new initiatives—the Sustainable Coffee in Brazil Program and the Quality Coffee Circle Program—aimed at increasing coffee consumption and promoting the production of fine and gourmet coffees in the country.[11] Because gourmet coffees are up to twice as expensive as standard brands, sales of these products are marketed to higher-income consumers.[12]

There are two major coffee varieties in the global market: arabica and robusta. Arabica beans are used primarily in the production of gourmet coffee. This variety originated in Arabia, as its name suggests. It grows better in mineral-rich dirt at high elevations and produces a full-bodied and full-flavored coffee with a rather low caffeine content.[13] Differentiation in taste is achieved through different crop varieties. In contrast, robusta beans grow quickly at low elevations, have double the caffeine content of arabica beans, and, if overproduced, can have a bitter taste.[14]

Maria Helena's Monte Alto estate (Figure 6.1) is well-suited for growing arabica beans. The plantation is at an altitude of 705–732 meters. During the summer, the temperatures range from 18°C at night to 30°C during the day (64–86°F). In winter, they range from 6°C at night to 20°C during the day (43–68°F). The region also enjoys plentiful rain, which eliminates the need for irrigation systems. In addition, four lakes surround the estate, providing even more natural sources of water that form into streams. Finally, the terrain is rich in red dirt.

Figure 6.1 Monte Alto Plantation
Source: Maria Helena Monteiro.

Deciding to focus on gourmet coffee because she did not want to simply produce a commodity without any added value, Maria Helena opted to produce four varieties of high-quality coffee from 100 percent arabica beans: Red Catuaí, Yellow Catuaí, Acaiá, and Obatã. She makes three blends with arabica beans and two blends with coffee cherry exclusively.

Coffee cherry refers to the coffee seed that forms the pit of a coffee cherry. The cherries are collected when they are ripe and bright red in color.[15] The pulp and mucus are removed, and the seeds are either set to dry or sent to a fermentation tank. They are then sorted by density—the greater the density, the better the quality.[16]

As Maria Helena explains, gourmet coffee is appraised and classified in a way akin to wine, mostly on the basis of body, flavor, bitterness, and sweetness. Good marketing, promotion, and distribution can fetch much higher prices.

Using one of the coffee cherry blends, Maria Helena developed her own brand: Café Helena. She gave it her name and added to the logo the year 1813, when the plantation was originally founded. Thus, Monte Alto plantation first began by just growing and harvesting and then added roasting, grinding, and packaging under Maria Helena's leadership. She invested close to BRL3 million (US$1.4 million) to equip the plantation for the roasting, grinding, and packaging processes.[17] The bulk of her output is exported by a third party. She also sells her branded coffee through distributors around São Paulo. In addition, she has developed a website (www.cafehelena.com.br) with an eye to selling her coffee online.

Maria Helena faces intense competition, as Brazil's coffee industry is very fragmented and regionalized. According to Euromonitor International, in 2007 there were 1,229 coffee companies and 2,512 brands in Brazil. About half these companies are located in the southeastern states of Minas Gerais and São Paulo.[18] According to the Coffee Industry Union of the state of São Paulo, in 2005 the state accounted for 43 percent of ground and roasted coffee—approximately 40 million coffee sacks.[19] The three leading multi-national players—Sara Lee, Melina, and Nestlé—together had a 28 percent share of the retail volume in the Brazilian market in 2008.[20] The Pilão brand, from Sara Lee, leads in retail volume and value according to 2008 data. In addition, a survey conducted by the Qualibest Institute reported that this brand has the highest consumer awareness.[21]

The Market for Quality Coffee

Maria Helena's decision to focus on gourmet coffee dovetails with the general trend in the market. Consolidation among the leading players has driven smaller domestic competitors to invest in fine and gourmet coffees to sustain profitability. High value-added coffee has enormous growth potential in Brazil because there is no dominant gourmet brand on the market.[22] Maria Helena has organized several meetings to attract more coffee growers to produce gourmet coffee. Her efforts have contributed to an increase in the number of specialty coffee producers in her region—from six to eleven.[23] In the future, she would like to see the formation of a "Coffee Club" to recognize the central part of São Paulo as a region that produces high-quality coffee.

Retail sales of coffee are predicted to grow in the Brazilian market by 6 percent annually between 2008 and 2013, with arabica and fresh coffee beans expected to show the fastest growth.[24] Specialty coffee shops in Brazil—such as Starbucks, Suplicy Cafés Especiais, Nespresso, and Espressamente Illy—are stimulating the consumption of fine and gourmet coffees in both the on-trade and off-trade channels.[25] Thus, consumer preferences are changing, with more people wanting to taste different varieties of coffee and then buying the beans or ground coffee at supermarkets or specialty shops to replicate the experience at home.[26] As a result, the appearance of more on-trade outlets will play a key role in stimulating the consumption of gourmet coffee.

Coffee growers and producers have invested in new distribution centers and signed agreements to offer more regionalized products and to expand points of sale by extending their reach in supermarkets.[27] As more consumers search for new flavors for home consumption, supermarkets are dedicating more shelf space to gourmet coffee.[28] For instance, in Pão de Açúcar, a prominent Brazilian supermarket chain, half the shelf space assigned to coffee is now occupied by fine and gourmet brands; and the supermarket has launched Qualitá, its own private gourmet label.[29] The chain is also developing new marketing strategies to support the gourmet coffee sales. For example, it has created an exclusive website dedicated to improving consumers' knowledge of fine and gourmet coffees.[30]

Euromonitor International reports that there are two growth opportunities in the Brazilian coffee industry. The increasing demand for espresso coffee machines has prompted manufacturers to offer a wider portfolio of higher-quality products to cater to affluent consumers, the only ones who are in a position to purchase the relatively expensive machines. The rapidly expanding college population also offers new opportunities for specialty coffee.[31] According to ABIC, most coffee consumers tend to be adults aged 36 and older. Younger consumers prefer creamy beverages such as cappuccino and mocha.

Looking to the Future

Maria Helena's efforts received national recognition when, in 2005, she was acknowledged as Brazil Woman Entrepreneur of the Year by SEBRAE, a government agency that provides support to micro- and small enterprises. She remembers crying when, at the time, she wrote the story of her journey to entrepreneurship. She called it, "Past and Future in a Cup of Coffee."

Maria Helena's most important challenge continues to be further developing brand recognition. One of her current strategies includes developing partnerships with manufacturers of espresso machines as a way of encouraging coffee-shop and restaurant owners to carry Café Helena. In the meantime, she sells the unroasted and unbranded coffee from Monte Alto to distributors for export to international markets, where it is processed and sold by roasting companies. Ideally, she would like to export her branded coffee to markets such as the U.S., where demand for gourmet coffee is high and growing rapidly.

She has considered different channels, mainly selling through a distributor. However, language barriers and her lack of knowledge of international markets make her wary of embarking on internationalizing her brand at this point. She is not sure if she should pursue foreign markets at all or just focus all her resources and efforts on expanding her share of the Brazilian market.

Maria Helena's future plans also include entering the field of "rural tourism." However, she does not envision transforming the plantation into a hotel. Rather, she wants to give visitors to the region the opportunity to experience life on an authentic coffee plantation. She has been careful to preserve the traditions of the plantation while incorporating modern techniques. The high ceilings, century-old walls, and antique balconies, tables, and wooden chairs in the main building make for a warm and inviting environment that recreates the period of the old coffee plantations.

This project is still in its implementation phase. Maria Helena plans to offer a tour around the entire plantation, beginning at the coffee plants, moving to the roasting and sorting areas, stopping in the family's solar room, and ending in a cafeteria where visitors can taste—and purchase—the different coffee varieties. She envisions offering other regional food products, as well as magazines and books providing information about the culture surrounding coffee. She is seeking partnerships with artisans in the region to promote this type of tourism. While she acknowledges this new endeavor falls outside the realm of her expertise, she believes tourism will provide added support to coffee plantations and hotels in the region.

QUESTIONS

1 Did Maria Helena do the right thing in leaving her husband and children to pursue her dream of becoming entrepreneur?
2 Was her decision to focus on specialty coffee the correct one?
3 Given that the Brazilian economy is growing very quickly, should she abandon her plans to pursue foreign markets?

Notes

1 Interview with Maria Helena Monteiro Alves in São Paulo, Brazil, by María Fernanda Trigo Alegre, May 21, 2009.
2 Ibid.
3 Prefeitura Municipal de Dourado, "Prefeitura de Dourado Responsabilidade de Todos," April 2010, www.dourado.sp.gov.br (accessed April 10, 2010).
4 Ibid.
5 Ali Ahmad Hassan, "Um Toque Femenino No Agronegocio," in *Historias de Successo. Mulheres Empreendedoras Pequenas Empresas Região Sudeste*. Brasilía, Brazil: SEBRAE, 2006, pp. 17–34.
6 Interview with Maria Helena Monteiro Alves.
7 Coffee—Brazil: Country Sector Briefing, Euromonitor International, September 2009.
8 U.S. Department of Agriculture, "Coffee: World Markets and Trade," Circular Series, June 2009, http://ww2.fas.usda.gov/htp/coffee/2009/June_2009/2009_Coffee_June.pdf (accessed April 18, 2010).
9 Ali Ahmad Hassan, "O Passado e o Futuro na Xícara de Café," in *Batons, Sonhos e Determinação. Jeitos Femeninos de Empreender*. São Paulo, Brazil: SEBRAE, 2, 2005–2006, pp. 12–19.
10 Hassan, "Um Toque Femenino No Agronegocio," pp. 17–34.
11 Coffee—Brazil: Country Sector Briefing.
12 Ibid.
13 Coffee Basics, "Front Porch Coffee and Tea Company," November 21, 2006, www.elysfrontporch.com/coffeebasics.html (accessed December 11, 2009).
14 Ibid.
15 Reg Coffey, "Coffey's Coffee—The Dark Side of Coffee," n.d., www.coffeyscoffee.com/thecoffees.html (accessed December 11, 2009).
16 Coffee Basics, "Front Porch Coffee and Tea Company."
17 Interview with Maria Helena Monteiro Alves.
18 Coffee—Brazil.
19 Hassan, "Um Toque Femenino No Agronegocio," pp. 17–34.
20 Coffee—Brazil.
21 Ibid.
22 Ibid.
23 Hassan,"Um Toque Femenino No Agronegocio," pp. 17–34.
24 Coffee—Brazil.
25 Ibid.
26 Ibid.
27 Ibid.
28 Ibid.
29 Ibid.
30 Ibid.
31 Coffee—Brazil.

Part II

Growing the Business

Research indicates that businesses owned by women tend to grow less rapidly than those owned by men, especially in developing countries and emerging economies. The difference is due to the fact that women often run their businesses out of the household, have difficulties accessing finance during the early stages of growth, are limited in their networks of contacts, and face tougher tradeoffs when balancing family and work (see Chapter 23 for a summary of the research findings). In this section we will see how a South African airline businesswoman, a Brazilian restaurateur, an Argentine tour operator, a Mexican media personality turned entrepreneur, and a Chinese digital-media geek managed to overcome the various challenges confronting them as they strived to grow their businesses.

7 Sibongile Sambo and SRS Aviation

Dalila Boclin

In spite of having no experience in the industry, Sibongile Sambo dreamed of founding an aviation company in South Africa. After years as a human resources manager, she secured a small amount of money from her family and established a company to broker contracts between aviation companies and clients. Soon thereafter she started to charter flights and lease airplanes, mostly for cargo. Her background loomed large when reflecting on her entrepreneurial voyage and thinking about the importance of networking, mentoring, and leading.

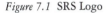

Figure 7.1 SRS Logo

For some people, the sky is the limit; for Sibongile Sambo, it was the frontier.

It is hard to imagine a time when Sibongile, founder and CEO of a burgeoning aviation company, would wave at airplanes overhead, hoping some gazing passenger would see her and wave back. Her story paints a picture of how a child's curiosity is more than a set of questions and answers, but also a seed of motivation that when nurtured with determination and passion, can flower into a life filled with success and dreams come true.

SRS Aviation, South Africa's first and only fully empowered, Black-woman-owned-and-operated airborne services business, flew its first flight in 2004. However, its foundation was laid years before the idea of a woman-owned corporation was even legal in South Africa. Sibongile grew up with a curiosity about airplanes—from how they were built to where they were going—fueling an aspiration to one day be more than just a spectator on the ground. Early in her life she began to chip away at the boundaries between herself and aviation. She laughed as she reminisced about her teenage demands on her parents: "I would actually force them to put me on a plane once a year so I could have a ride on an airplane." Those rides, she claimed, provided the momentum that carried her passion and interest for airplanes into her adulthood.

Background

After the treacherous reign of apartheid, Nelson Mandela dedicated his presidency to reforming South Africa. He worked to rectify social injustices, grounded in the nation's infamous past, and produced sweeping social reforms. His government did not try to simply overwrite the nation's harsh past; rather, in establishing the Truth and Reconciliation Commission (TRC), Mandela attempted to peacefully incorporate apartheid's history and influence into South Africa's national narrative and identity. The TRC's success is evident in the people: after 1994 political violence decreased dramatically and had virtually disappeared by 1996.[1]

The African National Congress inherited remarkable political, economic, and cultural challenges when it assumed power and took over from the tyrannical apartheid government. In 1994 South Africa was a country marked by racial segregation, unemployment, widespread poverty, and poor health and education. Since then the country has made incredible strides in improving economic and living standards.[2] To meet the enormous challenges, the Reconstruction and Development Program was created to improve living conditions and integrate marginalized groups into the population, providing housing and basic civic services, education, and health care to disadvantaged individuals.[3]

In an attempt to revitalize the South African economy, the new government paired this domestic social spending with a pronounced commitment to neoliberal free markets and privatization through the Growth, Employment and Redistribution (GEAR) strategy.[4] GEAR reduced the budget deficit and stabilized inflation, giving birth to a "healthy, robust, and resilient" banking system and providing the nation with the stable financial infrastructure it needed to flourish.[5] Despite these gains, formal employment issues of limited opportunity and mobility for the black population, as well as the racially biased distribution of the country's wealth, continued to plague the nation.[6] To combat this inequality, South Africa passed the Black Economic Empowerment Act (2003)[7] to try to assimilate the black community into South Africa's growing market. Following the fall of apartheid, South Africa embarked on a new chapter in its history: from social welfare to economic enfranchisement, the nation reborn was able to nurture its people and produce stunning achievements such as the case of Sibongile Sambo.

Starting Slow

Sibongile first attempted to break into aviation as a flight attendant but was always limited by the height minimum most airlines required. As luck would have it, her first job offer coincided with her first cabin-crew application. In 1997 South Africa's national airline offered her a position as a flight attendant on domestic flights on smaller aircraft with smaller cabins. Following advice from her family, she declined this long-awaited opportunity and decided to fall back on her degree in human resources, reserving her true goal for a later date.

Sibongile spent the next 7 years in human resources, working for SA Telkom and DeBeers, until the time was ripe for her entry into the aviation industry. In 2003 the post-apartheid state passed the Black Economic Empowerment Act, enabling people from previously disadvantaged backgrounds to enter and participate in economic life as entrepreneurs. Through the Women's Economic Empowerment Policy, which aimed to economically enfranchise South Africa's poorest group—its women—Sibongile felt ready to break out not only from human resources, but also from life as an employee.

Taking Off

In 2004 Sibongile invited her sister to be a partner in her quest to own an aviation firm. Investing in aircraft, however, required tremendous amounts of capital, to which neither Sibongile nor her sister had access. Sibongile did not take on any formal debt to finance her project; rather, she relied on the people who had always supported her life-long dream: her family. Sibongile's mother and aunt lent her the money she needed for SRS to take off. Still, with such limited funds and no experience, she was not disposed to buying or leasing her own planes. Rather, this small family loan enabled her to broker contracts between aviation services and those with air-transport needs.

SRS found its first opportunity with a government tender, which invited aviation firms to bid on a contract for cargo transport. The contract was ceded as a joint venture to SRS and another firm. Although a collaborative project appeared as a golden opportunity to wade into the industry, the other firm soon withdrew from the contract, leaving an untrained Sibongile to learn the contracting process on her own.

> It was very challenging, I had to learn the different background operational needs before a flight. I had to call around and find out from different people what I needed to do. Even the clients themselves assisted me because they had run [similar] contracts before.

Sibongile reflected on the challenge of this initially stressful situation as a tremendous learning experience that quickly gave her the knowledge she needed to navigate the industry.

Sibongile could have entered into aviation cautiously by becoming a flight attendant and learning gradually through observation, but her journey led, instead, to a bold entry as an owner with her own agency. Listening to her story of how she learned the process of chartering flights, it becomes clear how that same initiative was responsible for propelling her along the steep learning curve of the aviation industry. Neither the industry nor her company could accommodate a slow trial-and-error learning strategy.

> I had to actually spend time with different people who were willing to teach me how to run this business. I had to ask around in the industry. Some contractors didn't want to help, but others were more than willing to assist me. It was a matter of approaching people.

These informal teachers helped Sibongile learn the details of organizing a flight: from giving her leads to telling her which clearances she needed and where and how to get them, to knowing how much fuel a particular type of aircraft needed, these informal mentors guided SRS through a smooth take-off and landing.

Finding a Niche

SRS operated a model different from conventional airlines by tapping into the economic potential of airplanes on the ground: "An aircraft on the ground is money down the drain," Sibongile said. SRS evolved from its earliest model of brokering contracts, to leasing airplanes as it needed them. Most of SRS's contracts involved moving cargo, which, Sibongile explained, returned a greater profit in a shorter time, and with less of a headache than moving people. As a result, SRS did not generally encounter competition with commercial airlines; rather, their models complemented one another, as SRS employed standing aircraft that would otherwise be absorbing money. However, SRS did contract to transport people when returns were high enough: a small percentage of the business was contracted with exclusive travelers, who chartered SRS's private jets rather than purchasing a first-class seat with a commercial airline. This type of contract varies more compared to standard cargo transport: since the economic downturn in 2007, SRS has lost some of its business chartering private jets, as people have opted more prudently for first-class tickets. Cargo, on the other hand, has remained relatively stable, experiencing only a minor decline in 2007, with contracts resuming relative normalcy in 2008.

After merely a year of brokering flights, Sibongile's eager entrepreneurial spirit emerged again, and so began the first steps of her company's growth.

SRS managed to accumulate capital early on by maintaining very low overhead costs, with only four employees and no office space. Sibongile applied for licenses to become a full operator in the industry, which would authorize SRS to actually contract and pilot its own flights, promoting it from a go-between to a true player in the game. As a charter company, SRS had not been responsible for the flights themselves, but was concerned mainly with marketing, securing clients, and negotiating with licensed airlines and, ultimately, applying a mark-up and handing off the client. With Pat 121, 135, and 127 licenses, Sibongile's company leased aircraft under its own title and bore responsibility for all the logistical arrangements, from managing fuel to pilots' learners' permits. Although SRS progressed mainly to using leased aircraft, from time to time it provided some purely brokering services. Sibongile hoped to eventually move to a Fleet Management Model, by which she would contract with various fleets to maximize the utilization of their aircraft. Instead of leasing individual planes according to demands for transport, larger airline companies would contract with SRS to manage their fleets, in full or in part, out of South Africa. With more aircraft under SRS's control, the Fleet Management Model would grant Sibongile much greater leverage in negotiating the comprehensive costs of commissioning a flight.

SRS's clientele ranged from corporate or government work, to heads of state, to animal lifting, and beyond—"Anything and everything an airplane or helicopter can do . . . besides military work!" The majority of her contracts were made with the public sector, moving mostly cargo and flying within the African continent. SRS had no legal boundaries to what or where it could fly; 90 percent of its business took place predominately within the African continent, the other 10 percent comprised occasional flights to Europe, the United States, Asia, or the Middle East.

Sibongile's unique attitude and ability facilitated her success as an entrepreneur.

> I didn't fear anything. Inside, I was confident that I wanted to get into aviation. I love it. I've done enough research, and I think I would be able to make it in the industry. No, it wasn't easy, but because of the love and passion I have, I've persevered.

Resources Scarce and Plentiful: Financial and Human Capital

During her 7 years working as a human resources manager, although technically an employee, Sibongile assumed a leadership role and always worked above the standard, winning awards and recognition for her exceptional work. However, what stood out most, even as she was describing her time as an employee, was that she regarded it not as a deviation from her true goal, but as a constructive and integrated experience on the path toward aviation. This unique openness to learning and growing distinguished Sibongile as a natural leader. "Taking up that corporate job in 1997 in HR was a very good decision, because I do believe that I needed that corporate foundation to venture into entrepreneurship." She learned many critical skills about how best to manage people and decode human behavior. "When you run a company, your biggest assets are the people that work for you. My career in HR actually helped me to transition into an entrepreneurship role."

Moreover, working in human resources also gave Sibongile the opportunity to learn about herself. "I discovered that I'm actually more of an entrepreneur than a corporate person, and I came to that conclusion because of the natural characteristics that I have." Every year she discovered qualities about herself that magnified her desire to eventually have her own aviation firm.

> I come up with ideas very quick[ly], I see opportunities where most people might not necessarily see an opportunity, and I really get frustrated when I have to do one and the same thing all the time. I get frustrated when I come up with a new idea, and I want that idea to be tested and implemented, but it just gets blocked without even testing.

Ultimately, Sibongile learned as much as she could from human resources until she felt it was stifling her growth: "I was not being given an opportunity to unleash my full potential."

Not everything came as naturally as Sibongile's ability to lead. Aviation is a very challenging field and particularly capital-intensive. "One of the biggest challenges which we are still faced with today is capital and cash flow within the business." Despite the post-freedom economic reforms, entering the market was by no means seamless. "We were more like a guinea pig, I would say, within South Africa, as a small company looking for a big loan." Financial institutions would react with reservation to Sibongile's plan:

> "Aviation is risky," they would tell us. We've still never had any official funding, but because of my passion and my love and my vision for this business, I decided that I was not going to let that stop me from achieving my dreams and my goals.

Access to credit remained especially difficult for black women. Only 38 percent were bankrolled, compared to 44 percent of black men, 91 percent of white women, and 94 percent of white men.[8]

Sibongile met this challenge with the true resources she had on hand: She created a network of family members and friends willing to lend her money, promising to pay them back with interest within a reasonable period of time. SRS continued to rely on that lifeline. "It is not at all the most convenient way of running a business—it's very stressful and cumbersome to follow people to get them to lend you money." Business growth did not ameliorate but, rather, exacerbated this issue: the more flights SRS had on order, the more money it needed to operate the business. There was an even greater demand for money, and still investors were weary.

Despite Sibongile's resourcefulness, SRS had to turn away some projects because the company lacked sufficient capital. However, Sibongile did not see this financial model as conclusive for SRS.

> The network hasn't stopped me from looking for bigger investors. Right now I am working with consultants to package the company to attract investors. I've waited this long to create [a] strong foundation and something that is attractive to the investor: now, we're ready to go out to formal financial institutions [and] private or organizational investors to look for funding.

In 2007 Sibongile began strategizing with an external board of directors—comprising financial consultants, legal professionals, and marketers—to plan and direct the expansion of SRS. Although she was not ready to disclose any specific plans, Sibongile saw expanding her presence outside Africa as a possibility for growth. Her business flourished in Africa, where there were still a relatively limited number of aviation firms. Sibongile noted that there were several similar companies, but not that many—especially compared to the United States. "Competing with the American market would be a huge, huge challenge," she said; but her ambition enabled her to see beyond the horizon: "but I'd like to enter eventually into that market." Sibongile and her directors did not see any major challenges ahead and saw the sky only as opportunity.

Despite its optimistic outlook, SRS continues to face some significant challenges. Sibongile noted that her work relied heavily on contracts with the public sector, and she was trying hard to engage more private clients. Despite SRS's tremendous success, without any official credit or investors, expansion was a relatively slow process. In addition, a capital-intensive strategy would have invigorated the company as a competitor in Western markets. Sibongile was not discouraged, maintaining an attitude and approach that seemed assured of SRS's future promise and success.

Although SRS made a stunning entry into the industry, challenges waited behind the gates as well.

> Aviation is a very community-based type of industry. People know each other globally, and penetrating the industry is not exactly very easy. Most people saw [my entry] as very awkward, and initially, people never took me seriously. I had to prove myself more than ten times.

Ultimately, Sibongile got her message across: "I told them I'm here, I'm here to stay, I'm here to grow this business, and I'm here to make changes as well, because I'm young, I'm very innovative, and I want to bring a new spice into the industry."

In addition, the aviation industry did not have many young, female, or black entrepreneurs. Sibongile recognized that she faced some discrimination despite her skills and knowledge. "Discrimination is something that I don't think can just disappear overnight. There are some contracts that I didn't get purely because I don't go play golf with some of the guys." At times, some of her secured contracts were hampered by racial tension: "I have partnered for some of the work with other male-owned businesses, and I have found that most of them would really take advantage and want to run the show [and] deliberately exclude us from participating on the contract." Although these incidents occurred infrequently, they echoed South Africa's divided past and prolonged a turbulent racial environment.

Sibongile broke these barriers by ensuring she always had the best tool at hand for this industry—knowledge. She had to study quite a bit to keep herself informed, to learn the lingo and jargon of the industry, and to actually understand the ins and outs of aviation.

> In the end, [it] doesn't matter [about] the color of your skin, how tall or short you are, or where you come from[;] what matters in this business is the amount of knowledge that you've got and the ability to execute it. I really strive to make sure that I empower myself with knowledge and the ability to run this business.

It is not a common feat to be a strong woman in South Africa, but Sibongile felt that it was not only her dream that she had carried since childhood, but her strength as well.

> I guess my background actually gives me that platform to become a strong woman. I started living away from my parents from the age of 5 or 6 years old, which gave me a lot of independence. For high school, I went to a girls-only boarding school. I think those things have given me the confidence and also have actually shaped those strong characteristics that I have.

Moreover, Sibongile always had strong women as role models. "My mother and my aunt are very strong women as well. They both lost their husbands very early, and they took care of us as single mothers. For me, managing in an environment that is very male dominated just comes natural. I think it just comes from a confidence and willingness to learn, but also from the willingness to make mistakes, learn from them and move on."

Entrepreneurial Reality: Life on the Ground

Facing the world as an entrepreneur inevitably brought personal challenges as well. First, Sibongile had to face the new reality that, "If I don't work, there's no food on the table." But she averted this uncertainty by adding discipline and structure to her passionate goal. "I've tried my best to be disciplined. I try to get to work as often as possible, working like someone who works for someone else, from 8:00 to 5:00." But sometimes, discipline and determination themselves could be an obstacle: "If I feel sick, and I need to take time to rest, unless I really need to, sometimes I try to avoid that. Sometimes I push myself maybe way too much because I just want to see this business working."

Although Sibongile's confidence in herself as a woman and encouragement from her family were key to her success, at times they posed awkward stumbling blocks to SRS's operation. "Giving [my family members] duties sometimes has been a challenge." "You know," she said giggling, "acting as a boss, giving instructions to my elder brother." Moreover, juggling the roles of mother, business owner, sister, and friend took a toll on Sibongile's personal life. "I have lost quite a lot of friends because as soon as I started running a business, I needed to spend time with other business people." Other times, being independent cut into her family life. "I know there are times when my son, who's just seven years old, needs me, [but] I would have something for this." Sibongile gave an example of how being a responsible CEO could compete with being a mother: she cited a time when she was to attend her son's concert at school, but because she had a meeting with a potential investor, who was leaving the country first thing the next morning, she had to miss the opening night. Although she was able to see the show on a different night, her story provided some perspective on how she negotiated compromises between her lives as a mother and a businesswoman.

Being an entrepreneur challenged Sibongile in the industry, at home, and within herself. But what characterized her as a truly comprehensive leader was her keen recognition and ability to derive strength and knowledge from others. Despite her tremendous success, Sibongile still looked to her heroes for guidance, from former President Mandela to her mother, to both American and African women entrepreneurs, and to her clients. The diversity of her role models was indicative of the broad personal development Sibongile was constantly striving for. She cited President Mandela's "heart of *umbunto*"—compassion for other people—as a quality she truly admired, and she has been lucky enough to have chartered flights for him a few times (see Figure 7.2).

> I've moved quite a lot of people, from Harry Belafonte to heads of state. And those people are my role models too. I find that most of my clients are people I can actually learn from, and therefore I draw a lot of strength, energy, and knowledge from them.

Figure 7.2 Nelson Mandela and Sibongile Sambo
Source: Reproduced with permission from Sibongile Sambo, December 10, 2009.

Sibongile had also been paired with Louise Francesconi, former president of Raytheon, through an international mentorship program that matched women from developing nations with American businesswomen. "The experience has been so amazing. The mentorship that I've gotten and I'm continuing to get from her—it's brilliant. I talk to her either by phone or by email, it's a really, really empowering program."

Sharing her Strength

Having personally experienced the benefits of mentorship, Sibongile took on another personal goal, to share the aviation industry with those with the potential to pilot its future—namely, South Africa's children. She was engaged in a project to not only teach students from local schools about the opportunities in aviation, but also show them first-hand the promise of an empowered, determined individual. This project involved visiting SRS at its headquarters in Randburg or meeting with Sibongile at one of Johannesburg's main technology centers, to provide students with a real-world glimpse into the exciting opportunities in science and technology. Sibongile wanted to encourage children to focus more on mathematics and science and, obviously, to consider aviation as a career option. She wanted to package this as a formal social entrepreneurship initiative that could gain government funding and be extended to more students. Her own personal experience of realizing her dream not only made her an incredible role model for children, but also gave her a unique insight into the importance of inspiring children and adults in a way that was more personal than a policy and more fulfilling than money or profits.

Aviation was a male-dominated sphere: Sibongile was the only female CEO in South African aviation, although the industry saw women entering from different angles, from airport and traffic management to more technical jobs such as aircraft engineering. Since her childhood as an entrepreneurial dreamer, Sibongile persevered to realize her dream, appreciating every chance and challenge as an opportunity to expand her knowledge and personal strength. She and her company have traveled far and shocked the world with their success. They continue to plan, fly, and dream as if only the sky was the limit.

QUESTIONS

1   What were the key resources that Sibongile Sambo accessed in order to launch and grow her business?
2   Did the fact that she was the only female entrepreneur in the industry play a role?
3   What are the lessons in terms of mentoring?

Notes

1   U.S. Department of State, Bureau of Public Affairs, "Background Note, South Africa" (Washington, D.C.: U.S. Department of State). http://www.state.gov/r/pa/ei/bgn/2898.htm (accessed January 25, 2009).
2   Vivek Arora and Luca Antonio Ricci, *Post-Apartheid South Africa: The First Ten Years* (Washington D.C.: International Monetary Fund, 2005), p. 2.
3   U.S. Department of State, Bureau of Public Affairs, "Background Note, South Africa."
4   Ibid.
5   Arora and Ricci, *Post-Apartheid South Africa*, p. 3.

6   U.S. Department of State, Bureau of Public Affairs, "Background Note, South Africa."
7   Republic of South Africa, "Government Gazette, Broad-Based Economic Empowerment Act." (Cape Town, Republic of South Africa) www.info.gov. za/view/DynamicAction?pageid=545&sdate=%202003&orderby=act_no%20desc (accessed January 25, 2009).
8   The World Bank Group, "Flying High: SRS Aviation," *Doing Business: Women in Africa* (2009): 19.

8 Aldaci (Dadá) dos Santos' Recipe for Success

The Flavors of Building a Culinary Brand-Name in Brazil

Maya Perl-Kot

Poverty was both a motivation and a resource for Aldaci dos Santos. She built her restaurant business from the ground up drawing on the lessons in scarcity she learned while growing up. She faced, however, significant challenges when managing restaurants located in different cities without delegating decision making.

Figure 8.1 Sabores da Dadá

Aldaci dos Santos, better known as Dadá in her native Brazil, embodied the spirit of a true entrepreneur. Born to a poor, black, single mother in the highly segregated Brazilian northeast, Dadá managed to transcend her circumstances and create a thriving brand name in Brazil's culinary and entertainment industries. Despite a lack of formal business education, she avoided the typical professional route for women of her background

Figure 8.2 Aldaci dos Santos
Source: Maya Perl-Kot, January 2010.

—becoming a domestic worker, maid, or caregiver—and, instead, utilized her cooking talent to build her own thriving restaurant business. Her unique personality and risk-taking appetite allowed her to develop that vision further into a multidirectional venture that included catering services, high-end party productions, and media products. Dadá became a regional celebrity and an example of an entrepreneur from a socio-economically disadvantaged background who challenged traditional norms and independently moved up the social ladder.

Defying Demographics

Dadá was born in 1961 in Conde, a rural town on the northeastern Brazilian coast 120 miles from Salvador, the capital of the state of Bahia. For a black woman from a rural area, statistical predictions forecasted a future very different from the one she ultimately achieved; her geographic, racial, and gender groups were all significantly disadvantaged or under-represented in economic and entrepreneurial endeavors. Still, Dadá was able to become a successful businesswoman: In 2010 she was the owner, head chef, and general manager of two restaurants in Salvador—with over twenty employees in each—offering traditional Bahian cuisine in an upscale setting. She was also the producer of yearly carnival events, the director of a catering service, the co-author of a successful cookbook, and the star of a DVD film about her life.

Although Brazil was not as poor as some of its South American neigh-bors, with an average yearly income of just under US$10,000, the country was polarized and significant gaps existed between the rich south (where the capital of São Paulo was) and other regions. The northeast was the country's poorest region, consistently scoring lowest on various social and economic indicators. It also had the highest concentration of blacks: Bahia, at 16 percent, and Salvador, at 29 percent, for the highest state and metro-politan concentrations, respectively.[1] Thus, the state was one of Brazil's most polarized: The differences between the black and white populations were starkest and most severe across a range of fields: education, employment, earnings, and business ownership.

While Brazil's illiteracy rate in 2007 stood at 7 percent (14 million of Brazil's 190 million people), it was 14 percent among blacks nationally and 23 percent in Bahia—more than three times the national rate.[2] The average length of education across the nation was 8.1 years for whites and 6.3 years for blacks; but in the northeast the median length for blacks was only 5.6 years.[3] Nationally, black employees earned just over half the median hourly wage of white employees; but in Bahia they earned just over a third of the national average for whites: BRL8.0 versus BRL4.5 versus BRL3.7 (US$4.50, US$2.50, and US$2.00, respectively).[4] Unemployment was three times higher among blacks, who were three times more likely to be among the bottom 10 percent of earners.[5] Finally, social mobility—as measured by intergenerational improvements in education and employ-ment trends—was rare. Illiterate parents were six times more likely to have illiterate children and four times more likely to have children who would be unemployed once they reached working age.[6] Correlations also existed between parents' years of education, professions, and levels of earnings (benchmarked against the period's minimum wage) and those of children. Black Brazilians—who were consistently at the bottom of all of the above indicators—thus had much less of a chance to break away from the patterns of their families.

Women, too, faced significant impediments in business. Their unem-ployment rate was higher than that of men; in Salvador in January 2010, the difference was 15 percent and 9 percent, respectively.[7] Even when employed, women typically earned less than their male counterparts. As of 2000, when the national legislated minimum salary was BRL151 (US$85), Bahian women earned a median of BRL150, compared to nearly twice that amount for men.[8] This was due to differences in occupations: Women were more likely to work in services and without official employ-ment status, while men had more roles in commerce, civil services, and construction—which were all more lucrative.[9]

The poverty cycle was perpetuated by familiar trends: Women were twenty times more likely to be single parents and heads of households.[10] The poorer women were, the more children they had—a fact often related to the gap between urban and rural populations, where large families were the norm.[11] For many women in these situations, escaping the familial burdens in order to increase their earnings was impossible.

In the managerial and entrepreneurial dimensions, women were also significantly under-represented. In 2005 only 36 percent of Brazilian entrepreneurs heading their own businesses were female,[12] and those enterprises were usually smaller and had been started for the purpose of survival—rather than opportunity, growth, and expansion. Entrepreneurship was generally reserved for those who had prior experience as managers in the private sector, as public officials, or as independent freelancers in a related field: 75 percent of all entrepreneurs in 2005 reported one of these as their prior occupation.[13] Women, however, were much less likely to pursue any of these activities. In Bahia, women held less than a third of managerial positions in companies.[14] Public offices were generally reserved for men; and independent businesspeople (who made up 19 percent of the work force in Salvador[15]) were predominantly male (with the exception of women providing services, such as domestic workers).[16] When women did start businesses, they reported the reason as survival rather than opportunity more frequently than men (60 percent for women compared to 40 percent for men).[17] Credit and assistance resources to obtain investment capital were scarce, and starting—let alone growing—a business was extremely difficult for Brazilian women.

Entrepreneurship and the Restaurant Industry

Despite these formidable challenges, and against all odds, Dadá opened her first commercial restaurant in the early 1990s. Although she expanded on the concept and eventually developed additional products, the restaurant industry—particularly the Salvador and Bahian markets—remained her primary focus throughout.

In Bahia, restaurants and hospitality (excluding hotels and tourism) comprised a nearly BRL2 billion market as of 2007.[18] These businesses, which numbered over 10,000, employed around 70,000 people across the entire state.[19] Beyond the scope of the specific industry, the overall entrepreneurial environment in Brazil was also difficult. The cost of starting a new business in 2008, as a percentage of average income, was around 10 percent (compared to just 1 percent in the United States) and required a minimum of eighteen procedures (compared to six).[20] Micro and small-sized enterprises—categorized, respectively, as businesses with up to nine employees and BRL244,000 in revenue (US$135,000), and 10–40 employees and up to BRL1.2 million in revenue (US$670,000)—had particularly high mortality rates: Between 7 percent and 19 percent of them closed each year; the younger the business, the less the likelihood of survival.[21] Although low entry barriers made it relatively easier to penetrate the services industry (to which restaurants and hospitality belonged) compared to the industrial sector—as there was no need for machinery or very large equipment—surviving in the competitive environment was challenging. Still, Dadá managed not only to survive that environment and defy the statistics, but also to surpass all expectations and achieve success on a scale rarely attained by people from her background.

Early Influences

To understand Dadá's success, "one needs to understand [my] early life," she said. "It is a fundamental part of who I am today, and that's why I focus on it during interviews. Life as a child was not easy, and taught me about how to be tough in life—and in business." Dadá was the older of two siblings and grew up with her brother Renato and mother Julia. Her father left when the children were babies, and the traditional community in their small town—who knew every last detail of the affair—made life as a single, black woman incredibly hard for Julia.

> Although it wasn't her fault, my mother took the blame for my father's leaving. She was never fully accepted back into the black community in our town, let alone among white employers. After she couldn't secure permanent employment as a house worker, she had to resort to seasonal farm labor that left our family not only poor—we would have been poor either way—but also very unstable. Income was sporadic and unpredictable. Mother worked from 5 in the morning until after dark each day but, still, we only had meat once a year. That period was the most influential of my life; that's why I always speak of it. Where I come from is a part of who I am. I learned a lot from it: how to be frugal, negotiate to the bone, not let social expectations deter me from my dream. Most importantly, I learned that I want to work for myself, not anyone else, and that I should appreciate everything that I now have.

From a very young age, Dadá would accompany her mother to work. "Washing pots and pans while Julia was in the field was my first task," Dadá said, "and the one that introduced me to a new world that was previously foreign: a world of flavors and seasoning rising out of the dishes in front of me." The rich Bahian cuisine, which combines European, African, and Native American influences, charmed her immediately. It was occupational love at first sight. Her lack of inhibition and timidity allowed Dadá to approach her mother's employers and ask if she could help the cooks in the kitchen. Gradually, after observing and learning her surroundings, she began preparing food on her own; and it was not long before her inherent knack for preparing unique combinations and extravagant dishes was discovered. At age 10, she prepared her first real meal: a dinner for fifteen guests at the home of a local judge in Conde. As Dadá recalled, "Dinner was an instant success, and I realized then that cooking is what I want to do."

When Dadá was 13, Julia received an employment offer in Alagoinhas, a nearby small city, to be a full-time domestic worker. But the employers would not accept Julia with two children of her own. Renato, who was only 5 at the time, was permitted to come; but Dadá, the family decided, would not be. When it became evident that the only other alternative was to put Dadá in an orphanage, Julia decided it was time to send her away. They received word of a position for her as a *baba*, or au pair, in Salvador, a role typically reserved for young girls from the interior. Dadá went to live with a rich family in the big city to take care of their two young children.

Dadá's new employers provided her with board and paid her BRL130 ($US73), less than the minimum salary at the time. That was more money than she could hope to make anywhere else, and she was thrilled to be able to buy simple things and clothes for the first time ever. While tending to the babies, Dadá spent as much time as possible in the kitchen, assisting the cooks. That was how her new patrons learned of her nascent skills: her dishes were spectacular and became renowned among the couple's circle of family and friends.

The Business Building Blocks

Several years went by, and the family's babies were now old enough to no longer require a full-time caregiver. The couple worked primarily in real estate and, when they had an opening at a commercial beach-front location, they offered Dadá the opportunity to open a *lanchonete*, a small cafe, where she could cook and sell food to tourists. Dadá was thrilled and set up shop in the port of Barra, Salvador's main tourist area and the city's central carnival icon. She dressed in the customary Bahian outfit for black women and sold traditional delicacies—but with a twist. While many women were vending similar products in the area, Dadá altered the recipes to create new combinations. Her cooking gained an exceptional reputation and, together with her hospitable and entertaining personality, drew attention and business to her *lanchonete*. "I became known in the neighborhood, and everyone kept telling me to open a restaurant—to use the skill I had been given," Dadá said. However, "Just as I was gaining confidence and really contemplating the idea, a personal challenge arose."

Renato, Dadá's younger brother and only sibling, was killed in a car accident. And shortly thereafter her mother Julia was diagnosed with cancer. Dadá abandoned the cafe and life in Salvador to care for her, but Julia passed away 3 months after Renato. After she had lost all of her immediate family, Dadá decided she wanted one of her own. "I felt alone in the world, and, although I wanted nothing more than to have my own business, I also had to sacrifice if I wanted a family," she recounted.

Dadá reached out to an old boyfriend—one she knew from her years growing up in and visiting Conde. Several months later, the two were married; and daughter Rafaela was born in 1985, followed by Daniella in 1992. But life back in Conde was frustrating for Dadá. It held none of the growth potential that Salvador did.

> The time after my mother passed away was a crucial turning point in my life. Everything was set up for me to give up and resign to the cards I had been dealt and the life everyone was expecting me to lead: working day and night [for others, almost like a slave]. Even my husband believed that we were black and poor and probably hopeless. I was the one who did the convincing, who had the confidence that I can make it as something more.

Her husband was not fully convinced, but Dadá managed to talk him into moving back to Salvador, promising that the area would hold more opportunities for them. She contacted an old friend and asked to rent a room in the favela (shanty town) of Alto das Pombas. Her old employers, who were still fond of her, agreed to let her return to run the *lanchonete*. Her husband found employment in construction and, while he was at work, Dadá took Rafaela with her to the cafe. She kept her, quite literally, under the table and nursed her in between dealing with clients and cooking.

"Life wasn't unbearable; we managed to keep afloat. But that wasn't my goal in returning to Salvador," Dadá explained about that period. The cafe, by virtue of its location and purpose, was limited to specific dishes, and she did not have a free hand in making creative new dishes. Moreover, she had to pay remittances to her old employers—approximately 40 percent of the revenue—which significantly affected her profit. "The desire to do something more, something bigger, simmered in me."

The First Restaurant

After another year in the Barra area, Dadá was already a neighborhood celebrity, known for her effervescent personality and tasty food. Living in an extremely limited space allowed the family to save some money, and they were finally able to move into a larger home in a better part of the same Alto das Pombas neighborhood. That was when Dadá's entrepreneurial spirit truly emerged. The house had a big backyard that was largely unused. In the year-round warm Bahian weather, it would make a perfect restaurant space. "It would also allow [me] to save additional rental costs and stay at home with the girls as they grew older," Dadá said. Everyone around her, however, was skeptical.

> They claimed the location was impossible. The neighborhood was hardly a popular destination: it was poor and had one small supply store, one pharmacy, and one bar. Alto das Pombas wasn't very receptive to culinary adventures, entertainment or nightlife. But the more I thought

of it, the more I was convinced that an at-home restaurant would be a good idea.

Dadá began strolling through bookstores on her way to Barra and browsing through cookbooks on international cuisine. She used all of the family's disposable income to purchase spices and expensive ingredients at the market, and experimented with different dishes at home as she developed her soon-to-be menu. In 1987, she opened O Cheiro da Dadá: Comida Baina e Francesa ("The Smells of Dadá: Bahian and French Food").

> I picked French cuisine, and included the word in the title, for several strategic reasons. I probably didn't know the first thing about business strategy at the time, but I had a few concrete targets in mind. I wanted to set the place apart. Rather than another rice-and-beans lunch joint for men around the neighborhood grabbing a bite before their afternoon shift, I wanted to attract a richer crowd and offer them the opportunity to dine in a favela, as a cultural and culinary experience. I wanted to infuse a distant flavor into the traditional Bahian cuisine and prove to people that, contrary to popular belief, northeastern Brazilian food had more to offer than the typical pepper and *dende* [palm-tree] oil. So I chose a name—and a menu—that I thought would appeal to the middle-class clientele I wanted to attract.

Dadá bought four tables, plates and silverware for ten, twelve additional plates, and opened her restaurant for business. But she did not remain idle and waiting; she publicized her restaurant. She also approached her old employers and asked them to recommend her to their friends, all of whom were among the local social elite. She marketed her restaurant to an upscale clientele as a chic, bohemian place to visit in the middle of the favela. Salvador was an important center for artists, musicians, and authors from all over Brazil—and attracting the artistic community, she knew, would prove integral to her success.

The charm was in the place's simplicity, as laundry ropes hung above dining tables, combined with a sophisticated menu that Dadá kept improving by reading and accumulating more knowledge. In addition to being a restaurant, O Cheiro da Dadá was an entertainment and cultural experience. And it soon gained fame and recognition as such. Local news teams and reporters would frequent Dadá's house, and she became the model of a successful black woman entrepreneur who had risen from poverty independently against all the odds.

Horizontal Growth: Increasing Volume

Two years went by and, while the four tables had increased to six and the business was thriving, Dadá wanted to expand its dimensions beyond the backyard and open a restaurant in a commercial space. Her next big move was an ambitious one. Antonio Carlos Magalhães, the long-time governor of the state of Bahia and a highly influential public figure (often dubbed "The King" among Bahians), announced that he was renovating Pelorinho, Salvador's historic colonial downtown neighborhood. The plan was an attempt to modernize the neglected area and attract tourism, and many businesses vied to be part of this potentially lucrative project.

Dadá asked to see Magalhães, who had already heard of her through acquaintances and colleagues in the state government. Dadá met with him and showcased the business potential of an authentic Bahian restaurant in the heart of the new tourist center. Her appeal was both well substantiated and well presented. Magalhães was not only convinced, he was won over. He issued a grant from the state agency for small businesses for US$20,000. Dadá borrowed an additional $50,000—with the same agency acting as a guarantor—and, in 1993, opened Temperos da Dadá ("Dadá's Flavors"), her first commercial restaurant.

Temperos da Dadá was no longer a small-scale operation. Its twenty tables could accommodate up to 100 people. Now Dadá needed help in the kitchen and, naturally, a full front-of-house staff. She hired people whom she knew and trusted, including skilled servers who could represent the establishment professionally to tourists and upscale patrons. The restaurant was a huge success and drew a diverse but consistent crowd. Dadá became a public figure; newspapers wrote about her restaurant, providing publicity and free advertising. She continued to develop her key differentiator—cuisine that was Bahian in nature but infused with international influences. She entertained different themes, including French, Italian, and African, among others. With cultural icons such as author Jorge Amado and musicians Gal Costa and Caetano Veloso all frequenting the restaurant, Temperos da Dadá became a symbol of downtown Salvador and was operating at full capacity—hosting around 300 patrons daily, nearly year round.

As Temperos da Dadá gained momentum, Dadá received word of another wonderful opportunity: to open a restaurant in São Paulo, Brazil's capital. A close acquaintance alerted her to a vacant spot with the necessary infrastructure in a good location and a team of individuals with whom she could work. Despite the anticipated logistical difficulties, the potential was irresistible. São Paulo is Brazil's largest and wealthiest city. Making it there could mean national (and international) fame. Dadá applied for a loan and decided to pursue this new venture. She opened the second Temperos da Dadá in 1996 with a local partner.

Meanwhile, back in Salvador, demand was exceeding supply and Dadá began considering opening another local restaurant. After a careful analysis of the city, she chose Orla, Salvador's beachfront, as the next location. She again networked with Magalhães to assist with her liquidity limitations and borrowed money to fund the initial investment. The Orla branch, which opened in 1998, was smaller but still popular.

Differentiation

Dadá divided her time between the two cities, traveling frequently and spending long periods in São Paulo. Her restaurants succeeded because, despite offering a traditional Bahian menu, they created a completely innovative experience: the food was authentic but upscale.

> For my upper-middle-class audience, dining out was an opportunity to internationalize, to be non-Brazilian. My competitors were sushi, Italian and BBQ restaurants. People dined out to get away from the traditional food, which they considered inferior, mundane or simple. Bahian food, especially, was considered the quintessential Brazilian cuisine, because the state was so central to the country's cultural development—which made people think of it as even more plain or second-rate. My idea was unique because it took traditional cuisine out of the closet—and out of the kitchen. I managed to reinvent the way people thought of these so-called ordinary dishes that they were already acquainted with, and give Bahian food another dimension.

Dadá's differentiating factor was the ability to upgrade what people thought of as everyday food into an exquisite experience—and charge prices similar to (or even higher than) many foreign cuisine competitors.

> When I opened the restaurant in Pelorinho, no other establishment in Salvador had a similar business concept, with the same target audience in mind. Traditional eateries targeted day laborers and only operated during the lunch period. My idea was to use what I knew to evoke a "return to the roots" among a different set of people and offer competitors—other restaurants in the neighborhood and city—a new challenge.

Vertical Growth: Building a Brand

While focusing on the main line of business—her restaurants—Dadá began pursuing other revenue streams. She developed new products within the food industry, but also branched out into services that combined entertainment components with the culinary experience:

- Dadá started and developed a yearly *feijoada* event. Literally, *feijoada* in Portuguese is a dish of meat and beans; it also refers to the tradition in which extended families get together on a weekend day to eat the dish. Dadá's concept was initially a modest gathering at the first restaurant in Alto das Pombas. Gradually she built it into a popular annual summertime event, first at the Pelorinho restaurant and, over time, at ever-larger venues. A flavorful feast followed by an extravagant party, O Feijoada da Dadá took place during carnival season. It started in 1993 and celebrated its 15th year in 2008. With an average of more than 5,000 attendees, each paying over US$200 for the all-inclusive entrance ticket, the event was one of Dadá's most lucrative activities. Each year she employed around 2,000 people to organize, prepare for, and serve at the event. Volume at these events was substantial: in 2008, guests consumed 2 tons of meat, 1 ton of beans, 20,000 tamales, 15,000 skewers, 18,000 liters of beer, 1,200 liters of whiskey, and 600 liters of vodka.[22] The event became an integral part of Salvador's carnival celebration and received media coverage that constantly increased its popularity.

- Dadá approached her friend Paloma Amado, the daughter of Brazil's renowned author Jorge Amado, and asked her to collaborate on a cookbook. The result was *Tempero da Dadá* (Dadá's Flavor), featuring Dadá's most popular dishes with Paloma's commentary. The book was published in 1998 and was later translated into English.

- In collaboration with the State Ministry for Social Affairs, Dadá created a DVD about her life, entitled *E aí Negona?* (So What Now, Woman?).[23] Part documentary and part plot-based, the DVD featured illustrations of Dadá's life as a child as well as scenes from her adulthood. The directors interviewed Dadá's clients, employers, and acquaintances—all of whom provided insights into her unique life, talent, and personality.

- Dadá developed an additional business unit that offered large-volume catering services. She targeted mainly upscale clientele—the same political community and artistic crowd who had frequented her restaurants initially. Although she had established this line of business separately from her restaurants, she still used the connection between the two to her advantage: she exploited the restaurants' popularity in marketing the catering service, and the economies of scale concept when purchasing supplies and conducting administrative tasks.

- Continuing along the same line of domestic appearances in magazines and on television shows, Dadá contacted a public relations firm and pursued international opportunities. She became a well-known figure in the culinary world, traveling to France, England, Italy, Spain, and New York, among other places, to take part in cooking shows, forums, lectures, or conventions.

The Lessons of Over-expansion

Dadá's management style was more than hands-on; it was all-inclusive. In the beginning, with only the Pelorinho restaurant to tend to, Dadá was always on site, making all the decisions herself. In addition to designing the menu and cooking, she also took care of supplies, managed most of the staff, and decorated the restaurant. (As an homage to her beginnings in Alto das Pombas, she kept the original decor that became her trade-mark—laundry ropes with clothes hung above tables—at all of her locations.

Problems arose when her business grew but the organizational structure remained simple and limited. Dadá's lack of business education eventually caught up with her. The additional restaurants, in Orla Salvador and São Paulo, functioned poorly without Dadá's constant presence. Volume decreased and did not live up to expectations at either branch. Revenue declined and her profit, determined largely by fixed costs that remained high despite the shortage of clients, fell significantly. Dadá was not well versed in the process of hiring and training managers to do work similar to hers. Rather, she was accustomed to doing it all by herself. As additional ventures—the catering line, productions, appearances, and trips abroad—consumed even more of her time, it was evident that Dadá could not continue traveling to São Paulo or dividing her time between the two Salvador locations. In addition, she was going through a divorce after a long period of faltering relations with the father of her daughters. With the Pelorinho restaurant still her primary source of revenue, focusing on it was the best strategy. In 2000 she both finalized her divorce and closed the two other locations.

> This was a period of endings in my life. In addition to the end of my marriage, I had to let go of things that I worked very hard to establish. Antonio Carlos Magalhães, who was a big supporter of mine, had died—and I no longer had someone to rescue me. I had to let go nearly 100 people. It was very painful. But, in the end, it made me a better businessperson by forcing me to reach some very important conclusions.

Dadá realized that things were less under her control than she had thought. She decided to hire a personal manager, and the ideal candidate was not far away. No one was more qualified than her daughter Rafaela, who had studied business at Salvador's national university and abroad in Texas, was closely acquainted with her mother's established operational methods, and knew the priorities that required immediate attention within each business line. Rafaela was eager to apply what she had learned in a practical setting, and quit her office job to come work with her mother.

Developing a Management Style

Rafaela was able to bring structure and organization to the Dadá brand name. She set up operational procedures for hiring qualified managers, outsourced certain activities (such as the preparation of catering orders), and managed Dadá's time so that it reflected the most important tasks that she had to do herself—interviews, speeches, and TV appearances. Dadá still spent time at the restaurant and never abandoned the kitchen; but she now had more time to balance the various demands of the different business units.

After several years of Rafaela's stabilization efforts, Dadá was once again ready to open another branch; and she picked Pituba, a thriving middle-class neighborhood. In 2009, Sabor da Dadá (The Tastes of Dadá) opened for business with the same concept, decor, and menu as the other restaurants. Rafaela developed an operational scheme whereby Dadá's schedule was divided regularly between the various ventures and still left enough free time to accommodate special demands.

Dadá was the general manager and head chef of both restaurants. In the mornings, she alternated between the two, usually for 6 days of the week (Monday was her free day, as weekends were particularly busy and required her supervision). In her absence, each restaurant had a head sous-chef as well as a floor manager to handle back-of-house and front-of-house issues, respectively. Rather than training managers, Dadá hired experienced people and immersed them in the particularities of her business. Either she or the managers trained the general staff. Dadá herself purchased supplies for both locations (as well as the catering business unit) on a weekly basis.

During the afternoons Dadá either gave interviews, conducted meetings with potential catering clients, or communicated from her home-office with various partners and vendors. Rafaela accompanied her mother to business meetings and screened all calls on her mother's agenda. All accounting and financial functions were outsourced to a firm that also handled Dadá's rental and leasing arrangements for the restaurant properties.

With these new standards in place, profit margins improved and Dadá's overall income increased. The Pelorinho location grossed BRL400,000 (US$225,000), of which BRL200,000 (US$110,000) was net income; and the Pituba restaurant, still in its infancy, grossed BRL100,000 and netted BRL50,000 (US$56,000 and US$28,000, respectively). Revenue from all other products diminished somewhat and stood at BRL20,000 (US$11,000) at the beginning of 2010.

Growth Aspirations

Some additional expansion ideas were in the pipeline: Dadá was again collaborating with Paloma Amado, planning *O Dia Dia da Dadá* (Dadá's Everyday), a book that would include more recipes but also provide a glimpse into Dadá's early life and personal development—based on the success of the DVD that told the same story.

Dadá was also planning to get into the entertainment industry more seriously. Already a recognizable TV personality, she was procuring channels and production companies to start her own cooking show, to supplant her frequent guest appearances elsewhere. In addition, she was thinking internationally, looking into the possibility of opening a restaurant in

New York, where demand for international cuisine was strong and where she had good connections to get her foot in the door, having learned the appropriate lessons from São Paulo.

Dadá's final business aspiration was one intertwined with a personal desire: since her adolescence, she had wanted to start an NGO to house and educate poor children from her native Sitio do Conde. Her roots always influenced her hiring decisions, as she paid particular attention to her employees' personal and family circumstances and "was particularly sympathetic to women." Having an impact on the same community from which she came was a life-long dream that Dadá was striving to achieve.

Self-fulfillment

Dadá loved her occupation. "Cooking was my first love, and remained the most important one throughout my entire life," she said. "My clients are like a husband; getting compliments from them is more satisfying than anything."

Although she divorced her husband, Dadá remained in contact with him for her daughters' sake. Family, in general, remained the most central, most important, and most significant aspect of her life. Even years after her mother passed away, Dadá still spoke of Julia as the most influential figure in her everyday life.

> I learned from my mother how to be a versatile, well-rounded individual in spite of any impending circumstances: Mother was an architect—building the leaf roof of our house by herself, a decorator—using scraps of artifacts to give us a homely feeling, and a negotiator—always bargaining for the best price whether for our family or on behalf of her employers. I aspire to be like her in everything that I pursue: do things well, do them right, and be a noble woman about it. I was lucky to move ahead where many women like me stay put, and I am always grateful that I can do what I love for a living.

Business Challenges: Innovation

Volume at Dadá's restaurants decreased because of the financial crisis of 2007–2009, which had an impact on many of her patrons as well as on domestic and international tourism to Salvador. The Pelorinho volume fell by around 40 percent, and the catering business was particularly hard-hit. Although Dadá was able to restore the restaurant's performance, a more fundamental problem was undermining the situation.

As time passed, Dadá's fame among Bahians created certain business conflicts. The food industry was a fast-paced, constantly changing environment. Innovation was necessary in order to stay afloat and not become outdated. Coming up with these fresh ideas proved to be a real challenge.

At some point, it becomes difficult to create something from nothing —people get very easily bored when it comes to their restaurants and favorite "celebrities." Popularity is much harder to maintain, in the longer run, than quality food.

Dadá and Rafaela were thinking of campaigns and methods to get things back on track and to keep coming up with new Dadá products to keep the public interested in her market presence. In addition to typical food industry strategies (e.g., weekly buffet dinners and periodic promotions), Rafaela worked on obtaining sponsorships and inviting celebrities to the yearly *feijoada*, pre-marketing the upcoming potential TV show, and alerting the media to Dadá's various activities. Although it was a hard task, Dadá remained confident that "what [I have] learned throughout my lifetime will allow [me] to think up new ideas and not only survive, but excel, in business."

QUESTIONS

1　Should Dadá have chosen to grow her business more slowly? Why?
2　How did Dadá's personality influence her management style?
3　What are the best ways to ensure that growth of an entrepreneurial venture does not become chaotic?

Notes

1　The Brazilian Institute of Geography and Statistics, "Summary of Social Indicators 2008: An Analysis of the Brazilian Population Life Conditions," 2008, www.ibge. gov.br/home/estatistica/populacao/condicaodevida/indicadoresminimos/sinteseindic sociais2008/indic_sociais2008.pdf, p. 215.
2　Ibid., p. 209.
3　Ibid., p. 212.
4　Ibid., pp. 226–227.
5　Ibid., p. 228.
6　The Brazilian Institute of Geography and Statistics, "Social Mobility Statistics," 1996, www.ibge.gov.br/english/estatistica/populacao/mobilidade_social/default. shtm, tables 1 and 6.
7　The Brazilian Institute of Geography and Statistics, "Monthly Employment Surveys: January 2010," 2010, www.ibge.gov.br/english/estatistica/indicadores/ trabalhoerendimento/pme_nova/default.shtm, p. 19.
8　The Brazilian Institute of Geography and Statistics, "Profile of Female Heads of Household in Brazil," 2000, www.ibge.gov.br/english/estatistica/populacao/ perfildamulher/default.shtm, tables 7 and 8.
9　The Brazilian Institute of Geography and Statistics, "Summary of Social Indicators 2008," p. 245.

10 Ibid., p. 238.
11 Ibid.
12 The Brazil Support Service for Small and Micro Enterprises (SABRAE), "Conditional Factors and Rates of Initiation and Mortality Among Small and Micro Enterprises," 2007, http://201.2.114.147/bds/BDS.nsf/8F5BDE79736CB994832 57447006CBAD3/$File/NT00037936.pdf, p. 18.
13 Ibid.
14 The Brazilian Institute of Geography and Statistics, "Summary of Social Indicators 2008," p. 233.
15 The Brazilian Institute of Geography and Statistics, "Monthly Employment Surveys: January 2010," p. 26.
16 Global Entrepreneurship Monitor, "Entrepreneurship in Brazil," 2007, www.gem consortium.org/document.aspx?id=672, p. 78.
17 Ibid., p. 76.
18 The Brazilian Institute of Geography and Statistics, "Annual Survey of Services," 2007, www.ibge.gov.br/english/estatistica/economia/comercioeservico/pas/pas2007/ default.shtm, p. 165.
19 The Brazilian Institute of Geography and Statistics, "@States," 2007, www.ibge. gov.br/estadosat/temas.php?sigla=ba&tema=estruturaempresarial2007 (accessed March 19, 2010).
20 The World Bank, "World Development Indicators Report," 2009, http://web. worldbank.org/WBSITE/EXTERNAL/DATASTATISTICS/0,,contentMDK: 21725423~pagePK:64133150~piPK:64133175~theSitePK:239419,00.html (accessed March 1, 2010).
21 The Brazil Support Service for Small and Micro Enterprises (SABRAE), "Conditional Factors and Rates of Initiation and Mortality Among Small and Micro Enterprises," pp. 17–19.
22 UOL. "Fejoiada da Dadá Brings Revelers and VIPs to Bahia," January 28, 2008, http://translate.google.com/translate?hl=en&sl=pt&u=http://carnaval.uol.com.br/ noticias/2008/01/28/ult5682u12.jhtm&ei=Qm5zS—cK5TSM_unof4J&sa=X&oi= translate&ct=result&resnum=1&ved=0CA4Q7gEwAA&prev=/search percent3Fq percent3Dfeijoadapercent2Bdapercent2Bdadápercent26hlpercent3Den percent 26clientpercent3Dfirefox-apercent26rlspercent3Dorg.mozilla:en-US:official percent 26hs percent3DoCk
23 Literally, *Negona* means Negro in English, but is a term of endearment for black women. It is used colloquially and is not offensive.

9 Maita Barrenechea and Mai10

Building a Travel Business

Gregory Gilbert

Currency devaluations, financial crises, and global recessions did not deter Maita Barrenechea from building her customized tours business in Argentina and other South American countries. She hit upon the idea almost by chance, and soon realized that it enabled her to bring together some of her passion for the outdoors and her desire to help her country develop a competitive industry.

The name Mai10 is intriguing.[1] It is associated with the maiten tree in Patagonia, an area of spectacular natural beauty that, for many people, defines their image of Argentina. Mai10 also combines Mai, a nickname for the name Maita, and the number 10, which in Argentina signifies the top or best within any category. This unique combination of meanings and images wrapped into the company name of Mai10 was highly appropriate for the destination management company (DMC) that Maita Barrenechea founded in 1982 and nurtured and developed into the paradigm of tourism in Argentina. DMCs were the face of Argentine tourism for many of the world's key executives, celebrities, and political leaders and for many ordinary foreigners seeking a customized travel experience within Argentina. The company's name was appropriate because the business first began in Patagonia, and, while it had expanded to operate trips throughout South America, it remained firmly rooted in Argentina and, specifically, in the country's areas of great natural beauty.

One of Barrenechea's major goals in developing her company was to promote Argentina and its tourism industry and to show the country in the best possible light so the industry could grow for the good of all Argentines. Furthermore, the company unequivocally belonged to Barrenechea and was always her project and lifelong passion. She dedicated her life to ensuring that Mai10 offered the absolute premium, personalized travel experience to its clients without exception. As a result, the company began without any true competition in the industry, and the list of its accomplishments and accolades was long and impressive.

Mai10 specialized in tailor-made trips that were highly customized for free and independent travelers (FITs) and groups. Barrenechea stated,

"A lot of time is invested in personalization . . . It's a vacation and you are selling a dream." During conversations with her, one got the sense that this principle was not only a business philosophy but also something that she personally believed in. She firmly believed that her clients worked very hard for their success in life and that their goal and reward for this effort was to have the free time and ability to truly enjoy the most incredible vacation possible. As a result, Barrenechea and her staff felt personally responsible for ensuring that each client's interests were catered to and that all of them had the best vacation of their lives while under the care of Mai10. This passion to provide the perfect experience and the willingness to go to any length to satisfy her clients allowed Mai10 to expand its offerings and drove the company's amazing growth over its long history. With twenty-five full-time employees and dozens of other long-time trusted freelance affiliates, the Mai10 operation grew into a large and smoothly functioning company that generated $3–4 million in annual revenues in 2008.

Early Development

Like most entrepreneurs, Barrenechea never intended to start her own business when she began her career. As a native Porteño (resident of Buenos Aires), she attended university in the Argentine capital and chose to study business administration. As might have been expected in Argentina in the 1970s, Barrenechea said that she was one of only two or three women in her class at the business school. As a result, from a young age she was used to independently following her goals and being something of an anomaly in the male-dominated world of Argentine business. After graduation, she went to work for her father in the family ranching and agriculture business. However, she soon sought greater challenges and moved on to work as a simultaneous translator between English and Spanish, eventually heading Argentina's leading simultaneous interpretation school. Around this same Barrenechea married her first husband, Carlos Sanchez, who, like her, was very active and an enthusiastic participant in outdoor sports. Together they spent a significant amount of time hiking, fishing, skiing, and visiting the spectacular wild areas of Argentina. This personal interest, combined with her facility for languages, enabled her to establish and expand her business.

The business itself began by pure chance. Knowing her personal interests and knowledge of Argentina's spectacular natural areas, in May 1982, a friend asked Barrenechea if she could help another individual organize a fishing trip to Argentina. Since her friend did not know of anyone or any organization capable of doing this, Barrenechea offered to organize it herself as a favor. The individual was so impressed that, the following year, he recommended Barrenechea to another friend but insisted that she charge for her services. This pattern of word of mouth marketing continued, and the number of trips Barrenechea organized increased. Initially, the trips were a hobby for Barrenechea and her husband, with their first trips being organized around fishing, primarily in Patagonia. Skiing was also a cornerstone of the early business, as it was a personal passion for Barrenechea and it was easy for her to bring clients to international ski competitions in the area around Bariloche.

Initially, the business was focused on Patagonia, where there was virtually no tourism development. Barrenechea had to be creative in establishing an infrastructure. Although there were no high quality hotels, there were beautiful, private second homes called *estancias* that wealthy Argentines allowed their friends to use when they were not living in them. Because these homes were expensive to maintain, Barrenechea convinced the owners to allow her and her paying guests to use their homes for a fee. This was challenging at first because the homes were not designed for guests, and the owners were not accustomed to the discriminating clients she was bringing to Patagonia. Barrenechea had to convince the owners that it was worth the money she was paying them to close off entire wings for her guests or to make other accommodations.

Barrenechea also encountered similar challenges in finding fishing and hunting guides. Because there were no professional guides in Patagonia, she had to teach local fishermen how to handle the highly demanding international clients she was accompanying. They needed to learn how to be guides; they were not permitted to fish with clients but rather had to teach the clients how to fish. Eventually, she was able to hire several full-time fishing guides stationed in Patagonia. At this time, a specialized tourism company in the U.S. that was promoting her fishing tours and supplying her with clients asked if she could also organize bird shooting tours. Although Barrenechea knew nothing about bird shooting and hunting, she assumed she could learn the necessary information through some research. At that time, doves were considered a plague in Argentina, as they ate crops in the area, and the owners of the estancias were killing them by using poison. Since doves had been overhunted in the U.S., Barrenechea recognized an opportunity and was able to convince the estancia owners to stop poisoning the birds and, instead, allow her clients to shoot them, along with ducks and partridges. In 1990 she and her first husband opened her grand hunting lodge in Patagonia. For many years that lodge was considered the best in the country, although Barrenechea's involvement with the lodge ceased following their separation in 1993.

Just as Barrenechea's business had expanded from fishing and skiing into hunting, clients asked her to plan other trips, and she branched out into organizing trips for individuals or small groups that were focused around special interest activities. These activities multiplied to include golf, horse riding, polo, tango, photography, bird watching, horticulture, literature, architecture, opera, cattle study tours, grain tours, and art tours. For most of these special interest tours, Barrenechea used her contacts to personally learn about the activity and the location as well as to establish an infrastructure. In many areas, her personal interests and knowledge helped her significantly. She had studied art and architecture, had attended the opera with her grandfather since childhood, and was well versed in the grain and cattle industries through her family's business. In general, all of her clients' special interests were of interest to her, and she was therefore willing to invest the time to learn about them, or had appropriate contacts that enabled her to organize a memorable trip.

When organizing the first trip for a new special interest tour, Barrenechea invested a significant amount of time in researching and learning about the subject and determining the ideal itinerary for the trip to meet her clients' desires and needs. She always visited hotels and facilities, such as golf courses and museums, to ensure that everything would be up to the standards that her clients expected. As her business grew, it was less critical for Barrenechea to accompany her guests because she had cultivated trusted, freelance guides in various parts of Argentina who took on this responsibility for her. As a result, even though she was able to run the business from Buenos Aires, she never stopped participating in business development.

While developing the business for small, special interest groups, Barrenechea began taking on FITs—families or individuals who were not interested in traveling with a larger group. Given the high level of quality and service that Barrenechea provided, these clients tended to be wealthy, although she was always able to offer a range of cost options so that not every tour was at the high end in terms of prices and services offered. Instead of focusing on cost and luxury, the guiding principle behind this business—just as it was for the special interest groups—was to customize each trip according to the needs and interests of the clients. While it might not have seemed worth the effort from a business angle to plan highly personalized trips for a single individual or small group, Barrenechea realized early on that these clients were her best form of publicity through word of mouth advertising. They always brought her new clients and were instrumental in helping develop the group portion of her business. As a result, even as the company grew over time to become a much larger entity, Barrenechea maintained the FIT business as a major component of Mai10.

In 1987 a former Kenyan client requested that Barrenechea organize a trip for a much larger group, the Young Presidents' Organization (YPO), a global organization of CEOs under the age of 50. These were over-stressed, highly active, demanding individuals who were used to personalized attention, and they easily fit within Barrenechea's typical clientele. Just as she had done previously with new types of groups, Barrenechea immediately accepted the offer and assumed she could organize a trip for a group of between 900 and 1,000 people. Since the trip was not scheduled to take place until 1989, Barrenechea had 2 years to organize all of the events, which were designed to be distinctive, impressive, and of the highest quality, given her highly discerning audience. Over ninety activities were arranged for the group, including a talk by the Dalai Lama, as well as individualized pre- and post-tour activities for many of the participants.

The YPO trip was a huge success and gave Barrenechea the confidence to cater to large groups. Around the same time, she organized a similarly high-profile event for a summit of vice presidents, finance ministers, and associated staff from every country in Latin America. She took on the challenge with her now well-recognized entrepreneurial approach and organized a successful tour.

Despite the success of these large group trips, in the early 1990s Barrenechea returned to her core business of special interest and FIT groups. She had never wanted to build a large group business and the complexity and intensity of planning these events to her exceedingly high standards would have made it difficult to incorporate these types of trips as a regular part of her business without growing Mai10 significantly and risking a decline in overall quality. Furthermore, the large group business was irregular in timing and group size, making it a risky prospect to focus on this type of business. During this time she marketed her business primarily through word of mouth, augmented by several trips each year to Europe and the U.S. These trips were initiated by individuals who invited her to their clubs or homes to speak with friends and associates who were interested in Argentina and Barrenechea's services. Barrenechea felt that by promoting Argentina, rather than her tours and her company, her business would grow through highlighting the opportunities to travel in Argentina, rather than through an aggressive sales pitch. As a result, Mai10 grew organically.

Expanding the Business

While Mai10's growth had been consistent, by 1993 it was still a relatively small company and operating it was time-consuming for Barrenechea. Despite the YPO and the Latin American vice presidential group tours, the business primarily comprised fishing and hunting trips and a small component of special interest and FIT clients. In addition to Barrenechea and her first husband, there were only one or two full-time employees working in Buenos Aires, and the business was seasonal. Ultimately, that year brought dramatic changes for Barrenechea and Mai10. Barrenechea separated from her husband—she later remarried—and chose to remain in Buenos Aires with her three daughters. After dividing up the business with her first husband, Barrenechea continued to run Mai10, while her ex-husband kept the hunting lodge in Patagonia.

At that time, Barrenechea decided it was time to take truly proactive steps to expand and organize her business. She developed a business plan, a marketing plan, and an operations manual detailing business practices for Mai10 employees, formalizing and codifying the company's principles and procedures. She also invested her own money to create marketing materials to bring to conferences. Part of her marketing plan included the commitment to build a corporate business and market the Argentine tourism industry and Mai10 in more professional and formalized forums. Instead of depending solely on word of mouth marketing, Barrenechea traveled to the U.S. and Europe to actively promote her business.

Despite this focus on building her company, Barrenechea's marketing philosophy remained the same. She consistently focused more on enhancing global awareness of Argentina as a tourist destination rather than selling her company. She believed that by expanding the Argentine tourism industry in general, she would increase the overall market and Mai10 would benefit as a consequence. This attitude extended to her frequent inter-actions with foreign media who came to see her when they visited Argen-tina. When speaking to or meeting with these reporters, Barrenechea always focused first on promoting the country. She viewed reporters' recommendations of her services as a fortunate by-product.

In marketing Argentina and Mai10, Barrenechea had first begun attending fishing shows and then general travel shows. Initially, she went mainly to Europe to increase awareness. Prior to 1993, approximately 90 percent of her clients came from the U.S., but Barrenechea recog-nized that she could not focus solely on the American market and needed to target other markets as well. As a result, she began to travel to England, Germany, France, Spain, and other Western European countries to garner business. Her efforts ultimately yielded a pool of clients who were nearly evenly divided between Americans and Europeans. She also had a signifi-cant number in Australia and South Africa. Barrenechea continued her intensive marketing abroad, traveling to the U.S. and Europe about five times a year for large travel conferences and other marketing events. These events were typically forums to meet with travel agents or tour organizers in order to enhance Argentina's image as a tourist destination and to inspire clients to seek out Mai10.

From 1993 onward, Barrenechea's efforts to enhance the global profile of the Argentine tourism industry and to expand her business paid handsome dividends. Mai10 grew much faster than she had expected, and Argentina itself benefitted from significant tourism booms. The country became a hotspot of global tourism and the subject of countless travel articles, many of which mentioned Barrenechea. The business also expanded beyond Argentina, as demand from previous clients warranted, with Mai10 running trips to every South American country except Colombia and Venezuela. By 2008, Mai10 had twenty-five full-time employees working in the Buenos Aires office, all of whom were managed directly by Barrene-chea and her second husband, José García Calvo, whom she married in 1998 (see Figure 9.1). In addition, there were countless part-time and freelance employees who served as guides, greeters, and drivers through-out Argentina and South America. Whenever Barrenechea hosted a

Figure 9.1 Maita Barrenechea
Source: Reproduced with permission from Maita Barrenechea, July 29, 2012.

particularly large group with a complicated itinerary, the company might have as many as 200 different people working simultaneously under the Mai10 name.

In the Buenos Aires office in 2008, employees comprised two divisions: the groups division, which organized trips for groups of twenty or more people, and the FIT division, which organized trips for independent travelers or much smaller groups. Since a larger percentage of Mai10's business was with smaller groups, there were more people employed in the groups division. Within each division, employees were also divided into two functional groups: planning and operations. The former group worked directly with potential clients to plan and sell trips to fit their needs. Barrenechea and Calvo were very involved in the planning group, with Barrenechea focusing on FIT clients while her husband focused on the larger groups. After a trip was sold, it was passed along to the operations group which then handled all of the bookings and reservations. These employees then also ensured that the trip was successful and problem-free. This was an area in which Barrenechea and Calvo had much less involvement.

Because Barrenechea continued to broaden the spectrum of trips that she offered by adding new locations or developing new types of specialized trips, she had to continue to train new specialized guides. She said, "The most fun part of my job is inventing new, different, and original programs, and this process carries with it the need to train those who will actually run the trips." Fortunately, the Argentine tourism industry had advanced significantly since the early 1980s, and there was little need to continue to train guides about general tourism and how to interact with guests. Being a tour guide had become an institutionalized career with a range of specialized courses and training programs available, and this development certainly enhanced the process of choosing and training guides to work for Mai10.

Keys to Success and Challenges

Profitability for the business ranged between 8 percent and 15 percent, depending on which groups ultimately decided to travel with Mai10 and which trips they eventually chose. Costs were more or less fixed and different products and services had different profit margins, making overall profitability relatively variable. Not only did Barrenechea invest significant effort and her own money into formalizing and expanding the business in 1993, but, like most entrepreneurs, she was involved in every aspect of her business. At first she performed all tasks, and, although she had a great deal of help in virtually all capacities, she continued to maintain close control over all aspects of the business, along with Calvo. Either one of them personally answered any query that Mai10 received from a potential client, and one of them was often in the office on weekends and always on call to take care of any emergencies that might arise.

Despite the fact that she ran a business that provided people with the most memorable vacations of their lives, Barrenechea and her husband rarely ever had time to take a vacation of their own. Their intense focus on providing their clients with the highest level of personalization and customer service required a significant amount of time, with Barrenechea always wanting to be personally involved in ensuring that the expectations of every client were always exceeded. While she was able to pass along some responsibilities to her employees and Calvo, Barrenechea's focus on marketing and planning for her growing company also became more time-consuming, and finding a way to balance these demands with her personal life was sometimes challenging.

With a larger business and an expanding Argentine tourism industry, Barrenechea and Mai10 had to confront other challenges that arose (see Tables 9.1 and 9.2). Competition grew over the years. As of 2008, there were many other DMCs sending FITs and larger groups to Argentina for a variety of trips. Mai10 maintained its advantage, however, by focusing on the personalization and superior service that its larger competitors such as Abercombie & Kent lacked, while the smaller competitors could not match Barrenechea's reputation as an expert on Argentine tourism. Her competitive edge was also enhanced by the recommendations of her former clients, with word of mouth advertising consistently bringing Mai10 50 percent of its new clients. Although she wanted to continue to expand her business, she became discriminating about whom she accepted as clients, carefully screening each and every potential new guest. Additional challenges arose from the Internet, as it provided individuals with the ability to plan their own trips and created more transparency regarding pricing, something which negatively impacted profit margins over time. Nonetheless, Mai10's focus on superior service and attention to detail, as well as Barrenechea's longstanding relationships with hotels and tour operators, enabled the firm to continue to grow.

Competition from other DMCs and shrinking profit margins were not the only difficulties that Barrenechea encountered over time. Operating a business in Argentina brought other challenges. As Barrenechea stated, "The primary difficulty was the lack of infrastructure that persisted in the country." When she ran her first trip in 1982, Buenos Aires's iconic Alvear Palace Hotel was closed and the famous Llao Llao Hotel in Bariloche was in disrepair, leaving the country with no luxury hotels. While the variety and quality of hotels and restaurants multiplied dramatically after 1980s, there was still a notable lack of helicopters and private jets available for charter, and a railroad network did not exist. Furthermore, there was a scarcity of domestic commercial flights, and the domestic airline company, Aerolineas Argentinas S.A., had a terrible reputation, was massively inefficient, and was a target for government takeover.

This threat of nationalization highlighted another major challenge to doing business in Argentina. The country had long been avoided by major

Table 9.1 Annual Tourist Arrivals to Argentina

	U.S. and Canada	*Europe*	*Total*
1990	161,016	232,956	1,930,034
1991	138,058	201,873	1,708,183
1992	140,366	206,551	1,703,910
1993	137,832	196,210	1,918,462
1994	158,218	217,971	2,089,414
1995	178,180	248,348	2,288,694
1996	221,255	298,858	2,613,909
1997	242,193	319,787	2,764,226
1998	264,297	344,323	3,012,472
1999	249,781	336,676	2,898,241
2000	252,384	354,050	2,909,468
2001	179,832	370,933	2,620,464
2002	152,620	323,729	2,820,039
2003	224,472	455,998	2,995,272
2004	302,255	546,184	3,456,527
2005	369,753	630,888	3,822,666
2006	400,090	661,694	4,172,534
2007	445,410	737,634	4,561,742
Annual CAGR	6.2%	7.0%	5.2%

Source: National Institute of Statistics and Censuses (INDEC).

Table 9.2 Annual Foreign Tourist Expenditures in Argentina ($ million)

	U.S. and Canada	Europe	Total
1990	167.5	273.4	1,130.9
1991	173.6	289.9	1,241.1
1992	197.6	335.4	1,413.0
1993	207.6	332.1	1,625.1
1994	246.4	381.5	1,862.0
1995	285.0	449.1	2,144.1
1996	356.6	547.6	2,541.5
1997	391.0	580.6	2,693.0
1998	429.8	629.3	2,936.2
1999	407.8	609.8	2,812.7
2000	412.1	628.8	2,817.3
2001	293.4	652.5	2,547.5
2002	152.9	314.9	1,476.4
2003	246.9	528.7	1,942.3
2004	323.4	641.9	2,162.7
2005	414.7	782.5	2,640.9
2006	489.9	925.2	3,249.5
2007	647.8	1,190.3	4,218.1
Annual CAGR	*8.3%*	*9.0%*	*8.1%*

Source: National Institute of Statistics and Censuses (INDEC).

international investors, largely due to its economic and political instability. While this view has long been pervasive in the consciousness of the Argentine public, since 2001 the greatest concern has been over how the government would treat bank deposits. In that year the government prevented Argentines from withdrawing their deposits, an action known as *el corralito*. At the time, the Argentine peso was fixed at 1-to-1 with the U.S. dollar, and *el corralito* was followed by a devaluation of the peso. As a result, many Argentines saw their savings cut by two thirds. Fortunately, Calvo anticipated the devaluation and Mai10 took the necessary actions to protect their capital, averting disaster for the company. Nonetheless, the constant fear that the economy might easily collapse again or that the government might take drastic measures that would tremendously damage businesses was a constant and very real threat for Barrenechea and her company. As a result, Mai10 maintained most of its capital in foreign currency.

Another challenge for Mai10 that was unique to operating a business within Argentina was the exposure to inflation risk. Inflation was typically quite high in Argentina and had long posed a problem for local businesses. Since Mai10 often quoted and booked trips over a year in advance, Barrenechea had to manage the risk that her profits would be eroded by inflation in the interim. Fortunately, most hotels and other service providers quoted her fixed rates 6–12 months in advance, assuming the inflation risks themselves. Whenever this was not the case, Mai10 inserted clauses into its contracts indicating that costs and prices in Argentina were often subject to sudden change and that clients needed to be prepared to assume any potential cost increases. While this minimized Mai10's risk of price hikes in flights or other services, Barrenechea did not want to pass on large increases to her clients indiscriminately. Furthermore, it was difficult to pass on any necessary increases in her employees' and freelance guides' salaries that were due to inflation. Mai10 therefore estimated the likely inflation, charged her clients by installment and also paid service providers and other creditors in this way, coordinating the timing and scale of the corresponding inflows and outflows of cash so that the minimum amount of money was held in Argentine bank accounts and exposed to inflation. In addition, Mai10 took great care to draw on foreign currency deposits or payments to pay the costs of trips only when absolutely necessary. These measures served as important hedges against both inflation and potential capital seizure by the government.

In addition to the economic problems that appeared to be endemic in Argentina, Mai10 was also exposed to other risks and challenges that were specific to the tourism industry. As Barrenechea stated, "Tourism is an industry that is very sensitive to the political, economic, security, and health problems that very often afflict countries such as ours and the global or regional issues impacting the countries from where our clients arrive." Certainly, the great security fears generated by the terrorist attacks on New York City on September 11, 2001, hurt tourism globally and also affected travel to Argentina.

Another example was the global news generated by *el corralito* in 2001, which resonated with many Europeans and North Americans and damaged the image of Argentina as a tourist destination. As a result, tourism declined and one of Mai10's groups canceled its trip. However, the devaluation of the peso also had the benefit of making the country less expensive for foreign travelers, and in the end this counterbalanced the fear of traveling to Argentina and helped to encourage and expand the country's tourism sector.

Gender as a Challenge

Perhaps the greatest potential challenge for a woman running her own company in Latin America was the fact that she was functioning within a male-dominated business society. For Barrenechea, however, this factor was never a major impediment during her impressive trajectory. In speaking with her, one felt that she had never really considered the issue, either because it was never even a minor challenge or because she was so driven in her path that such distractions had never caught her attention. While Argentina was certainly a society where the macho culture was prevalent, the tourism industry was more heavily populated by women. For example, Barrenechea observed that the general manager of the Alvear Palace Hotel, the finest hotel in Buenos Aires, was a woman and that there were many women working in marketing within the industry. Nonetheless, Barrenechea had been working with and dealing with men throughout the development of Mai10, from owners of estancias to fishing guides, hotel owners, and managers. These individuals may at first have been skeptical of such a strong Argentine woman making demands of them, but her natural charisma and talent ultimately won them over. As a result, Barrenechea never felt that being a woman was a challenge in growing her business, and, perhaps, her personal nature was such that the challenge was not as noticeable to her. It was also true that, since the industry was still in its infancy when she started Mai10, Barrenechea was not yet operating within an established system or male-dominated industry. Instead, she helped to develop tourism in Argentina and made Mai10 a major pillar in the industry's foundation.

Looking Toward the Future

Mai10's success as a business resulted in increased tourism to Argentina. Over the years Barrenechea has received various awards and repeated recognition by publications such as *Travel + Leisure, Conde Nast Traveler*, and *National Geographic*. In 2009 Barrenechea was continuing to strive to refine her business. While the global recession and increased competition within the South American tourism industry continued to present difficulties for Mai10, Barrenechea was considering the different ways she might adapt her business to prepare for the challenges ahead.

QUESTIONS

1   What were the main challenges Maita Barrenechea faced in growing her business?
2   How can an entrepreneur protect his or her business from the volatile environment of a country like Argentina?
3   In what ways should Maita change her marketing strategy to attract more customers?

Note

1   Most of the information presented in this case is based on interviews with Maita Barrenechea conducted in December 2008.

10 Martha Debayle's bbmundo

Helping Parents and Their Children

Mauro F. Guillén

Martha Debayle was a TV and radio personality, and a divorced mother of two young children. She realized that Mexican women like herself needed advice and resources pertaining to rearing children and taking care of the various aspects of family life. She launched an Internet portal and, later, a magazine, hired a small staff, including her sister, to run the business, and put together a roster of seventy doctors, psychologists, therapists, educators, nutritionists, and other professionals to generate content and field users' questions. Her revenue came from magazine sales and corporate sponsorships, but could stagnate unless she paid more attention to the business, and pursued new growth opportunities.

Figure 10.1 Martha Debayle

Source: Martha Debayle, January 2009.

"I am blunt, very direct, and very real," said Martha Debayle, the Nicaraguan born, New York raised, Mexican television personality, and entrepreneur. An accomplished communicator and divorced mother of two, she hit upon the idea of setting up a company to provide useful content and advice to parents and families, while facing, in her own life, the enormous challenges of managing the demands of work and children. In addition to her daily radio and weekly television shows, Martha was the founder and top executive of bbmundo, a company that, in 2008, generated 5 million dollars in revenue, sold nearly 90,000 copies of its lavishly illustrated monthly magazine aimed at parents and families, and boasted 690,000 registered users of its free Web site.[1] Armed with an inexhaustible passion for what she did, Martha learned the ropes of entrepreneurship through experience—not at school. And yet, she became a master at the game of growing and diversifying a business that did enormous good while doing well.

Martha was a gifted communicator. She was especially adept at pronouncing all of the key management buzzwords with a remarkably funny and scornful tone: business plan, cash flow, barriers to entry, competitive advantage, and all the rest. Her body language complemented her spoken English, Spanish, and "Spanglish" seamlessly. She remembered being scheduled to speak as a guest lecturer at Columbia Business School on entrepreneurship after two male entrepreneurs gave presentations using the customary PowerPoint slides. She stated: "I realized I had not prepared. It was my heels and me confronting the audience. I just spoke about my business, my passion, and how I make decisions." The result was that the MBA students loved it.

The Entrepreneur and Her Environment

Martha's radio and television career was built on the basis of conveying direct messages in straightforward language to women, in general, and mothers, in particular. She was often dramatic and very resourceful when using metaphors, but she did not let the ornament overshadow the substance of what she had to say. bbmundo's headquarters mirrored the founder's philosophy. It was located in a two-story, modernist-looking building in the central district of Polanco in downtown Mexico City, not far from the ruins of the Aztec capital, Tenochtitlán. The decor was minimalist throughout. White, unadorned walls predominated. Windows were large and provided almost no separation from the bustling street outside. Her office was unassuming. A couple of Bauhaus-style white leather sofas arranged in the shape of an "L" provided for a comfortable seating area. A large desk surrounded by six chairs sat at one corner, almost as an afterthought and with no obvious signs of activity. Martha, however, was full of ideas and enthusiasm for what she did. Or, rather, as she liked to put it, "My ideas come direct out of my soul. I do not let rational models drive my business decisions. I let my instincts reign free."

Martha's trajectory was strikingly unconventional. Her early childhood took place in Nicaragua. Her family then migrated to New York City before she was barely a teenager; her father was then transferred to Mexico. While her male siblings pursued MBA degrees, she enrolled in an undergraduate program in graphic design and advertising in Mexico City. Disillusioned with academia, she quit. She yearned for a career in communication and music, but had no patience for schooling. As a child, she was the one in the family who made and sold things. Her father used to say, "You will be a great entrepreneur." She did not believe him at the time.

In 1990, she landed a job on a radio program called *DJ Live*. She then moved on to other shows, including hosting the Grammys, the World Music Awards, the Oscars, and various beauty pageants for Mexican audiences. In 1992, she switched to television, and, in 1997, she persuaded executives at Televisa, Mexico's largest media group, to air a 20-minute segment on child rearing called bbtips. The idea came from her early experience as a mother—her first daughter was born the year before. "Why not do something about raising kids?" she asked herself. She worked enthusiastically—researching, writing, and presenting the show all by herself. She then gave birth to a second daughter. Her marriage floundered and she returned to her parents' house with her two children. But, by the late 1990s, she had become an opinion leader among mothers throughout Mexico, with an average viewership of 1 million.[2]

Getting Started

However, television was not the ideal medium to realize Martha's goals. While it gave her tremendous visibility and fame, it did not allow for the kind of user-initiated interaction that the Internet provided. It was early 2000 when Martha became obsessed with the idea of launching a Web portal to provide Mexican mothers with the content and advice they needed to improve their lives and those of their children. One night in early 2000, she decided to use her credit card to purchase the bbmundo.com domain. She then got in touch with México Analítica, a Web services provider. Within weeks, GBM Grupo Bursátil Mexicano approached her with an offer to pay 1 million dollars for her company, which did not really exist, did not produce any goods, and did not generate any revenue. Kimberly-Clark de México approached her within days with another offer. But Martha was not ready to sell her idea to anyone. She wanted to pursue it by herself. It took her no more than 24 hours to dismiss both suitors. Various Internet companies, including AOL México, Terra, and Starmedia, received the same answer. She even resisted Televisa's Es Más portal division which offered $750,000 for 75 percent of the company. And so a stubborn Martha, aided by twelve employees, launched the bbmundo.com Web site on September 4, 2000, months after the NASDAQ had collapsed and Internet startups were rapidly depleting their last reserves of cash.

She stated, "Maybe I was naïve, but I resisted the temptation of selling out. It just did not sound right."

bbmundo.com did not sell banners; rather, it offered businesses microsites that they could use to convey as much information as they desired to their customers. Martha stated, "We did not want to become a marketing site but rather one in which women could become better mothers." Within a few weeks of its launch, she had 40,000 visitors to her Web site and reached breakeven after 8 months of operation.[3]

The bbmundo.com Web site offered a variety of services, including bbnombres (to search baby names and their origins), bbpensamientos (to share thoughts and feelings), bbdudas (for frequently asked questions), bbchats (to exchange advice and information), bbdirectorio (for a directory of businesses), and bbrecetas (for recipes), among others. The site also offered interactive tools that enabled the user to obtain and tailor information to their needs, including diaper calculators, height and weight tables, and vaccination calendars, among others. Its flagship service was a free 24/7 online advice and support system which provided assistance on any medical, psychological, or legal issue, and was staffed by a group of specialists. The service processed 3,000 consultations per month. Many bbmundo services required user membership and registration in bbclub, a user's club.

Initially, Martha relied on ad hoc advertising from the microsites to generate most of her revenue. She quickly realized that a more systematic approach was needed. Her family was not very supportive at the time: "'Martha you are going through a divorce, you have two daughters, you just signed up to be the brand image for Pantene shampoo in Mexico, and they paid you well . . . Stop wasting time and money on this business . . . it is going nowhere . . .'"

"But I insisted that it would all work out in the end," said Martha, and went on:

> It's a logical thing, don't show me any numbers, it's just common sense; I could not believe the people surrounding me were so blind. So I used any money at my disposal to pay off my debts, and I remember my Mom saying, "But whose mind could possibly conceive this business that does not turn out a cent and look how exhausted you are, how irresponsible! You're everything your two daughters have in this world . . ."

Growing the Business

In April 2001, she approached Nestlé SA and asked for $9,000 a month over 1 year in exchange for advertising space. Her argument was that brands needed to establish direct communication and rapprochement with the user—this was a radically new concept in Mexico at the time. She then struck a deal with Ford Motor Company, which wished to reach parents who were concerned about the safety of their children in automobiles.

Gerber Products, Disney, Johnson & Johnson, Wyeth, Seguros Monterrey New York Life, and a few others followed suit. Martha stated: "I simply made the sales pitch straight out of my soul, and it worked. They believed in the potential of my business."

Martha admitted to having received some help during 2001 from two former consultants who founded LabRed, a business incubator, although they delivered far less than the expectations they raised. In exchange for a 9 percent stake, they gave Martha some office space, $60,000 in cash, and a promise to help her raise more capital. But the timing was not great, and fresh money did not come in. By 2002 she owed $15,000 to various service suppliers and 3 months in back wages to her seven employees. The non-profit venture capital firm, Endeavor, provided some further advice and legitimacy beginning in 2002, but Martha overcame the initial difficulties by pressing forward. "I was living in anguish," she recalled. She was evicted from her office, so she moved the computers and files to her parents' home. The employees continued to work out of their homes.

In 2005, with few resources on hand, she made the most momentous decision: to launch a monthly magazine targeting "women who are smart, awake, and have self-respect." The slogan was "Inspired by love, guided by knowledge." She enlisted the collaboration of two designers who had founded Mapas, as well as back up from Endeavor. They advised Martha that she would need about $100,000 a month to survive in the difficult and unforgiving world of magazine publishing. She decided to call on her corporate sponsors. Disney, Wyeth, Kimberly-Clark, and Brystol-Myers Squibb responded positively. The most successful Mexican magazine in the parenting and family category was born, replete with attention grabbing photos, trendy articles written by experts in plain prose, and tips on a wide variety of topics. An annual subscription was 330 pesos (about $25). However, given Mexico's poor postal system, most copies were sold through newsstands for 30 pesos (about $2.30). Ninety-five percent of revenues came from advertising. In February 2005, Martha launched the bbmundo card with some 120 participating companies that agreed to offer discounts on baby-related goods to cardholders. This new product helped propel the magazine's circulation.

bbmundo Magazine relied on a roster of seventy doctors, psychologists, therapists, educators, nutritionists, and other professionals who wrote articles for free in exchange for accessing its readership. Some of the articles were written in-house. Topics included pregnancy tips, sleep deprivation, autism, obesity, nutrition, time management, and recipes for having silent sex, all of which addressed the obvious and pressing needs among parents of young children. A typical article would first frame the issue at hand, and then offer different ways of reframing or resolving it:

> Although they tend not to admit it, moms and dads usually have some gender preference concerning their soon-to-arrive babies. These preferences do not form overnight; rather, they are constructed over one's

lifetime. . . . Gender preferences have many different causes, from childhood games to the family's social situation. Although many parents-to-be keep their preferences to themselves, most have an answer available to the inevitable question of "Do you want your baby to be a girl or a boy?" These fantasies are natural and will not necessarily carry negative consequences for the baby. It all depends on how one manages the contrast between the imaginary baby and the real one. . . . It is entirely O.K. to feel frustrated, guilty, sad or angry: just help each other identify your emotions and talk about them without feeling scared. At the same time, try to build together new fantasies about the actual gender of your baby, think about the positives, imagine possible games, choose a name, and start decorating the baby's room.[4]

Over the years, the structure of the magazine changed. Article topics were classified under the rubrics of development, pregnancy, nutrition, health, psychology, sexuality, and fashion. A series of short sections were introduced, including:

A calendar of relevant chats and radio shows.
Editorials written by Martha or her sister on important issues affecting parents.
Readers' letters.
News about ways of getting information or new products.
Questions and answers in which complex parenting topics were broken down into specific issues and how to address them.
"Numbers": generally about milestones in the development of babies and children.
"Shopping": new trends, stores, and product offerings.
"Don't Torture Yourself": damaging myths regarding motherhood and childrearing.
"Entertainment": tips on books, movies, and music.
"Mom": tips for the various roles that mothers play in the household.
"The Doctor in the Home": health issues and minor illnesses.
"Ellos": advice for dads.
"Shop Directory": topic-focused listing of stores.
"Picture of the Month": pictures submitted by readers.
"Tips": other suggestions not covered elsewhere in the magazine.

In August of 2006, Martha returned to television with the show *Cerca de Ti*, sponsored by Avon Products. It covered a wide range of topics, including family, health, emotional well-being, fashion, beauty, sexuality, and personal finance. The show ended in December 2007, and Martha then started a daily, hour-long radio show which featured a bbmundo segment every Monday—the show averaged 1.4 million listeners. She also led a Thursday morning television show on Televisa's Channel 2 which was written, casted, and produced by bbmundo.

Martha liked to say that her greatest virtue was being generous, while her biggest fault was impatience. She ardently argued that the most important feature of an entrepreneur was having "a certain degree of craziness. If entrepreneurs analyzed everything that can go wrong, they would not accomplish anything." And she added that persistence and a strong will were essential:

> Losers make excuses, winners make a way and there is always a way. My leadership style is authoritarian but very inspirational, close, loving; I like spending time with my people and I care deeply about them—I have a big heart. At bbmundo we are a big family, passionate for what we do, which translates into new forms of communication, alternative marketing paths, innovative products, and support for our community.

Growing Pains

Until late 2007, bbmundo lacked what most business textbooks would identify as the attributes of a serious company. After experiencing annual growth rates in excess of 60 percent, Martha finally caved in. The company now employed accountants, marketing experts, designers, editors, and even a CEO—a concession to her father, an investment banker who spent a couple of days a week providing advice. Her younger sister Eugenia started as marketing director in 2003 and, beginning with the September 2008 issue, became the magazine's editor. In her first editorial, she explained her view of the magazine:

> Something I've always liked about bbmundo is that we have contributed to strengthening the new mom, that of our times, a redefined mom, the one who has opinions, who questions things, the one who likes to read about topics in-depth, and wants to be a better mom.

That issue also saw the launch of the 26-page bbKIDS section which responded, in Martha's words, "to my own needs." She stated:

> My daughters have grown: Antonina is now 12 and Camila 9. Just as when they were babies I felt I did not have the information available to me, now I am coming across another set of questions. They ask me about sex, they talk to me about the boy they like, I see them getting exposed to so much information; they disagree and want to negotiate with me, they talk about bullying at school, and they demand my attention more than ever. I quickly realized that I needed to be more prepared than ever, especially for what's to come. It is in this context that bbKIDS was born, for all moms and dads of kids between the ages of 6 and 12, who, like myself, have many unanswered questions.

The contents of the September 2008 issue included articles titled "Bullying," "Mom, I have a girlfriend," and "Tips to motivate your kid to do the homework." The success of bbKIDS led Martha and Eugenia to entertain the possibility of launching an entirely separate magazine.

In 2004, Martha received several awards: *Gatopardo* named her one of the ten most successful Internet businesswomen in Latin America, *Mujer Ejecutiva* designated her Businesswoman of the Year, and Mexico's leading business magazine, *Expansión*, named her one of the ten most outstanding female entrepreneurs. Her role models were Oprah Winfrey and Martha Stewart, though she had no intention of going through any up-and-down cycles of obesity or of acting on privileged financial information.

Martha was not shy about discussing the challenges facing her company: "Should we try to decouple bbmundo from the Martha Debayle brand image?" "Should we hire a professional CEO?" "Should we launch a line of branded baby clothing and accessories, or focus on expanding our multimedia offerings to include books, videos, and podcasts?" "Does it make sense for bbmundo to pursue the rapidly growing Hispanic market in the U.S., which is already 44 million strong?" "Should we perhaps become a magnet for women of any age and life situation as opposed to just focusing on mothers?" While pondering these options, Martha stretched on the sofa as if she were waking up from a dream. But it was all very real for her, and for the million-odd Mexican women who followed her on the radio, on television, over the Internet, and in print. She declared that "In order to succeed, you need to believe in yourself, in your dream."

QUESTIONS

1   Which of the strategic growth options entertained by Martha Debayle make the most sense in the short run? And in the long run?

2   What types of resources would Martha need to secure in order to pursue product diversification? How about international growth?

3   Should bbmundo pursue these growth opportunities by itself or in collaboration with other companies?

Notes

1   Martha Debayle, Personal interview, Mexico City, Mexico, December 16, 2008.
2   Ibid.
3   Ibid.
4   *bbmundo Magazine*, November 2008, pp. 67, 70.

11 Angela Chan's i-Vision

"Killing Me Softly"

Christine Chang

An investment banker by background, Angela Chan, together with her friend Ivy Zhang, launched i-Vision to capitalize on China's rising digital media market. Starting as a provider of interactive TV solutions, i-Vision realized that the future lay in offering a TV channel through hand-held devices such as 3G phones featuring trailers and synopses, micro-blogs, aggregation tools, and sharing programs. In order to pursue this strategy, Angela counted on her contacts in the government, a partnership with a state-owned enterprise, and the funding and advice provided by a venture capital firm.

Figure 11.1 Angela Chan and Ivy Zhang
Source: Angela Chan.

Angela Chan is the well-respected and thoughtful founder and managing director of i-Vision, a leading technology company in China's mobile television industry. She blushes when she talks about herself during our conversation, and speaks softly as she presents her company. She is a graceful and quiet woman whose appearance is as understated as her personality.

Since its inception, i-Vision has earned a number of high-profile awards. In 2007, it was named a Red Herring Asia 100 winner and a Top 50 Innovator for the Mobile Innovation Summit (Asia). The company has also received the Sony Ericsson-sponsored Golden Olive Award for "the best mobile phone advertising platform," and a Top 100 Fast Growth Company Award from China's *Business Watch Magazine*. Despite these accolades and the huge potential for the business going forward, Angela does not label herself a "success" just yet. Instead, she is modest and still considers herself a striving entrepreneur.

In 2004 Angela partnered with her engineer friend, Ivy Zhang, to form i-Vision. They took a leap of faith that their then-two-person team could build a successful media technology business based on the combination of their engineering know-how and business acumen. They believed China represented a vast marketplace of new digital media consumers and leapt at the challenge. Angela left her high-powered career in the financial/ investment banking industry, while Ivy left her senior management job at a Japanese IC software design company in Beijing. The pair began their foray into entrepreneurship by launching i-Vision. Angela also garnered the support of family, friends, and former colleagues who provided the seed money to jump-start the new venture.

Market Background in 2004

When they established i-Vision, Angela and Ivy's objective was to bring interactive services to cable digital television by integrating services on one-way broadcast with two-way telecommunication networks. In 2004 China was already the world's largest cable television market, with around 100 million subscribing households—representing almost full penetration in the large cities. At that time, nearly all cable television subscribers received analog cable signals, and the central government was pushing an aggressive plan to digitalize the entire country, thus cutting off analog television signals by 2015.

Analog television was traditionally a one-way, vertical media experience. Consumers watched programs at set broadcast times, with little interaction with their televisions. In contrast, digitalization defined a whole new horizon for this mass-media platform by providing the audience with a variety of additional experiences and services via set-top boxes. Angela and Ivy envisioned that home consumers could enjoy new interactive services, such as choosing program enhancements, checking public information, voting, and even shopping—all while being entertained. The idea of "inter-activating" the nationwide cable television households seemed to hold unlimited possibilities and became too exciting to pass up.

Guanxi

Guanxi is the Chinese word for "relationships." Historically, *guanxi* are the crux of how business is conducted in China. You know someone who knows someone who knows someone. This is how deals are still made in China. In fact, it was through her *guanxi* at the investment bank that Angela gained an entry point for i-Vision into one of China's largest state-owned enterprises (SOEs). This former client owned one of the nationwide cable companies—a backbone of China's cable television infrastructure. The SOE planned to work closely with China's government to finance the digitalization process and further involve local cable television operations afterwards. Angela immediately identified this as an opportunity for i-Vision.

As she leveraged her relationships to set up introductions and meetings throughout the SOE, Angela's strong reputation as a marketer in invest-ment banking worked to her advantage. Her old *guanxi* assured decision-makers at the SOE that Angela and i-Vision were solid, reliable business contacts. Eventually, i-Vision found both its first client and business partner in the SOE. As Angela reflected,

> In China, people have to trust or even like you before they start talking business with you. (This is somewhat different from the west where business can be transacted based on an understanding that there are mutual benefits.) This kind of trust may take years to build up, but very often it is more important to have trust than to have a written contract on paper.[1]

Although the scope of i-Vision's initial project with the SOE turned out to be limited, it allowed the company to begin developing and testing its product while generating revenue. Although Angela and Ivy's vision for their company was greater, they viewed the project as both a learning opportunity and a stepping stone toward a larger objective. Their relationship with the SOE opened more doors for i-Vision to work with other top industry players, including China's licensed broadcasters, telecom operators, and internationally renowned technology companies. The initial project also enabled i-Vision to evaluate the technologies and products it developed side-by-side with top companies in the value chain of the industry. The project with the SOE also legitimized the company in the eyes of other potential business partners, clients, and investors. This part-nership provided increased credibility that enabled i-Vision to gradually emerge as a leading digital media technology solution provider in China.

Venture Capital Partnership

At the same time, Gobi Partners, an early-stage venture capital firm focused on digital media investments in China, was also paying attention to the same SOE's activity. The firm observed that the SOE already had significant exposure to the digital media area and had been watching it to measure the pulse of the digital media landscape. Although Gobi Partners was unable to invest directly in an SOE, it was aware of this particular SOE's assets and relationships. After following the standard due-diligence process, Gobi Partners invested in i-Vision, becoming its primary institutional investor.

Gobi Partners not only provided much-needed capital as an investor, but also served as a business advisor, helping to develop Angela and Ivy's vision into that of a sophisticated business objective. Angela describes herself as "naïve"[2] compared to Gobi Partners. However, both parties shared a similar vision for digital media in China. As Angela described the exchange, "We were looking from the ground up, [and] they were looking down from a higher plane [with a] fuller picture. [Gobi Partners] was able to see a bigger value the team could create than we saw ourselves."[3]

Gobi Partners had already been studying the digital television market and understood the labyrinth of China's government policies as they related to the digital media market. Having already invested in 60–80 digital media companies, Gobi Partners had key expertise and real exposure to the industry. A venture capital firm such as Gobi Partners—that had already been analyzing the market, the latest technologies, and the environment of an industry—was able to advise its portfolio companies, providing additional business perspective. With i-Vision, Gobi Partners was interested in helping the company find a way to turn its technology into a business advantage by generating an entire business ecosystem.

When venture capitalists evaluate companies to invest in, they are concerned with two main factors. First, they are interested in whether the business is viable. Gobi Partners, focused as it is on technology and digital media, views technology mostly as a Trojan horse that gives the business a head start in the larger game. Second, and perhaps more important, a venture capital firm such as Gobi Partners evaluated the quality of the business manager(s). This firm believed that, although the specific technology is important, actual business skill is still very necessary. According to Wai-Kit Lau, founding partner of Gobi Partners, "we watch the same old movie over and over."[4] Throughout their work as venture capitalists, Lau and his partners observed the reasons why some businesses fail while others succeed. Lau believes that when businesses fail, "most of the time it is because the manager didn't deploy [effectively]."[5]

A Heavy-Duty Team

In i-Vision, Gobi Partners saw the assets as both i-Vision's technology platform and services business and its unique business team. Lau recounts how he was intrigued upon meeting Angela and Ivy. As he led the pre-investment due diligence on i-Vision, Gobi Partners sought to uncover why and how i-Vision was able to accomplish all that it had to date. Lau concluded, "I think a lot of it has to do with their personalities."[6] Ivy was an extremely competent and well-respected engineer. While she focused on the technical aspects of the business, it was Angela who led i-Vision's business development. Lau described Angela as sophisticated, pointing to her "relationship management" capabilities. He said, "this does not mean 'wining and dining.' Those times are long gone."[7] Instead, Angela's style of relationship management was centered on integrity and consistency.

In fact, Angela was by no means a flashy CEO. Rather, she came across as a quietly confident woman with a strong business focus. Lau believed that the straightforward and trustworthy management style of Angela and her team allows i-Vision to consistently stand above the crowd, especially in the Chinese environment. He proudly described i-Vision's management team as "killing you softly" (referring to Roberta Flack's 1973 song). He explained that the Chinese technology market was a male-dominated community where others may underestimate the potential of the female team of i-Vision and see it as a threat to viablity. i-Vision may appear to be "soft, but they are strong . . . heavy-duty."[8]

This management ability also lent itself to Angela's skill in enabling i-Vision to respond swiftly to changes in the market. Indeed, Angela has led i-Vision to significantly change its original business from that of set-top boxes for cable television to today's focus on mobile television services. Lau pointed to Angela's experience in working at the investment bank/multinational company. He believed this gave Angela the general background to lead business development for i-Vision. The company benefited from Angela and Ivy's partnership—while Ivy is a talented engineer, Angela is a business person who keenly understands the continually evolving business needs of a rapidly changing industry.

The Evolution of i-Vision

i-Vision began as Angela and Ivy's brainchild during the digitalization process of cable television in China. Ivy was paying attention to the Japanese digital television industry and drew inspiration from the additional services provided to consumers through set-top boxes. As China's cable television digitalization developed, Angela and Ivy sought to create a technology platform to provide similar services in China. i-Vision also joined the working group the SOE had formed with other top technology partners, moving on to develop digital set-top-box solutions to target the next generation of cable television consumers.

In 2005 i-Vision completed the first version of an open interaction platform to deliver services and applications through cable television set-top boxes. This platform enabled service operators, content providers, and advertisers to develop and implement interactive television applications, including government public information services, enhanced and interactive television content, television shopping, online surveys, and interactive advertising.

In the same year, i-Vision, together with the SOE and other partners, ran the first commercial trial of interactive digital cable television in the Chinese municipality of Dalian. i-Vision's iTV solution facilitated services through cable television, including an interactive program guide, voting, television messaging services, and interactive stock services. i-Vision also developed a television payment solution, in collaboration with Dalian's local partners, which enabled Dalian's consumers to shop and make payments through their television sets by simply using their remote control units.

While working on the project with the SOE, i-Vision gained the attention of a European technology company that was working on another project in Taiwan. The iTV solution was what the client, a Taiwan cable television operator, was looking for in its digitalization project. With this new partnership, i-Vision's product began to find its way into the commercially sophisticated Taiwan cable television market. Throughout 2006, i-Vision dispatched engineers to Taiwan and Seoul, South Korea, several times to integrate its technology solution with that of its project partners. In addition to generating revenues, the Taiwan project was an important learning experience and milestone for i-Vision because it involved international partners. It also helped i-Vision gain additional credibility as a technology company.

Back in mainland China, however, the cable television industry presented challenges. First, the market was highly fragmented, with thousands of local operators each guarding their own territories. This made technology standardization almost impossible. (Unlike the industry in the United States, China's cable television is a government-controlled, government-sponsored operation used for party propaganda purposes.) At that time, monthly cable subscription fees ranged between 12 and 18 RMB per household for network maintenance while content was free. The sometimes-manual billing systems/mechanisms created money-making opportunities for small local operators. The central government's digitalization efforts were seen by some local operators as a threat to these systems. In addition, set-top boxes were sponsored most often by cable television operators who were looking for only the most basic versions. These operators had no incentive to upgrade to the technology to which i-Vision's interactive services were tied. Furthermore, consumers were not in the habit of paying to upgrade their cable television set-top boxes regularly, as is the practice with mobile phones, for example. As a result, by the end of 2006, i-Vision decided to redirect its efforts from cable television to mobile television.

This willingness to make changes to their business has enabled i-Vision to survive in the rapidly changing technology industry in China. Entrepreneurs often become too attached to their original business plans or technology solutions and fall prey to the force of inertia. As Lau notes, "Some local entrepreneurs are not as open-minded because they are holding on to one concept. i-Vision is very open-minded and listens [to suggestions from business partners]."[9] i-Vision's switch to mobile media represented a major change, as Angela's strong desire to succeed and survive motivated her to lead the i-Vision team in this new direction.

The Growth of the Chinese Market

In 2006 China had already overtaken the United States to become the largest mobile telecom market in the world. By the end of that year, the mobile population in China had surpassed 461 million, with penetration at around 35 percent. This remarkable growth rate was expected to continue. Studies also showed that it was very common for urban mobile consumers to upgrade their handsets every 12–18 months.

At the same time, the Chinese government, determined to showcase the country's advanced technological capabilities to the world, was pushing for widespread mobile television availability for the then-upcoming 2008 Beijing Olympics. A mobile television service was promised to be available to help distinguish the Beijing Games from previous Olympics.

Mobile television is generally understood to be television that is watched on personal handheld devices. It can be either pay video services via telecommunication networks, or broadcast services via terrestrial networks. It can also be in the form of Internet streaming video delivered over the wireless network to handheld devices.

In the run-up to the Olympics, the market was expecting Chinese regulatory agencies to grant 3G operating licenses and decide which mobile multimedia broadcast standard China would adopt. There were a number of competing mobile television technology formats, and it was unclear which one would prevail in China. The market was also waiting to see which entities would get the official licenses to operate mobile television services. Complicating things even more, the new digital media service of mobile television was sitting in the middle of the overlapping territories of mobile operators and the broadcasters/licensed content providers, under the jurisdiction of two traditionally "competing" government authorities.

Throughout this time of uncertainty, i-Vision continued to move forward by completing the development of a server-to-device mobile television operation system and participating in as many trials as possible for various technologies. This allowed i-Vision to continually cultivate relationships with business partners and to remain up to date with new technologies. Angela and Ivy continued to believe that mobile television would soon become one of the most influential new media formats in the country with the world's largest and still-expanding mobile population. They aimed to be ready when the uncertainties cleared up and the technology standard was finally set in China.

i-Vision also recognized that the future of mobile television was not limited to the delivery of video content to mobile devices. To become successful in operating mobile television services, there must be a smooth convergence of both rich video content and interactive personalized services. Mobile television would become a whole new media platform, distinct from traditional home cable television or IPTV. i-Vision's mobile television technology solutions have been focused on how to integrate relevant interactive services intelligently to complement video content viewed on small and large screens.

Before the final decisions were announced on technology formats and operating entities, i-Vision decided to work with various parties advocating different standards to maintain a flexible market position. As the company's open technology systems were compatible with all the major standards and offered a unique value proposition to the other partners, the team was involved in almost all major mobile television tests and trials with different collaborating parties along the value chain. These included broadcasters, telecom carriers, systems providers, device manufacturers, and government agencies. During this challenging period, i-Vision managed to build its reputation as a reliable and advanced mobile television technology solution provider. Angela believes this is also the kind of relationship—or *guanxi*—building that would be useful for future developments and opportunities.

During the Olympics in August 2008, i-Vision partnered with BTVM (the subsidiary company of the Beijing TV station responsible for the new digital media business) to run a mobile streaming television channel called *Jia You Zhan* (meaning "gas station") on China Mobile's network. Mobile subscribers in Beijing could use their cell phones to access the channel, which continuously aired videos of behind-the-party scenes and social events going on around Beijing, with celebrities chanting "*jia you*" to the athletes. i-Vision secured the participation of Olympic sponsors, public relations companies, and international brands by showing their events on the mobile entertainment channel. The only problem was that 3G was not yet available in China. Thus, the video quality on the wireless devices was not as good as i-Vision had hoped. Nevertheless, the channel did gain the attention of a number of top consumer brands that returned to ask i-Vision to cover more of their subsequent promotional events in the country. This trial run confirmed that users, operators, and sponsors were, indeed, interested. It also confirmed to i-Vision that the market players were starting to pay attention to this new media platform.

By the end of 2008 it had become clear that China would adopt its home-grown technology, China Mobile Multimedia Broadcast (CMMB), as the country's mobile broadcast television standard. In the first week of 2009 the government also finalized the issuance of 3G operating licenses after a restructuring of the country's telecom industry that resulted in three operators providing full-range services, including fixed line and mobile. The market anticipated that operators would boost investment in the Chinese telecom market to upgrade the infrastructures. The convergence of telecom networks, digital television networks, and the Internet—combined with deployment of 3G and CMMB networks—would create tremendous opportunities for industry players, especially technology providers, in the next few years. For i-Vision, this also meant that the technology development and relationships cultivated in the earlier years had started to pay off as they generated licensing revenues from the company's mobile television technology products. Angela believed that, without the team's continuous hard work and *guanxi*-building at all levels with the clients over the past few years, it would have been nearly impossible for a small company like i-Vision to win such contracts.

> In China you have to do multi-level relationship-building if you want to do business with the big organizations. It is not enough just talking to the top guys. Sometimes it is more important to win the trust of the middle managers.[10]

Although China was right on the cusp of a government-led investment cycle in upgrading its telecom infrastructure and i-Vision's business volume has been growing, Angela and Ivy are feeling far from complacent. After carefully evaluating the market, the team decided the time was right to change direction from a technology company to a mobile Internet application/service company.

The Decision

i-Vision decided to focus on building a mobile Internet video-centric social networking service platform, taking what it believes is a bet on the development of 3G and the mobile Internet market. Angela believed that the mobile Internet would be a more successful network for mobile television for several reasons. First, mobile Internet users were growing rapidly, and there were more handheld devices with browsers embedded. Second, with 3G and mobile broadband networks, the quality of wireless video services has improved tremendously. i-Vision believed it should capitalize on its own mobile television solution to develop innovative mobile television applications and services to build its consumer user base to generate recurring revenues. The company called this new product "Pocket TV," a video-centric mobile Internet social networking service platform. i-Vision did not expect most mobile users to watch 1-hour soap opera episodes on their handhelds. Instead, with the Pocket TV platform, users could discover entertainment news, view trailers and synopses, micro-blog, aggregate their own personalized channels, and share with their friends via the mobile Internet. The management team hoped this decision would help i-Vision prosper.

QUESTIONS

1 What were the most significant challenges faced by Angela Chan when attempting to grow her business?
2 What roles did *guanxi* play in the process?
3 Should i-Vision grow by itself or pursue even more partnerships?

Notes

1 Interview with Angela Chan, August 4, 2009.
2 Ibid.
3 Ibid.
4 Interview with Wai-Kit Lau, August 8, 2009.
5 Ibid.
6 Ibid.
7 Ibid.
8 Ibid.
9 Ibid.
10 Interview with Angela Chan, August 4, 2009.

Part III

Organizing and Leading

Research on entrepreneurs and managers has failed to find any consistent and systematic differences between women and men when it comes to leadership style and ability to organize. Some women entrepreneurs do exhibit specific preferences for choosing, organizing and managing their venture, and may define success in terms of goal achievement, a better work/family balance or community benefits as opposed to growth, profits and fame. Overall, however, research has documented a great diversity of approaches to leadership and organization on the part of women entrepreneurs (see Chapter 23 for a summary of research findings). In this section we will examine the leadership and organizational qualities of an Egyptian jeweler, a Mexican pottery maker, a Kuwaiti investment banker, and a Mexican caterer.

12 Azza Fahmy

Egyptian Jewelry

Maha ElShinnawy and Mauro F. Guillén

In Egypt, women were not meant to become apprentices in jewelry making, let alone designers and entrepreneurs. Azza Fahmy defied the odds and launched a high-end line of jewelry inspired by local traditions. Her initial success made it possible to expand the business, add new product lines, establish a large factory, and even pursue foreign sales. Rapid growth, however, led to inefficiencies and organizational troubles, which she sought to overcome by appointing an outsider as general manager, who failed to resolve the problems. The founder then delegated day-to-day management to one of her two daughters, while the other assisted with design. Their challenge was to ensure orderly growth through diversification and internationalization without compromising quality.

AZZA FAHMY

Figure 12.1 Azza Fahmy Logo

"It happened in 1974, at the first Cairo International Book Fair," recalled Azza Fahmy, the Egyptian jewelry designer and entrepreneur.

> As I stood leafing through an illustrated book on mediaeval European jewelry, new vistas seemed to unfold before my eyes: a world of beauty, art and intricate craftsmanship. I paid my month's salary to purchase the book, for I could not leave without it.

At the time she worked for the Egyptian Information Authority, designing book covers. She made inquiries about how she could become a jewelry designer and maker.

In the gold- and silversmiths' quarter of the Khan [market], I met Osta Ramadan, a man in his early thirties, dark and tall with curly hair. . . . I explained my wish to become an apprentice. . . . [He] thought it a very strange idea since it was the first time a woman had expressed such a wish. . . . He thought it over for a brief moment, then accepted with enthusiasm.[1]

"So I tied my hair back, put on my overalls and spent my days in a workshop full of men learning the tricks of jewelry making."[2]

Becoming an Entrepreneur

Entrepreneurs often lacked the encouragement of their social environment. Moreover, Egypt was a country that scored lower on many indicators of social development than other countries in the Middle East and North Africa. "My family was not very supportive at the beginning because they could not quite understand what I was doing, but I was very confident about my work,"[3] said Azza. "My mother was very sad," she recalled, "she thought I was crazy, sitting with ordinary workers when I had a good government job."[4] Thirty years later, Azza Fahmy was a US$4 million company, with some 165 employees, boutiques in Egypt, Dubai, and Jordan, and retailing agreements in Quatar, Bahrain, Dubai, and the United Kingdom. About a third of its sales were exports, and another third were sales to tourists visiting Egypt. Her collections included gold, silver, precious and semi-precious stones, and fashion jewelry, with pieces selling from as low as US$100 and up to US$40,000. The company made about 11,000 pieces each year, at an average price of US$330. In 2007 the *Financial Times* chose Azza as one of the twenty-five most influential businesswomen in the Middle East. The *New York Times* and the *Wall Street Journal* also published accolades of her work and business acumen.

"My new experience was out of the ordinary for any conventional, young Egyptian woman in a traditional environment, but I was determined to go on."[5] Azza graduated from Helwan University in 1965 with a degree in ornamentation and decoration. The British Council gave her a fellowship to study at the City of London Polytechnic School, where she sharpened her design skills and learned how to "translate designs into actual jewelry."[6]

"When one designs jewelry," Azza once said, "one has to know how to do it, not only how to draw it, but even more importantly, how to be able to work with the material."[7] Much of her work was inspired by Egyptian arts and crafts, with a touch of European influence. "Everything inspired me, and still does: palm trees, birds, flowers, and the motifs in a house or a piece of proverb."[8] A marketing brochure read:

Her inspiration stems from classical poetry, old proverbs and colloquial sayings—derived from the famous poets and philosophers of the Arab world—as well as her studies of various eras and civilizations with distinctive jewelry traditions–namely Bedouin, tribal, Mogul and Victorian. She then marries these influences with modern touches to create timeless pieces wearable by today's most contemporary women.

Azza had family ties to Turkey and the Sudan, having been born in the southern governorate of Sohaj. She stood on the shoulders of millennia of fine jewelry making by Egyptians, Armenians, and Turks living in Egypt.

Fahmy's necklaces capture Egypt's sights and sounds, intertwining silver beads with desert stones like those that once draped the Pharaohs. They embody the shocking silence of Egypt's deserts, the smiles of wandering nomads, the rushing palms of distant oases.[9]

Growth and Organization

The business grew very quickly during the 1970s and 1980s. As Azza noted,

> I found that I could not go on alone. I had to create a company, have a production plan and use quality control experts. I used to dream that my work would expand and suddenly I realized that I had a growing business.[10]

In 1974, she organized her first exhibition and decided to become self-employed. The minister of economy, who happened to be a friend of hers, recommended her for a bank loan of 15,000 pounds (a similar amount in dollars at the time).[11] Her first shop opened in 1981 at the El-Ain Gallery in Cairo's upscale Mohandiseen district, in collaboration with her sister Randa, a designer of Islamic metalwork and lighting, and her then-husband, the architect Nabil Ghaly. In 1997 she opened the Azza Fahmy Boutique in Maadi, a suburb of Cairo, followed by another store in Heliopolis. There were five Azza Fahmy boutiques in Cairo alone. Her customers included the Saudi, Kuwaiti, and Jordanian royal families. For many years she worked out of a cramped workshop in a poor district of Cairo, with twenty people working in two small rooms. She opened a rather spacious factory in 2003—located in the Sixth of October district of Cairo, not far from the great pyramids of Giza—which was later expanded. The ground floor comprised the main workshop area, the raw materials lock room, the planning and quality control sections, and the receiving area. The second floor housed the administrative offices, arranged around a balcony from which the craftsmen could be seen working below (see Figures 12.2 and 12.3). Azza's office was unassuming. The pictures on the walls reminded one of the many awards and distinctions she had received over the years. One was a signed photograph of Queen Rania of Jordan, a customer.

Figure 12.2 Factory Floor and Second-floor Administrative Offices, Azza Fahmy
        Factory in Cairo

Source: Mauro Guillén, January 2009.

By the early 2000s Azza realized that the necessary organizational and financial controls were not in place. She was also overwhelmed by the complexities of setting up her own factory and hiring large numbers of workers. In 2004 she decided to focus her energies full-time on design and to appoint an outside manager with experience at a multinational firm. He lasted only a few years, as he became increasingly frustrated by the lack of systems and organization. Upon his resignation, Azza turned to her daughter Fatma Ghaly, appointing her managing director. Her other daughter, Amina Ghaly, assisted her with design and later took on full responsibility for the fashion line and the St. Valentine's collection. As Azza noted, she did

> a fantastic job in bringing together two trends—a fashion style treatment which she combined with a technique that has been widely applied on leather and wood and adding a further edge by translating it using silver while capturing the brand's unique essence.

According to Azza, having her daughters leading the company "is a dream come true. Amina and I work very closely together. Our thoughts complete one another with her bringing in the modern touch to complement the brand essence." Fatma's role as managing director gave Azza

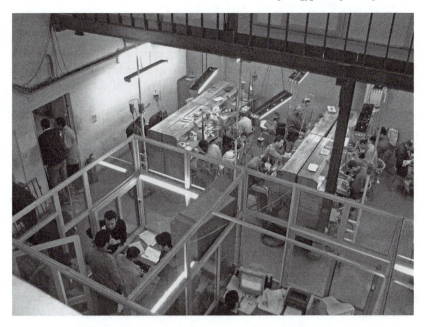

Figure 12.3 Factory Floor: Quality-control Cubicle on Left and Planning
Department on Right

Source: Mauro Guillén, January 2009.

"room to concentrate on the designs and undertake the research that goes with this process; we work very closely in terms of strategic business developments and I trust her views on related matters and the general running of the company." Amina added,

> Growing up with someone as passionate and hardworking is very motivating; witnessing her dream becoming what it is today and watching her continuous and tireless efforts makes me believe that I can get to what and where I want by simply working at it.[12]

Fatma was a fine arts graduate who began working in the marketing department in 2000. During several months in 2003 and 2004 she rotated through various positions to acquire an overall view of the business. In 2004 she became deputy general manager, at the same time Azza had hired the outside director. After becoming the chief executive, Fatma was horrified to find that eighteen different managers were reporting to her, including, for example, the cost-accounting head and the information technology head.

Seeking help, Fatma called her high-school friend, Nadine Okasha. Born in Northern Ireland to Egyptian parents, Nadine had returned to Cairo as a child, studied chemical engineering, started her managerial career in marketing at a local textile company, where she also helped create an operations manual, and then accepted a job at the French sales office of an Egyptian essential oils company. She restructured and ultimately dismantled that office. When Fatma asked her to join the firm in 2006, Nadine agreed on two conditions: access to all internal information and full backing from her friend and boss. She was appointed organizational development manager, with overall responsibility for hiring and organizational structure. One of her main challenges was to unveil hidden thefts. But the greatest task was to reorganize the entire firm. The organizational structure as it was made no sense, and there were no coherent profit and loss statements to guide the reform.

Nadine proposed a structure in which four key managers reported to Fatma: operations, marketing and retail, finance, and organizational development. The operations department, headed by Dalia Kandil, included the design (fifteen employees), planning (four employees), production (eighty-five workers), and warehousing (thirteen workers) sections. Fatma headed the marketing and retail department, where three people worked on marketing and public relations. The company had six boutique managers and about twenty attendants. A plan was in place to turn the boutiques into profit centers that would place orders for the factory. In fact, Azza Fahmy was incorporated as two separate companies, one of which comprised the boutiques. The finance department, run by a man hired specifically for this position, handled accounting, finance, and legal issues. Its offices sat toward the rear of the balcony floor, with plans to move to the expansion next door. This department produced myriad reports and statements. However, the company tended to buy equipment with cash and to expense it immediately, as opposed to amortizing it over its useful lifetime. The organizational development department, headed by Nadine, comprised two employees who also handled human resource and payroll issues.

The production department was highly stratified, following the Ottoman tradition of jewelry making. Four masters were at the top of the occupational pyramid. The highly skilled workers were aided by the apprentices and their helpers. In addition to the top management and administration, women worked in the warehouse, the raw materials area and the beading room. All workers arrived at 9 a.m. and stayed at the factory until 8 p.m. every day but Friday, taking several breaks for prayers and an hour for lunch. The design section included Azza Fahmy as chief designer and her daughter Amina. The design manager, Aleya Tawfik, was a mechanical engineer who had worked for BMW Egypt, quit her job to raise her two children, and was then hired by Azza. Aleya was also in charge of buying new equipment and tools, such as wax injectors, vacuum mixers, sanding machines, and continuous casting machines. The workers trained on the new equipment for about a month and typically used both the old and the new machines until they were fully comfortable with the new machinery. The quality control section manually inspected every piece, fixing minor problems and sending those with major defects back to production; this unit was located within a glass cubicle in the center of the production floor, adjacent to the planning section. It included three workers and a quality manager who reported directly to Dalia, the operations manager. Quality control was also involved in inspecting the "zero lot," a set of five pieces that were produced and scrutinized before launching any given collection.

Work Flow Organization and Decision Making

The work flow was quite linear. Aleya, the design manager, explained that it typically began with a brief from the marketing department. Azza or her daughter Amina then worked on a sketch based on research that was normally outsourced to local museums. Then marketing calculated a price range based on the sketch. The draftsmen in the design department on the second floor then used computer-based tools to produce a technical data sheet to specify the materials, dimensions, weight, and overall design. Based on this data sheet, the model makers and the workers on the ground floor produced a prototype that was evaluated by the entire organization, including the retail managers. The necessary dies for stamping the raw materials and applying inscriptions were also produced on the premises at that time. To ensure quality and feasibility, a second complete technical data sheet, called the "patron," was produced. After repricing by marketing, the design proceeded to the planning section and entered production. The typical lot size ranged between 50 and 80 pieces, each crafted by hand. Special orders for high-end customers or weddings, while relatively rare, were very profitable.

Fatma ran a very tight ship. Design met with marketing every Tuesday. Management meetings moved easily between Arabic and English, although English tended to dominate when the Turkish retail manager was present. All internal e-mail communications were in English. The incentive structure was quite clear and effective. Nadine recalled, however, that the incentive schemes in place in 2006 were perverse and often decoupled from performance. For instance, workers in charge of recycling and exchanging scrap for pure silver were paid a bonus each time they went to the *suk*, an incentive that led to more silver being wasted. As a result, Nadine linked all incentives and bonuses strictly to performance. Any new incentive schemes had to be approved by the top four managers.

Collections and Marketing

Azza Fahmy's collections comprised a variety of jewelry. One of her first collections, "Houses on the Nile," featured jewels shaped like small houses encrusted with palm trees or rocks. Next she turned to renditions of Salah Jahin's *Ruba'iyat* (colloquial poems). Later, she incorporated calligraphy from Arabic literature and was among the first designers to combine silver and gold in the same piece of jewelry. Another innovation was in the area of filigrees.

> Used as a form of decoration on metals from the earliest times across many cultures and traced all the way back to the Greeks, filigree was a very popular and intricate technique of jewelry making during the Islamic era. The filigree technique basically entails twisting very thin threads of silver or gold to form beautiful lace-like decorations. Due to its very time-consuming nature—it can only be done by hand— filigree was used less and less over the years until it was scarcely used. Today, even when used, silver thread rather than gold is employed as it is easier to shape.[13]

By 2009, Azza Fahmy sold four product lines: "culture," "exclusive," "fashion," and "gifts & men." Culture, considered the "trademark" line, each year introduced a new theme inspired by Egypt's rich history. The collection featured pieces in sterling silver and 18-carat gold and often incorporated semi-precious stones in its designs. The line married traditional workmanship, cultural motifs, and calligraphy to form a modern, stylish, and eminently wearable work of art. *Rumuz* ("symbols") was a more recent addition to the culture line. According to a promotional booklet, it

> goes beyond the boundaries of jewelry design and art by exploring ancient universal customs and practices to uncover the traditional and diverse symbols that have, over centuries, influenced beliefs ranging from safe travel and protection to good luck and power of revealing secrets.

The firm worked with experts on symbolism for 2 years to design the collection, which included items such as the eye, which

> represents a belief that a gaze from an individual thought to be motivated by envy can bring misfortune to the person or object envied. Wearing an eye amulet is used for protection since it serves as an intermediary by catching the evil eye's negative forces and diverting it from the wearer.

Or the scissors are "believed to grant protection from evil gossip . . . In ancient times . . . people snipped scissors over the heads of brides as if cutting off tongues of evil gossipers."

The exclusive collection, launched in 2001, represented the couture line at Azza Fahmy. Each serialized, limited-edition piece was traditionally handcrafted in 18- and 21-carat gold. These decorative pieces were adorned with precious stones such as diamonds, emeralds, rubies, and sapphires. The delicate filigree technique was especially highlighted in this collection with accents of precious stones. The subtle use of Arabic inscriptions, combined with the beautiful lace-like designs, made this a truly unique and eye-catching collection.

The fashion line was considered the trendy collection and, according to the company's website, was "seasonal and ever-changing depending on what is 'in' today." This silver collection incorporated vibrant colored stones and animal prints into a chic, young product line. The jewelry ranged from oversized cuff bracelets to eclectic necklaces to ornamental earrings and rings. This innovative, fashion-forward line targeted a younger audience and was designed by Amina Ghaly.

The "gifts & men" collection featured silver and gold merchandise for all occasions, including corporate gifts. Inspired by the culture line, it offered a selection of unique items for all price ranges. The choices included delicate silver spoons inlaid with gold calligraphy, silver and gold key chains decorated with cultural motifs, and elegant silver picture frames. For men, the line offered an array of jeweled and silver cufflinks and was expanded to include fine leather wallets.

While the company faced very little competition in its culture and gift lines, competition was quite stiff in the exclusive and fashion lines, especially from international firms such as Tiffany and Dior. Fatma observed that the company's role model was Bottega Venetta (part of the Gucci group) because it had managed to "grow without becoming mass."

Marketing efforts were focused on magazines, public relations, events, and direct marketing. Marketing expenses amounted to about 12 percent of sales. There was a "no sale–no discounts" policy in place. Launching a new collection in the culture line took up to 4 years. First, research was needed to ensure that the collection spoke to some aspect of cultural traditions. This process could take up to 2 years. Sketching and prototyping required 1 year. The fashion line's innovation cycle was much shorter.

The company faced a significant problem with copycats. However, Azza always liked to put a positive spin on this issue. "But, look, if someone is copying me, then it means that I'm successful," she said. "For the last four years we've made it difficult to copy us, because our work is very sophisticated, no one with a small workshop can do what we do."[14] Fatma corroborated this point of view by asserting that "it is annoying but not worrying." In effect, Azza's designs were very difficult to imitate. The firm had occasionally gone to court, although mostly as a public relations gimmick. As Fatma explained, "initiating legal action is a marketing expense, but you cannot overdo it."

Strategic Options for the Future

Fatma strongly believed that product diversification and international expansion were the best strategies for growth. She was thinking about and planning for a leather line of wallets and possibly purses and a pen and watch collection. She explained that these products were "natural extensions of jewelry." She was also considering a line of silverware.

Further foreign growth was a tantalizing possibility. Azza Fahmy faced significant challenges when selling her jewelry internationally. "It's so different. In Britain and here in the U.S., women don't like the big jewelry that we do in the Middle East. Once again, one has to understand what they—the customers—like."[15] In the United Kingdom, she collaborated with Julien Macdonald, a designer. "We were both interested in each other's markets, and fortunately we clicked."[16] She had to adapt her products in many ways. "Maybe [European women] will not understand the verses and not understand the words. For Europe [what] we are planning is taking motifs from various civilizations like Islamic and turning them into modern jewelry [that] people will understand."[17] International expansion also required thinking carefully about the sequence of markets to enter. "We realized that in order for us to do very well in the Gulf, we have to become an international brand," argued Fatma. "We need to go to Europe or the U.S."[18] Fatma explained that the relationship with Macdonald was great for branding and positioning, but that it was going to be discontinued so that the image of Azza Fahmy would not be perceived as being linked to someone else's in foreign markets.

Was Azza Fahmy a company prepared to undertake growth on a truly global scale? Should it have focused its efforts on product diversification or on international growth? Were further organizational changes necessary? Could the firm exist without Azza's design talent? As the top management team pondered the options, the workers meticulously put the final touches on new collections. Azza Fahmy's strengths as a company remained, after all, in design and craftsmanship.

QUESTIONS

1   What is Azza Fahmy's characteristic leadership style?
2   How do you evaluate her decision to delegate day-to-day operations to her daughters?
3   Which strategic options for further growth are more compatible with the company's organizational structure?

Notes

1 Azza Fahmy, *Enchanted Jewelry of Egypt* (Cairo: American University in Cairo Press, 2007), p. 3.
2 *Al-Ahram Weekly Online* August 30–September 5, 2001.
3 *Arab News* April 17, 2008.
4 *New York Times* May 1, 2004.
5 *Al-Ahram Weekly Online* August 30–September 5, 2001.
6 *Arab News* April 17, 2008.
7 Ibid.
8 Ibid.
9 *Times-Picayune* October 3, 1993.
10 *Financial Times* June 18, 2007.
11 *New York Times* May 1, 2004.
12 *Passion* no. 20 (Fall 2008), p. 126.
13 Azza Fahmy's Facebook page.
14 *Arab News* April 17, 2008.
15 Ibid.
16 *Financial Times* September 13, 2008.
17 CNN, May 9, 2008.
18 *Wall Street Journal* December 28, 2007.

13 The Spirit behind Talavera de la Reyna

Angélica Moreno's Pottery

Rajagopal, Roberto Solano, Felipe Burgos, and Lilia Gamboa

When it comes to pottery, almost everything has already been invented. Aspiring pottery entrepreneurs must first master styles and techniques perfected over hundreds of years, and then find a niche for themselves that sets their products apart from those of the competition. Angélica Moreno found such a way to differentiate her pottery by drawing from the most exquisite traditions in her locality and beyond.

ⓂⒶ

TALAVERA DE LA REYNA

Figure 13.1 Talavera de la Reyna Logo

In the early 1990s, Angélica Moreno, an elegant and action-oriented woman hailing from a family of average socioeconomic background in Puebla,[1] became one of the few businesswomen in this traditional and beautiful city in south central Mexico. Angélica always had a strong inclination towards art and aesthetics. She liked earthenware because it appealed to her sense of aesthetics and fueled her artistic passion. Pottery making is one of the oldest and most widespread of human activities, with a history that can be traced back to the Stone Age. Stylistic and technical changes over time reveal a great deal about the societies in which the pottery was made, so that clay vessels serve as essential cultural and dating indicators, as well as objects of individual skill and creativity.[2]

Angélica conceived the idea of developing an enterprise that established a milestone in the region for art lovers and also nurtured her entrepreneurial instinct. She opened a small pottery workshop in her hometown. She called it "Talavera de la Reyna," which later became an enterprise and commercial brand name for the products manufactured therein. Angélica had been inspired by a history book from which she learned that Talavera de la Reina is a city and municipality in the province of Toledo in western Spain, internationally known for its ceramics, which King Philip II used as tiled revetments in many of his projects, such as the monastery of El Escorial.[3] Angélica's plan was to combine the tradition of Spanish pottery with the aesthetic values of Puebla, a blend that may be termed *Talavera Poblana*—a fully hand-made ceramic craft. She took the pertinent step of developing pottery using an organic and eco-safe manufacturing process.

Puebla was not new to pottery making. In 1565, when trade opened with Asia, Spain began importing Chinese porcelain in large quantities, and by the mid-seventeenth century Puebla ceramists had succumbed to the fashion for Chinese blue-on-white porcelain. Around the time of Mexican independence in the early nineteenth century, the *Talavera Poblana* ceramic tradition experienced a decline that lasted until the early twentieth century.[4] Angélica's Talavera de la Reyna ceramics are tin-glazed earthenware that incorporate elements of foreign porcelain products from the seventeenth century to the present day. "When I founded Talavera de la Reyna, my goal was to produce the best ceramics in the state of Puebla," recalls Angélica:

> As time went by, I realized that this ancestral tradition had to be more formally acknowledged. In order to do so, contemporary painters, sculptors, ceramists and designers had to be involved. With a joint effort we achieved recognition for one of the finest artistic and traditional Mexican expressions.

Angélica rose to prominence as a handicrafts business icon in Puebla by sheer dint of her commitment to her goals, innovative skills, and her effective management style that drove her organization towards great success. She became known for espousing a set of humanistic values that were an extension of her kind and people-oriented leadership. She achieved her goal of turning Talavera de la Reyna into the most successful workshop established in her hometown, with some forty employees. Besides recalling the memory of the Spanish town that gave it a centuries-old tradition of ceramic production, Talavera de la Reyna is now a name recognized for its prestige in Mexico and abroad. Angélica believes that the art of *Talavera Poblana* is not only entrenched in the eyes of the public but also represents an important art movement among Mexican artists. Art is always changing and Talavera de la Reyna strives to achieve its craftsmanship by blending tradition and modernity and by a bridging dialogue between contemporary artists and local artisans.[5]

As part of Angélica's way of blending business, art, and socially responsible activities, she established a Talavera showroom called ALARCA, in order to give people the privilege of appreciating the traditional Talavera pottery as well as enjoying the unique collection of masterpieces of contemporary artists. This is a one-of-a-kind showroom in Latin America.

Starting a Business in Mexico

Traditionally, most Mexican women entrepreneurs get their start as part of a family business, and only in a few cases do women purchase, inherit or acquire the business as a gift. Culturally, it is evident that women entrepreneurs receive maximum support from their families for initiating and further managing their business. Thus, husbands or boyfriends constitute an important support role for women, while parents rank second followed by other family members and friends. Women in Mexico take the initiative to start their own enterprises for various reasons, which include a search for independence by owning a business, a need to improve their societal values and life style, a keen interest in the particular line of business, the fact that it was a family business, factors linked to need and the loss of employment, and the search for personal achievement.[6]

Besides personality factors conducive to taking initiatives, women in Mexico are also deeply concerned about economic empowerment in their lives. This is one of the major concerns in households headed by women. Since their position as women and heads of families places them in a vulnerable situation, they must combine activities to obtain income not only for uplifting the family values but also to support the raising of children. A survey[7] conducted in 2004 revealed that the status of typical female occupations in Mexico includes salespersons and shop assistants (20.3 percent), artisans and workers (14.8 percent), office workers (12.7 percent), domestic workers outside their homes (11.7 percent), and employees in services (9.2 percent). Some of the push factors compelling women to become entrepreneurs are poverty and the need to provide financial support to the family, while the pull factors include self-determination, desire for wealth, and self-fulfillment. However, some entrepreneurial motivations cross over income boundaries. Generally, women are most frequently motivated to become entrepreneurs by opportunity; however, necessity in entrepreneurship is a larger motivator for women in middle-income family segments in Mexico. The difficulties faced by women revolve around funding and family support. Despite a woman's level of education, corporate experience, and technical expertise, various business functionaries in areas like production, marketing, and logistics show lingering concerns about women's commitment to their enterprises, leadership of high growth businesses, and ability to garner crucial resources.[8] "When you reach an obstacle, turn it into an opportunity. You have the choice," Mary Kay Ash, founder of Mary Kay Cosmetics, once said. "You can overcome and be a winner, or you can allow it to overcome you and be a loser. It is far better to be exhausted from success than to be rested from failure."

Intrinsic Factors in Launching a Venture

Angélica Moreno was no exception to the familiar social and economic hardships faced by women entrepreneurs everywhere. Taking care of her family has been at least as difficult as dealing with her venture. For Angélica, her two children and husband have always taken priority over the demands of the business. She remembers the early days of working on pottery designs, setting up the workshop, and attending to small trade inquiries. Simultaneously, she was facing an uphill battle over clothing her children for school and helping them with school assignments and needs. However, friends stood by her throughout the adversities and encouraged her to move forward with her business and family objectives. Angélica received very valuable personal, family and professional assistance. Support rendered by loyal friends, colleagues, and craftsmen who believed in her goals and working philosophy had positively driven her efforts to shape the business culture and future of the enterprise.

Marriage and family were always the derived plans for Angélica. She was married several years after her workshop was established. With a growing family, combining work with her personal life was easier said than done. She had to play the quadruple role of wife, mother, friend and entrepreneur.[9] Initially, her professional work had isolated her and kept her from expanding her circle of friends and limited her involvement in parental activities at her children's school. "Though my grandparents had little resources, they helped me in taking a bold step to craft my dream," she recalls:

> I have learned many things from my grandparents such as dedication, responsibility, and human virtues. At the same time I got to know and enjoy a very intense home life that taught me to value the simplicity and charm of the most primary decorative, culinary and gardening arts. I took initiative to work on my dream factory making clay pieces, each one able to turn into a work of art, which gave me the necessary vigor to nurture my dream further; in this way I was able to carry it out. My grandmother and some friends gave me advice whenever I needed it.

The difficult dynamics faced by women entrepreneurs like Angélica can be summarized by the "LIFE" factors of liberty, intelligence, fraternity and equity.[10] Women entrepreneurs require persistence, awareness of personal progress, and a careful analysis of the obstacles that lie ahead. Pressures from intensive parenting and increasing professional roles leave women entrepreneurs with little time to socialize with colleagues in order to build professional networks and accumulate the social capital that is essential to women entrepreneurs who want to get ahead.[11]

Angélica constructed a sense of fraternity and equity in her business as she moved significantly ahead in her career path. People who work with

Angélica have always been loyal to her as they are true believers of her philosophy of life and work. She has also been successful in developing and retaining good employees at Talavera de la Reyna. Nineteen years after being established, Talavera de la Reyna is known as one of the best, most innovative and high-quality places to work in Puebla, which has given Angélica the highest social equity ever dreamt.

Extrinsic Factors

Angélica worked mostly alone during the initial 3 years of manufacturing pottery. Only on weekends did she have some help in painting some of the pieces. Under these circumstances there were only few family resources to support her professional growth. During these initial years she learned the basics of manufacturing pottery on a trial-and-error basis. Eventually, she started producing pieces of the expected quality and managed to get a small business loan.

The growth of Talavera de la Reyna was also influenced by other external factors which were sometimes beyond Angélica's control. As with many small and medium size enterprises, it was difficult to get financial assistance from government programs. Women face problems in starting and running a company that involves family funding and support. It is difficult for women to benefit from government funded programs because they need to acquire sophisticated knowledge and skills to deal with government bureaucracy. The knowledge and skills necessary for obtaining government financial support are very different from those normal everyday ones used in the family business.[12]

Angélica's tenacity paid off when she received government recognition and certification for Talavera craft. When the government issued an Official Mexican Norm that established the manufacturing procedures and characteristics that a product must fulfill, Talavera earthenware obtained the NOM-132-SCFI-1998; TALAVERA Official Mexican Norm, which protects its fabrication under the following criteria:

- Workshop located and clay obtained from the predetermined region
- Individual fabrication and articles to be painted by hand
- Diffused colors to be used
- The base glaze should be neither completely white nor transparent
- Talavera products may be relatively heavier than other ceramics
- Rigid and very hard constitution of craft articles
- Great resistance to wear and fading
- Total compliance with industrial regulations regarding the lead content in glazed ceramics.

Talavera de la Reyna obtained the certificate of authenticity with the code DO4–002 in 1998, and is one of only seven workshops that have been certified, and the only one that has achieved renewed certification continuously over time.

The Talavera Workshop and Its Products

Starting a business is difficult but Angélica made it even more difficult. She was determined to not only open a new business but also a business that was to design, manufacture and sell art made following ancient principles and procedures. She intended to make the best pottery in the state of Puebla and realized the need to reposition the value of the ancestral ceramics tradition. She engaged contemporary artists and invited them to work together and bring out the most beautiful expressions of Mexican aesthetic craft. On September 8, 1990 she formally opened the workshop on the site where it stands today. Since the very beginning, the artisans intended to go further than anything that had been done in *Talavera Poblana* before, proposing new designs based on the replication of details applied in antique pieces. The workshop of Talavera de la Reyna speaks to ancestral traditions, languages, and cultures and contributes to the dynamics of the contemporary art without losing the original values. Simplicity was preferred over visual saturation, a historical characteristic of this craft. Starting from this idea, the artisans working with Angélica Moreno created new exclusive designs for the workshop which are termed as *Casa Vieja*, *Las Américas*, *Mandarín* and *Células*. Other colors, yellow for example, were used instead of the traditional blue in the feather (*plumeado*) design. All these changes were implemented in order to offer something different and contemporary for its simplicity. The innovation was the proposal, not the decorative motifs themselves.

Angélica likes to say that art is always changing. The goal at her workshop remains to harmoniously blend traditional with modern art and make the workshop and the Talavera art gallery a collection of contemporary art and design. She began only with three employees, a thrower (*tornero*), a glazer (*esmaltador*) and a painter (*pintor*). Angélica's workshop was one of the original ten in the region that founded the Consejo Regulador de Talavera, an accredited organization designed to support the work of artists working in the traditional *mayólica*[13] technique producing high-quality traditional ceramics.

Talavera de la Reyna pottery is unique in that it is totally ecologically sustainable. "In making the best pottery, we use the traditional manufacturing system, careful selection of clay that is kneaded with the feet, manually shaping the clay, glazing and then decorating the pieces with organic colors prepared in the workshop distinguishes our products," Angélica explains. "Ours is one of the few workshops that follow the same steps of our ancestors in the production of Talavera without polluting the environment."

Figure 13.2 Talavera de la Reyna Pottery
Source: Lilia Gamboa, August 2009.

Since 1993, Angélica has invited artists to work with the artisans in her workshop to create new designs using the Talavera materials and process. She carefully explained that the remaking of the traditional glazed pottery from Puebla is not illegal copying because the workshop has the appellation of origin established by Norma Oficial Mexicana (DO4), which further envisaged legal security in 1997 on selling Talavera products to the buyer.[14] However, the initial 3 years were learning days in which to develop the innovative pottery manufacturing ideas for Angélica. During these years experiments were carried out with the quality of clay and raw materials to be used for colors. A special kiln had to be constructed for firing the products at a very high temperature. Six major colors—black, red, blue, green, yellow and brown—were also developed using high quality materials.

Talavera pottery is made with three kinds of clay which are mixed, strained and kneaded, then sent to the workshop. Each item is hand modeled and left to dry for 8–12 weeks. Once dry, the items are baked for about 8 hours at 1562°F (850°C). This process turns the grayish color of the clay into its traditional yellowish hue. In the next step each and every items is hand-dipped in a tin and lead mixture known as the traditional glaze. This glaze grants the Talavera pottery its traditional off-white background. After each coated piece is checked to ensure that the glaze is even and complete, the decorating stage begins. The stencil designs are sketched with charcoal powder as preparation for the painting stage. At this stage each item is hand-painted with natural mineral-based colors applied with mule hair brushes. Finally the pottery is fired once again, this time at 1922°F (1050°C), to reveal wonderful colors.[15]

Much time and effort was devoted in the early days to learn about painting Talavera products and also identifying efficient painters. The pottery is painted by hand using the six traditional mineral pigments to develop combinations of tones of blue, orange and purple. The pigments are made at the workshop following long-established formulas. The original Moorish technique was brought to Puebla by sixteenth-century Dominican monks from Talavera de la Reina in Spain, but seventeenth-century Italians introduced new colors, namely yellow, green and black, and Chinese imports inspired new designs depicting animals or floral scenes.

Workshop activities suffered during these early years because of the time devoted to learning the process of manufacturing high-quality ceramic products of various dimensions with cost effective propositions. Some of the major problems faced in building the workshop were location, land, installations for firing and clay mixing, and buying hand tools. Since financial support was not sufficient at first to build a fully equipped workshop, production capacity has been a sensitive issue throughout the story of Talavera de la Reyna in Puebla. Today, production is at one third of the workshop's potential capacity as estimated by Angélica.

Angélica and her team recognize that even though the business is going well, there is a tremendous need to update and enrich training and development activity for all workers, especially those with managerial responsibilities.

Driving Market Response and Business Growth

Managing people in organization and production is much easier than marketing the Talavera products in Puebla. There are hardly any organized outlets supported by public or private organizations. Most customers are buyers who informally hear about Talavera and its art products, and have the resources to travel to Puebla to purchase them. There is no brand promotion or publicity given to Talavera crafts because of limited financial resources and lack of marketing knowledge. The only way this craft is getting noticed among people in the region and Mexico in general is by word of mouth. Indeed, hearsay has become an increasingly potent force, capable of catapulting products from obscurity into runaway commercial successes.[16] Currently, the Talavera de la Reyna workshop is frequently visited by tourists. This has been generally good for the company, but insufficient, as the city of Puebla is not one of Mexico's top tourist attractions.

Angélica Moreno's Talavera de la Reyna is a place of art where ideas evolve and are aesthetically developed. However, it lacks the necessary business processes to further develop and grow. There is no set production schedule, no well-defined product line, no system to track raw materials, and no catalogue of products to promote in the marketplace. Consequently sales are low. In a more positive vein, the Mexican Ministry of Culture, in association with the National Council of Arts and Culture (Conaculta) has published a catalogue—*Alarca 54 Artistas Contemporáneos*—featuring the works of fifty-four contemporary artists, including Angélica, which serves both as a historical document with various images of artworks, and as a kind of commercial list for buyers.[17]

> Catalogues help buyers develop perceptions of the products who in turn can touch, feel and pick them up upon visiting the workshop in person. Though we have a corporate website[18] on the internet, we do not have the means to sell the products on-line. I understand the major source of growth for the catalogue marketing is expected to come from the internet where the on-line catalog can be placed and supplies can be supported by channels. We do not have the financial and human resources to develop this sales outlet.

As of 2009 sales of Talavera products greatly depended on walk-in customers who had learned about the workshop informally. Often it is difficult to explain to buyers that Talavera ceramics are worth the relatively high prices, especially in the case of the fancier patterns and larger pieces which take many hours of artisans' work and are unique as no two items are exactly the same.

Angélica feels the need to have a sales force to promote the *Talavera Poblana* products, and is engaged in lobbying activity with other Puebla ceramics producers to persuade the government to help, with some limited success. For example, Talavera ceramic designs and private collections were exhibited in China in 2005, which boosted the image of Angélica's products and helped motivate the artisans. This recognition helped in promoting exports of Talavera products to some extent. It is estimated that about 20 or 30 percent of the production at Talavera de la Reyna is exported to the United States, Canada and eventually Europe, to be sold at artisan craft stores. Exports began with a local trader who worked at the Amparo Museum, one of the most visited attractions in Puebla.[19]

Economic downturns have had a large impact on Angélica's business. Talavera de la Reyna flourished from 1992 to 1994 but declined steeply in 1995 as the Mexican economy went into recession. The global financial and economic crisis of 2008 also affected sales negatively. Nowadays, the income generated from the venture is just enough to meet the working capital requirements, barely turning out a profit.

Looking Ahead

Angélica Moreno's entrepreneurial life goes on with new challenges. She made her dream a reality and became a Talavera producer, turning her venture into a respectable business. Entrepreneurial growth is a process and innovation gets rediscovered as a growth enabler at every stage of development of an enterprise.[20] A strong commitment to goals and the sincerity of work has worked wonders for Angélica and her team. She is considering diversifying her art products from manufacturing historical replicas of Talavera ceramics to mass production of tiles. There is in Mexico a rapidly-growing market for Talavera-style tiles. Besides diversifying the product line, Angélica is pondering opening a 12,000-square meter showroom in a commercial street two blocks from Puebla's cathedral and main square. Though the initial cost of this proposal would weigh heavily on the venture, it would most likely make a huge difference in terms of sales.

QUESTIONS

1 How would you describe Angélica's worldview and leadership style?
2 Which were the critical resources that Angélica had to secure in order to launch and grow her business?
3 Should Angélica expand her business by diversifying into related product lines?

Notes

1 Puebla was built by the Spaniards in the sixteenth century and is located in highland wilderness some 2,100 meters above sea level. The walls of many churches in the town are decorated with a huge number of tiles. They are known as Talavera tiles and are a nostalgic reminder of the settlers' homeland.
2 Cooper, E. (2000), *Ten Thousand Years of Pottery*, 4th Edition, Philadelphia, PA: University of Pennsylvania Press.
3 Field, A. (2006), *Talavera: Wellington's First Victory in Spain*, Barnsley, UK: Penn and Sword.
4 McQuade, M. C. (1999), *Talavera Poblana: Four Centuries of a Mexican Ceramic Tradition*, Albuquerque, NM: University of New Mexico Press.
5 Lara, J. (2006), "El taller talavera de la reyna, parteaguas en la historia de este arte," Consejo Nacional para la Cultura y las Artes, Government of Mexico, press release, February 28.
6 Zabludovsky, G. (2002), "Trends in women's participation in Mexican businesses: The importance of small companies, family businesses and the increasing diversification of women-owned firms," *International Journal of Entrepreneurship and Innovation*, 3(2), 121–131.

7 Asia-Pacific Economic Cooperation (2004), *Report of Mexico on the Implementation of the Framework for the Integration of Women in APEC*, Gender Focal Point Network, Santiago, Chile, September 26–27. www.apec.org/apec/documents_reports/gender_focal_point_network/2004.MedialibDownload.v1.html?url=/etc/medialib/apec_media_library/downloads/otherfora_initiatives/gfnp/mtg/2004/word.Par.0027.File.v1.1

8 Mueller, S. L. (2004), "Gender gaps in potential for entrepreneurship across countries and cultures," *Journal of Developmental Entrepreneurship*, 9(3), 199–220.

9 Also see similar results in a large survey conducted on working women in Mexico by Zabludovsky, G. (2001), "Women managers and diversity programs in Mexico," *Journal of Management Development*, 20(4), 354–370.

10 Rajagopal (1999), "Empowering rural women's groups for strengthening economic linkages: Some Indian experiments," *Development in Practice*, 9(3), 327–330.

11 Eagly, A. H. and Carli, L. L. (2007), "Women and the Labyrinth of Leadership," *Harvard Business Review*, 85(9), 62–71.

12 Mueller, "Gender gaps in potential for entrepreneurship across countries and cultures."

13 *Mayólica* is the Spanish term for a specific method of glazing earthenware pottery. In Spain and Mexico it is often called *talavera*. For details see Museum of International Folk Art, www.internationalfolkart.org/

14 Quijas, F. P. (2007), "Creatividad e innovación, apuestas para impulsar la cerámica de Talavera," *La Jornada*, August 5. www.jornada.unam.mx/2007/08/05/index.php?section=cultura&article=a03n1cul

15 For details of ceramic manufacturing processes such as *talavera* see European Ceramic Art Center (2005), *The Ceramic Process: A Manual and Source of Inspiration for Ceramic Art and Design*, Philadelphia, PA: University of Pennsylvania Press.

16 Dye, Renee (2000), "Buzz on Buzz," *Harvard Business Review*, 78(6), 139–147.

17 Lara, *El taller Talavera de la Reyna, parteaguas en la historia de este arte.*

18 Talavera de la Reyna's corporate website can be viewed at www.talaveradela reyna.com.mx

19 Lopez, E. M. (n.d.) "La talavera, orgullo artesanal de Puebla es hoy fuente de ingresos y razón para emprender," *Soy Entreprenuer*, www.soyentrepreneur.com/home/index.php?idNota=3131&p=nota

20 Rosabeth, M. K. (2006), "Innovation: The Classic Traps," *Harvard Business Review*, 84(11), 73–83.

14 Maha Al Ghunaim

Building an Investment Bank through the Crash

Adrian Tschoegl

How can a woman leading an investment bank in an emerging economy such as Kuwait navigate the turbulent waters of the global financial crisis? Maha Al-Ghunaim headed a multi-billion dollar financial powerhouse—the only woman to do so in the Middle East—and grew it domestically and internationally. Her unique leadership style, corporate governance, and approach to strategic thinking proved essential to meet the challenge.

On June 28, 2008 Maha Al-Ghunaim, chairperson and managing director of Global Investment House (Global), the investment bank she had built with four friends, was on top of the world. The company was celebrating its 10th anniversary. In the space of 10 years it had grown from an entrepreneurial US$50 million company to a company with a market capitalization exceeding US$5 billion. It had a regional and international client base of over 6,500. In October, Global reported pretax profits of US$386 million for the first 9 months of 2008, an increase of 66 percent from the year-earlier period. Global's assets under management surpassed US$10 billion.

Global had grown from one office in Kuwait City to offering stock brokerage or investment banking services in Bahrain, the United Arab Emirates (UAE), Oman, Jordan, Tunisia, India, Qatar, Hong Kong, Pakistan, Sudan, Yemen, Egypt, Iran, Saudi Arabia, and Turkey. At home, Global had just moved into a new US$70 million headquarters building in Kuwait City, leaving behind its former modest and aging head office building a few blocks away.

Global's shares were listed on the Kuwait, Bahrain, Dubai and London stock exchanges. In May 2008 it had just had a successful offering of global depository receipts (GDR's) in London, raising £600 million (US$1.15 billion) in equity. This was the first such offering by a Kuwaiti company. The company was highly respected. In June *Euromoney* had named Global the "Best Equity House in Kuwait" for the fourth year in a row and *Asiamoney* had named it "Best Investment Bank in Kuwait" for 2008.

Maha herself had become chairperson of Global in March 2007 when Anwar Abdullah Al-Nouri, who had been chairman since the company's founding, had decided to step down from the position for personal reasons. She was the only woman at the head of an investment bank in the Middle East, and one of the top bankers in the Gulf. She had reached this position not by inheritance but rather by her own efforts. She had first risen through the ranks of the Kuwait Foreign Trade Contracting and Investment Company (KFTCIC), a government-owned investment firm, despite meeting some resistance from men who thought that a woman's place was at home. Then she had the courage to found her own firm.

Maha's success had also drawn media attention, and she won a number of accolades. She received the "Banker Middle East Industry Award 2008 (BME) for her outstanding contribution to the financial industry." In September 2008, the *Wall Street Journal* named her number 43 on its list of 50 "Women to Watch." Forbes (U.S.) ranked her 91 on their list of the "world's 100 most influential women," and Forbes (Arabic edition) ranked her second in its list of the Arab world's fifty best businesswomen. Though she had not sought the honors, the press was now proclaiming her a role model for Arab women and women in the Islamic world.

Maha Al Ghunaim's Professional Background

Maha was born in 1960 and is one of eight children, four girls and four boys. (She also has one half-sister and four half-brothers through her father's first wife.) Both her parents believed in education for all their children, girls as well as boys, and Maha attended a French-language boarding school. Her mother was educated and spoke English as well as Arabic. Maha describes her mother as independent and strong. Most of Maha's siblings went into engineering. She herself loved math and was in the top ten students in Kuwait in her year.

In 1978 Maha went to college in the United States. She chose San Francisco State University solely because a friend was going there. At the time she did not realize that the university was not among the more prestigious in the United States. Still, Maha graduated with a degree in math in 1982.

After graduating Maha returned to Kuwait and looked for a job. One man she remembers well suggested that she not bother: women should stay in their parents' home till they get married, and then should stay in their husband's home. Some years later Maha became this man's boss's boss.

Maha joined KFTCIC, which was not only the largest of the three Kuwaiti investment banks, but also 80 per cent government owned (in time the Kuwait Investment Authority came to own 95 per cent of its shares), and the only one to show an active interest in marketable securities, where it played a key role in trading bonds and shares in international markets. Working there provided her with an opportunity to learn. KFTCIC already had a good reputation for competence and focused on providers. The company was looking for educated staff and gave her the opportunity to choose her assignment. She began as a dealer in marketable securities, executing transactions, and then became a portfolio manager. This gave her the opportunity to travel to visit companies to see how they operated, which was itself an education.

In 1988 she became vice-president for portfolio management. She became a member of the asset allocation committee and a member of Al-Kharejeyah Umbrella Fund. In 1995 the Kuwait Investment Authority combined KFTCIC with Kuwait Investment Company (KIC) under the KIC name. Maha was appointed assistant general manager of asset management at KIC and was responsible for the local and international markets.

By 1998 Maha had arrived at the point where the next logical step was to found her own investment bank. She had had a model career in which she had worked her way up through the major areas of investment banking, and so had a good understanding of what was involved.

She also saw an opportunity. There was a need for a local investment bank that would meet international standards. There were few local competitors, and no foreign firms. The foreign firms would send in representatives from time to time to tout their latest product, but these representatives did not know the area or the clients. As a result, there was no one who produced equity research, or underwrote bonds, traded fixed income, or offered money market and bond funds. Maha decided that she would build a firm that would do all of this. The key to success would not lie in taking market share away from competitors but rather in introducing new products that would make the pie larger.

Maha believed that she had to work harder than her male colleagues. She was quick to credit her husband and family for their support. Her husband is the chairman and managing director of another company and understood the pressures she faced. She always worried about how the demands on her time of building and leading an investment bank would affect her children. When asked, they reassured her that they understood that her drive was a core part of her.

As far as acceptance by clients was concerned, Maha acknowledged that "first, clients look at you as a woman." But, as she puts it, the key issue is, "Are you competent? Investment banking is a field where numbers are the metric." Performance is measurable and visible, and clients respond accordingly.

Organizing and Leading Global Investment House

When Maha decided to establish her investment bank she knew she needed a management team. She brought in four people as co-founders. They were:

- Mr. Bader A. Al-Sumait, who had 19 years' experience and would be in charge of investments locally and in the member countries of the Gulf Cooperation Council;
- Mr. Omar M. El-Quqa, CFA, who had 16 years' experience and would be in charge of corporate finance and treasury;
- Mr. Sameer A. Al-Gharaballi, who had 16 years' experience and would be in charge of investment funds; and
- Ms. Khawla B. Al-Roomi, who had 16 years' experience and would be in charge of personnel and administration.

Maha brought Mr. El-Quqa, Mr. Al-Gharaballi, and Ms. Al-Roomi, with her from KFTCIC. In appointing Ms. Al-Roomi to a top management position Maha started as she meant to go on—giving women positions of responsibility. When Global started, it was a pioneer in hiring women for leadership positions in investment banking, though seeing women in responsible positions was more common in commercial banking. Today, Global is only slightly above average in giving women responsibility as the other firms have caught up. With the team in place, there was still one additional leadership role that needed filling.

One of Kuwaiti culture's distinctive features is the *diwaniya*. Originally, among the Bedouin, a *diwaniya* was the section of the tent in which male members of the family would meet with male visitors, separated from the women and children. In old Kuwait City, the *diwaniya* was the reception area of a house where a man received his male business colleagues and guests. Today *diwaniya* has come to mean both the reception area and the assemblies that take place there. For a Kuwaiti man, visiting or hosting a *diwaniya* is an important part of both social and business life.

When Maha and her colleagues established Global, she knew that she needed someone to represent the bank in the *diwaniyas* of Kuwait. She therefore invited Anwar Abdullah Al-Nouri to be chairman of the bank, a position he would hold for the next 9 years. His acceptance of the chairmanship gave Global immediate credibility. His role was neither symbolic nor only Global's public face. Maha referred to him as "The last gentleman on Earth." He provided the young founders of the bank with a voice of experience and wisdom. In addition to Mr. Al-Nouri (chairman) and Mrs. Al-Ghunaim (vice chairman), the board included Mr. Khalid J. Al-Wazzan, Sheikh Abdulla Al-Jaber Al-Sabah and Mr. Marzouq N. Al-Kharafi as board members.

Maha was able to establish the company within two weeks. The shares were over-subscribed, a testament to her reputation, that of her family, and that of her team. As a result, she was able to choose her shareholders and board of directors. Her initial board remained unchanged until 2007 when Anwar Abdullah Al-Nouri stepped down from the chairmanship. (Then Maha became chairperson and managing director, and Mr. Khalid

J. Al-Wazzan became vice-chairman. An Englishman, Mr. Alan H. Smith, joined the board as an independent member.)

A last issue was to pick a name. Stuck after considering and rejecting a number of ideas, Maha turned to a sister, who suggested "Global" as a modifier of "Investment House." "Global" embodied an ambitious goal, and so "Global Investment House" was born.

Business Strategy

Before the crash, Global built its growth on five areas: investment banking, brokerage, asset management, real estate and principal investments. It used research to build its brand name in new markets before it launched new products and operations. Also, research supported asset management, brokerage and investment banking. Investment banking created investment opportunities for asset management clients and could suggest opportunities for principal investments. Brokerage benefited from both the strong research base and from the asset management client base. For the purposes of this case, the discussion below looks only into some aspects of asset management and principal investments.

In the asset management area, most of Global's initial clients were its shareholders. They were also almost entirely male. Then between January 2001 and June 2005, Global started offering annual seminars for women in Kuwait. Global saw an opportunity in educating women to make decisions for themselves. In time, the wealth management client base in Kuwait grew from being about 3 percent women to about 30 percent. Global now plans to introduce such women's seminars in Saudi Arabia and elsewhere in the GCC area. Global's existing wealth management clientele in the Gulf is predominantly male but as in Kuwait, Global sees an opportunity in catering for women.

From 1999 on, the number of asset management clients grew at about a 22 percent per annum cumulative average growth rate, reaching about 7,600 in 2009. The amount under management grew at a cumulative average rate of 19 percent per annum, reaching US$5,087 million in 2010, after having peaked at US$8,587 million in 2007 (see Table 14.1).

Institutional investors accounted for about 79 percent of the assets under management. Retail investors accounted for about 21 percent. Global had a good history of client retention. One reason for this was that Global was the first investment bank in the region to have a client relationship department. Furthermore, Global kept staff numbers in line with the growth in clients and so kept service levels consistent. As a result, 85 percent of Global's clients from 1999 were still with Global as of mid-2009. In mid-2008, 8 percent of Global's clients had been with Global for over 8 years. Some 26 percent had been with it for a year or less.

The bulk of the assets under management were in in mutual funds. Global's best performing fund was the Global 10 Large Cap Index fund,

Table 14.1 Selected Financial Data for Global Investment House

	Assets	Y-on-Y (%)	Debt	Y-on-Y (%)	Gearing (%)	Revenue	Y-on-Y (%)	Net income	Y-on-Y (%)	Assets under management	Y-on-Y (%)
1999	18	—	0	—	0	—	—	—	—	—	—
2000	19	10	1	—	3	4	—	2	—	763	—
2001	27	37	6	974	30	5	20	2	19	1,539	102
2002	32	20	9	49	41	6	17	3	24	1,916	24
2003	50	56	16	75	48	18	187	12	300	2,576	34
2004	99	98	50	209	103	29	64	21	72	3,792	47
2005	301	203	172	241	133	80	174	62	189	6,698	77
2006	692	130	448	161	183	110	38	71	16	7,624	14
2007	913	32	590	32	183	154	40	91	28	8,587	13
2008	1,253	37	798	35	176	-41	—	-258		8,023	-7
2009	833	-34	579	-27	228	-46	-42	-149	-42	5,949	-26
2010	675	-19	566	-7	519	-22	-52	-75	-49	5,087	-14
2011	564	-16	518	-8	1,132	-11	-50	-59	-22	3,623	-29

Notes: All asset, debt, revenue and income numbers are in millions of Kuwaiti dinar (KD), except for "Assets under management," which are in millions of US dollars (US$). In 2010, KD1 was approximately equal to US$3.45. "Y-on-Y" means year-on-year. "Gearing" (or leverage) is the ratio of debt to equity.

Source: Global Investment House Annual Reports.

which invested in the ten largest companies listed on the Kuwait Stock Exchange. However, as an index fund, the fund simply depended on the Kuwaiti stock market for its performance. Its only innovation lay in bringing index investing to Kuwait. What was more interesting was Global's Global Buyout and Global Opportunistic private equity funds. Furthermore, Global has launched Global al-Ma'amoun fund in 2001, a unique income fund in the Kuwaiti market with two classes of shares, class A being owned by the Kuwait Investment Authority and class B by the public with a priority for the latter to receive the first 4 percent of the fund's yearly return. In return, class A shareholders get a higher share of the returns should the fund generate over 4 percent annually.

Already in 1999 Global put a little money into principal investments, that is, investments on its own behalf rather than for clients. The investments grew modestly through 2004, with growth becoming rapid from 2005 on, when annual gross income was 38 percent. In subsequent years, income averaged about 19 percent annually, before dropping to 12 percent (annualized) by the end of the third quarter of 2008.

To support this growth Global started borrowing. As it did so, the ratio of its debt to equity (its gearing or leverage) climbed. Not only was Global now more highly geared (levered) and more dependent on principal investments for its profits than in its early days, but the debt was relatively short-term.

In the Gulf, "long-term" meant a maturity of 2–3 years as medium term notes (maturity of 5 years or so) were not yet common. This 2–3 year maturity of its recent debt meant that Global had to refinance frequently, and in ever larger amounts. Furthermore, it was in the nature of principal investments holdings that they were not liquid. And these factors were the source of the start of the crisis, when Global could neither refinance to make its principal payment nor sell assets, and so had no alternative except to default.

Impact of the Financial Crisis

In 2007, oil prices started to climb steeply. The pace accelerated from March 2008 and prices peaked in August 2008, before starting to fall sharply. The run-up in the price of oil triggered problems in mortgage and lending markets in the United States. Much of the growth in residential construction in the U.S. was occurring in suburbs in California, Nevada and Florida. High oil prices discouraged people from buying in areas where they would face long and thus expensive commutes, reduced households' ability to service their debts, and caused them to tighten their budgets and reduce consumption.

The housing price bubble in the United States had already peaked, and started to collapse in 2006–07. This led to the crisis in the sub-prime mortgage market. When the housing market began to deteriorate and the ability to obtain funds from investors through investments such as mortgage-backed securities declined, the investment banks were unable to fund themselves. Investor refusal to provide funds via the short-term markets was a primary cause of the failure of Bear Stearns and then of Lehman Brothers on September 15, 2008.

Stock markets around the world, which had been falling for some time, sunk precipitously. This set off a panic in interbank markets, which froze. Banks stopped lending to each other, including short-term (even overnight) money. This was particularly problematic for investment banks, which relied on short-term financing that required them to return frequently to investors in the capital markets to refinance their operations.

Global Investment House was not immune. It had made many long-term investments that were relatively illiquid, but had funded them by relatively short term (2–3 year maturity) debt. When one of these debts came due, Global was unable to raise new debt to fund the repayment.

On December 15, 2008, Global announced that it would be unable to pay a principal payment that was due on a US$200 million international syndicated lending facility (that is, a loan extended by a group of banks). Global stated that it would continue to make interest payments, but the failure to make the principal payment meant that the firm was in default on its borrowing contract. Because debt contracts have cross-default clauses, default on one debt meant that Global was automatically in default on all its debt. Global announced that it was appointing a financial adviser to renegotiate the existing credit facilities' terms with lending banks.

The Growing Problem

Even before the bankers arrived on December 22 to discuss Global's future with Maha, its board and its top managers, the rating agency Fitch had downgraded Global's issuer default rating (IDR, an estimate of a borrower's ability to meet its financial commitments on schedule) from BBB to C, its short-term IDR from F3 to C, and its individual rating from C to E. Furthermore, Fitch had put all three ratings on Rating Watch Negative.

On January 9 Fitch further downgraded Global's long- and short-term IDRs from C to D. Global's KD long-term rating dropped to from C to D. Lastly, its individual rating dropped from E to F.

In April the Kuwait Stock Exchange barred Global from trading on the exchange for some days because it had failed to publish its year end results on time. Global eventually posted a net loss of KD257.6 million ($885.2 million) for the year 2008 after it had made impairment charges of KD297.4 million ($1 bllion). These impairment charges were due in large part to unrealized losses on the company's investments. The Gulf had thought that it was somewhat insulated from developments in the rest of the world, but as matters turned out, it was not. Problems developed in Dubai and elsewhere in the GCC and even in the wider Middle East and

North Africa ("MENA") region. Equity indices in these regions fell between 36 and 55 percent, an unprecedented decline that hurt Global's principal investment holdings.

The creditors established a steering committee to discuss how to restructure the US$1.8 billion in debt. Some fifty-three creditors appointed West LB, which had arranged two syndicated loans, to chair the committee.

A high-level steering committee chosen by Global's creditors was in talks to restructure Global's $1.7 billion debt. A Kuwaiti bank, representing local banks, and an Islamic bank, were also on the committee. Global, with its financial advisors, presented a comprehensive restructuring plan backed with financial forecasts, a detailed business model and an independent valuation of its assets.

Throughout the process, Maha and Global stayed in touch with the asset management clients, explaining what was going on, reassuring them that write-downs and impairment charges were only for Global's own holdings and did not affect the funds that Global was managing for the clients.

Changing the Strategy

To return to profitability Global had to undertake a number of difficult measures. First, it instituted salary cuts of up to 20 percent and canceled all bonuses. On the operational side it closed its operations in Yemen, Iran and Iraq.

The largest change was in strategy. Principal investments had been the source of the largest part of Global's losses. Henceforth, Global would return to its roots as a middleman, giving up acquiring companies purely for investment purposes. Although principal investments had suffered in 2008, fee income from asset management and the other activities had continued to grow.

Maha committed Global to exiting the principal investments business "in a orderly fashion" over the medium term. She also committed to using the proceeds primarily to repay Global's debt obligations.

The first step in the restructuring of Global's management consisted of changes in the management team. Mr. Bader Al-Sumait, who had been the executive vice president for local and GCC investments, became the chief executive officer. All the business groups would be reporting to him. Mr. El-Quqa was asked to resign.

There were also additions to the management team as featured in the annual report. In the 2008 report, Ms. Khawla B. Al-Roomi, the fifth of the founding managers, appeared as the EVP–personnel and administration, representing an elevation in the role she had occupied since Global's founding 10 years earlier. Ms. Nawal Mulla-Hussain, who had joined Global in 2004, was elevated to the position of EVP–legal affairs, a testament to the important role that legal matters now played in Global's survival. Last, Mr. Sunny Bhatia, who had joined Global in 2006, was elevated to the position of EVP–chief financial officer (CFO).

In 2010 Mr. Khalid J. Al-Wazzan, the vice-chairman and a member of the board since Global's founding, left the board. His replacement as vice-chairman was Hamad Tarek Al-Homaizi. Sheikh Abdullah J. A. Al-Sabah, who also had been on the board from the start, left. The board received several other new members, one Kuwaiti, Ali Abdulrahman Al-Wazzan, and two non-Kuwaitis, Bambang Sugeng Bin Kajairi, CEO of Reem Investments, Abu Dhabi, and Junaidi Masri, of the Brunei Investment Agency.

Financial Restructuring

In December 2009 Global arrived at a debt-restructuring agreement with its fifty-three creditors. The creditors agreed to reschedule the $1.7 billion debt and entered into new 3-year loan facilities. Global also undertook to make payments to reduce the outstanding principal.

Global transferred substantially all of its principal investments into the newly created Global Macro Fund, incorporated in Bahrain, and a Kuwait-domiciled special purpose vehicle (SPV) real estate holding company ("Real Estate Holdco"). Global would continue to own both, so their performance would continue to affect Global's financial results. Global undertook to wind down its investments in an orderly manner and apply the proceeds to repaying its debt.

David Pepper, from WestLB and chair of the Banks' Steering Committee, added:

> We are delighted by this successful outcome today and are highly appreciative of the tremendous efforts Global and its advisers, HSBC have demonstrated throughout this process. Global's professionalism and transparency throughout this process has been highly commendable and has set precedents for other restructurings in the region.

In May 2010 Global's shareholders approved a rights issue that would increase its capital by about 76 percent or about US$346 million. However, Maha has not implemented the capital increase.

Between August 26, 2008 and December 31, 2008, Global's share price fell 80 percent. Between 1 January 2009 and the end of October 2010, the share price had fallen another 67 percent, with the sharpest fall coming in the first quarter or so of 2009. From then on, the share price has simply trended flat to slightly down.

In November 2011 the Kuwait Stock Exchange suspended trading in shares of Global on the grounds that the company's losses had exceeded 75 percent of its capital. Global fought the ruling. Global is fighting the suspension, but the shares have not traded since November 14, 2011.

Then on December 13 Global announced that its lenders had agreed to defer certain mandatory minimum principal payments to June 10, 2012 and defer or waive certain covenants. Global would continue to pay interest payments as they came due, but would not have to start repaying principal. Global subsequently asked for another extension to November 10, 2012. More positively, Global won a US$250 million case against a UAE bank.

Global remains one of the most highly regarded investment banks in the Gulf. Maha is in an advanced stage in the negotiations with Global's creditors to reach a permanent solution that will reposition Global as one of the leading financial services providers in the region, capitalizing on its competencies: loyal and experienced management and employees, its presence in major regional capital markets, and the relationship Global enjoys with its loyal clients who have shown support, especially during challenging times.

Over the years, especially during the financial crisis, Maha has shown a great level of commitment and devotion to her employees, clients and share-holders. This is key in implementing the company's strategy moving forward, which focuses on offering services to its clients in asset management, investment banking and brokerage.

QUESTIONS

1 What were the factors behind Maha's success? Did it matter that she was a woman?
2 What were the factors behind Global getting into trouble? Did Maha being a woman play any role?
3 What is the role of corporate governance in the success and problems that face any firm where the founder also runs the firm? What are the tradeoffs involved?

15 Alicia Escobosa's Catering

Sustaining a Business

Roberto Tolosa[1]

She started a catering business out of necessity. She grew it through hard work, learning through formal courses and from other large-scale restaurant operations about the best ways to scale up. The economic and financial crisis posed many challenges, prompting her to revisit the assumptions underlying her business strategy.

Figure 15.1 Alicia Escobosa Logo

At the beginning of the 1980s, in Culiacán, Mexico, Alicia Escobosa managed her household and took care of her children while her husband was away for work. Whenever she found spare time, she would prepare some dishes for acquaintances and casual customers as a hobby and, occasionally, as an extra source of income. "Cooking had never been my strongest skill, and as a newlywed I often wondered whether I would even have enough time to cook for the family," Alicia commented. "But as time went on, I realized that I had good taste and cooking skills." The daughter of a locally renowned author of a cookbook, Alicia became known for her exquisite taste and delicious courses.

In the summer of 1992, a tragic accident led to the death of Alicia's husband. Suddenly, she was left with five young children to raise and support. "I was faced with one of the greatest challenges in my life. We had invested most of our life savings in a new house, and all the children were in private schools." In addition to helping her husband manage his business, Alicia had held a few teaching jobs. When she got married and moved to another city, she was less than a year short of earning her bachelor's degree. "I had no choice but to work hard to give them the best I could provide." After assessing her options, Alicia realized that she would have to commit fully to the food service business to raise enough money for her children. Her kitchen at home was a standard residential kitchen; but it was all she had, and it would have to do.

The Beginnings

Alicia started out by simply receiving small orders for family gatherings and small events, working on her own and occasionally hiring part-time workers. The plates were basically fixed and delivered, and customers served the meals themselves. "Initially, I felt uneasy charging people for the dishes, as my customers were mostly relatives and good friends," Alicia recalls. During the first years, she used small family-owned cars to transport the food and equipment.

Even though the small business relied on word of mouth to attract new clients, it became well known for its superior food quality and genuinely caring service. Soon Alicia started getting calls for larger weddings, conventions, and conferences; and she saw the need to expand, first by hiring full-time staff. As she recalled, "in my first years, most of the changes made to my business were small but constant, as I adjusted the business to the growing demand and the general environment." Some of her clients were also not skilled enough to serve the prepared food at their events or would make mistakes and spoil the food. At this point, Alicia noticed the great potential in her blossoming business and set out to become the premier food caterer in the region.

The first thing Alicia realized was that clients were eager to receive a full catering service instead of simple food delivery, and that they would be willing to pay a premium for it. In addition, they often wanted the event preparation to be as streamlined as possible. If the food arrived in poor shape because a waiter mishandled it, the caterer would be blamed, not the waiter. (Contrary to industry standards, caterers in Culiacán did not come with a team of waiters, but rather hired third parties.) As Alicia noted, "the quality of our service is just as important as the quality of our food." This meant that, even though it was outside the scope of her business, Alicia would have to meet with decorators, waiter captains, sound technicians, and even security guards to anticipate any contingencies and to coordinate the course of each event. "Recently, I have even been hired for a number of weddings as both an event planner and caterer, even though planning events is not necessarily my core focus."

Supplies are key to any business, especially one focused on food preparation. Fortunately, Alicia's business was located in one of Mexico's agricultural centers. With warm, sunny weather year-round, the city of Culiacán proved to be a very fertile ground for various crops and forms of livestock, giving Alicia's catering service cheap and ample access to high-grade, export-quality produce. Over the years, Alicia fostered a strong business relationship with a number of suppliers who specialized in areas such as vegetables, seafood, or meat and poultry.

> Once, in preparation for a special event where a large supply of high quality asparagus was needed, one of our suppliers went looking for contacts as far as Chile to obtain enough asparagus that would meet the desired quality. Our friendly, mutually beneficial relationships with our suppliers have come from a genuine interest in their businesses, which has translated into easier transactions and more flexible terms and prices.

Alicia also frequented large stores, such as Sam's Club, to purchase ingredients not easily found elsewhere.

Toward the end of the 1990s, after some years of proving to the market that her catering business had superior quality, taste, and hygiene, Alicia's company was successfully established as the top choice for premier events in the area.

> One of the early stages of our expansion came in 1999, when the state government requested a dinner for a 600 guest event. When they asked for an appropriate invoice, I replied that our business was not yet registered under Mexico's Internal Revenue Service. To this, the person replied, "Alicia, we are at the turn of the millennium, and with that flavor and service that you provide, you are telling me that you have not formally established the business? You are the number one choice in the region, but we cannot hire you if you are not registered." Three days later, my business was properly registered as "Alicia Escobosa Banquetes," and I was working on the government event. Before this, all bookkeeping had been done informally and only as needed to account for sales and costs. I now had to hire an accounting firm to go over my business and keep formal accounts.

Another important acquisition came in 1999, when Alicia took the savings she had accumulated for expenses larger than simple kitchen equipment and bought an SUV to transport food, equipment, and staff to the events. Before that, the only cars the catering team owned and used were smaller sedans. Not only did this allow for less frequent and thus faster trips between the business premises and client locations but, more importantly, the SUV allowed Alicia to travel to Arizona and California to access more food and equipment options.

Previously Alicia had been unwilling to make trips to the U.S. without giving her children the same chance. With enough seats for her children to go on vacation and sufficient cargo space to bring back new equipment, she traveled more frequently, she established key contacts, and her business began to see a constant influx of the latest catering equipment and high-quality durable ingredients, like spices or sun-dried fruits that could be stored, further setting Alicia's catering apart from that of her competitors.

In order to stay on top, Alicia decided to renovate all of her equipment, replacing her standard equipment with professional- and industrial-grade gear. Although she had considered eventually relocating the business outside her family's house, it was much easier to improve her current plant rather than undergo a more aggressive investment. At this point, only the portable equipment was the latest models, and the business plant still used some consumer-grade stoves and appliances.

Growing the Business

Despite her success, Alicia knew there was still room for improvement. Many aspects of her business operations had never changed and the workplace needed to be professionalized. She looked everywhere for opportunities to develop new ideas or improve the business.

> In 2004, while on a cruise to Alaska, I was allowed into the ship's central kitchen to figure out how the crew could cater to 4,500 passengers around the clock with different menus every day. The most striking feature was the highly organized, systematic approach to food preparation that allowed for gourmet food production [in] such large amounts. With the proper facilities, following a similar approach at home would be easy to implement. Just a couple years earlier I had also visited many cities in Europe, where I frequented the most distinctive restaurants to learn of gourmet cuisine firsthand.

In January 2005, Alicia attended Catersource, a professional catering conference in Las Vegas, Nevada, to learn the latest organizational and logistical designs. As with any other company in the catering business, Alicia and her employees had to work long hours for prolonged periods of time, especially when there were four events to be served in three different cities on the same day. Any logistical advances that Alicia learned or devised were instrumental in increasing the scale of her business.

"At the catering conference, I had the chance to compare every part of my business to other professional catering businesses around the world, and to see where I could improve the model," she recalls.

> After the conference, I returned with a firm goal to revolutionize the business. I was looking forward to the summer, when people are away and there are few events, so that I could carry out some kind of expansion. Every aspect of the company seemed to have performed remarkably over the years, and we had experienced sales increases of 20 to 25 percent for over 5 years. I never imagined what 2005 had in store for my business.

In April of that year "Alicia Escobosa Banquetes" catered for one of the larger weddings in town. Alicia coordinated the preparation and serving of a four-course dinner for 900 people, featuring Chinese and Thai fusion food to represent the bride's heritage. Later, at three in the morning, late-night snacks were served to 600 guests, and a post-wedding reception was held the next day for an additional 300 guests. "It was a very beautiful wedding, and people loved the food we served," Alicia remembered.

> Suddenly, on Monday, I received a call saying that some of the guests had fallen ill. I immediately contacted the bride's parents, who had not heard anything of the like. The following day, I spoke with a gastroenterologist, from whom I found out that people were turning up with what seemed to be salmonella. The first indication to the source was that all of the patients had stayed for the wedding's late night party. Without asking any more questions, I immediately hired a food testing laboratory to go over our premises and shut down all activity in the meantime, calling off at least ten upcoming large events.
>
> The analysis was going to take at least one week, during which I thoroughly considered what to do. Although there were no critical cases, 30 people had been hospitalized, and more people lay sick in their houses. I seriously considered closing up shop for good.

Later, the results came, and the source of the bacteria was identified as a batch of blue cheese shipped from Finland.

> Fortunately, people were very understanding, recognizing that the salmonella found in the blue cheese was in no way due to my own handling of the food, that it was virtually undetectable, and that it could have happened to anyone. At that point, I had two choices: yielding to this catastrophe and leaving the business, or taking the business and modernizing it to come out stronger. Since the business was still sound and people had behaved sympathetically, I decided to keep the business going. After giving my clients for upcoming events the choice of a refund or to keep me as caterer for their events, none of my clients cancelled, and three weeks later, we were serving a banquet for 600 guests.

With the business back on track and following through with her initial plans for the summer of 2005, Alicia expanded the business fleet with two pick-up trucks and planned for the most ambitious expansion to date.

> While I could have finally moved the business into its own lot, I decided to keep the plant where it was, right at home. Having my work right where my children are has proved invaluable in allowing me to perform both roles of parenthood.

With this in mind, Alicia began the expansion, revamping the office and storage space and scrapping the whole kitchen to replace it with top-of-the-line equipment and a professional design that would optimize worker productivity and ensure the best food quality.

> I hired experts to design the kitchen with efficiency and productivity in mind, and when the project went through, I had walls torn down, rooms built from scratch, and a complete transformation of half of my house. As I began to look for more space, the backyard had to give way to build a storeroom.

The house, with a floor area of close to 5,400 ft^2, underwent major changes and was divided into a house and a workplace. Approximately 3,200 ft^2 was designated for the business, two thirds of which was dedicated to food production. "By the end of the renovation, I had 8 industrial cooking ranges, a gas deck oven for up to 24 pans, separate cold and warm food kitchens, and a walk-in cooler."

Before the renovation, all the business growth had been financed through business earnings. As Alicia put it, "the business had always provided enough return to be able to expand with its own profits, but suddenly I was over $100,000 dollars short. I decided to take on a loan and set my business new challenges." The renovation ended up costing US$120,000 for new equipment and remodeling, US$60,000 of which was taken as a loan, leveraging the business substantially for the first time. All the profits were always reinvested, making Alicia's company a healthy business.

After a rocky and eventful year, the catering business was back much stronger than before. At the time of this expansion, Alicia usually employed from forty to fifty employees to prepare the food, although the number would rise when catering larger events. (Waiters, who were hired from different places, were not included in this tally.) Two years later, in 2007, another vehicle was purchased—a van for personnel transportation—for a total of one SUV, one van, and two pick-up trucks. Occasionally, cars or pick-up trucks were rented for specific events, including passenger buses for fifty people and refrigerated trucks for out-of-city catering.

Continued Professionalization

Growing from a small endeavor, the business began with no money to spare for what would have been considered secondary tasks at the time, such as advertising. Alicia's catering always relied on word of mouth as the most effective advertising medium for her business, with virtually no paid advertising. She always said that "our best publicity is our own satisfied customers." And her healthy relationships with her clients paid off in many ways. On some occasions, clients flew Alicia to certain restaurants in the United States, just to let her see and taste the specific entrées the clients wanted for their special occasions. Often, Alicia was allowed into the restaurant kitchens and received detailed explanations on how to prepare the dishes, along with a few helpful tips, all adding to Alicia's cumulative knowledge. Other times, chefs from Mexico City's most prestigious restaurants were flown to Culiacán to work with Alicia's team for specific clients. During these visits, Alicia had the opportunity to benchmark her business against external players. "Alicia Escobosa Banquetes" continued to utilize no advertising but relied instead on its well-established reputation and public exposure, which always enabled the company to excel. With the local media praising Alicia's company as the top catering choice for any event, her main advertising tools were food quality and customer satisfaction, which Alicia viewed as essential catalysts for effective word-of-mouth promotion.

The company's equipment ranged from stainless steel utensils to insulated food transporters, vacuum packagers, and food shredders. There was a refrigerated room, where all the food was stored, and a number of freezers, used mainly for seafood and desserts, among other items. Industrial-grade cooking ranges would together handle up to twenty different preparations at once, and there were enough ovens to cook up to twenty turkeys at the same time. Portable kitchens and other equipment owned by the company allowed for a catering capacity of over 1,500 people.

> Throughout the years, I have steered the organization into a premium catering business. In 2006, when I was approached by the organizers of a rotating national conference to serve food for the visiting crew of 2,000 workers at an accessible price, I replied that my business structure did not allow for low cost options at such a scale. Instead, we wound up serving the VIP banquet for speakers and key guests.

Kitchens were often set up at event sites under marquees ranging from 775 to 3,500 ft^2. Under Alicia's coordination, up to 1,500 people were served in less than 40 minutes, with 90 percent being served in the first 20 minutes. In Culiacán, other caterers typically served to only 500–750 people in the same time frame. Alicia always based her success on her employees, and they received pay notably higher than the prevailing industry wage. Ninety percent of the company's employees were female, with men hired mainly for carrying and transporting equipment. In addition, 70 percent of these female employees were single mothers or had families to support by themselves. While most worked in household services before joining the company, some had prior cooking experience and a few had university degrees. Of the business' employees, Alicia recalled that

> hiring and managing people initially became a problem. Because of the nature of the business, there would be no work for some days and

Figure 15.2 Alicia's Team at a Mobile Kitchen Set Up at a Catered Event
Source: Roberto Tolosa, September 2009.

intense labor the following days, so that the number of people I needed could change drastically from week to week. Plus, people complained about the late hours at which events could finish. One of my responses was to compensate my employees with higher pay.

Standard wages ranged from 35 to 70 Mexican pesos per hour (about US$2.80–5.40), depending on factors such as production stage and time of day, compared with the regional minimum wage of US$4.15 per day.

Years of a healthy relationship with her employees led to a low turnover rate and a high rate of satisfaction for Alicia's company. In general, a caterer's work schedule is unstable and can include some periods of very intense and hard work. Thus, it may not fit all personalities. But those employees who liked it stayed for years, adding to the company's human capital. As a result, Alicia's employees were able to take complete charge of some smaller events from production to delivery and serving without Alicia's assistance, as long as she mapped out the guidelines beforehand. This allowed her to leave the city for important business activities without disrupting the day-to-day operations, giving her the opportunity to travel to the U.S. to acquire special ingredients for an important event, meet with clients at their favorite restaurants to sample the courses they wanted her to produce on a mass scale, and also take courses and attend conferences while still keeping the business running.

Historically, few competitors, if any, operated in the same upper-level market or in the same quality and price range as Alicia. Most caterers offered lower priced and less elaborate banquets, practically serving different markets. In 2006, a gourmet restaurant opened and began offering a professional catering service, effectively posing the first same-level competition Alicia had seen in two decades. In late 2008, another local caterer was reported to have started offering similar menus.

> In reality, my toughest competition has come from upscale event centers with policies prohibiting outside caterers, thereby decreasing venue choices for customers who wish to have us as their caterers. There have been cases in which customers have paid the event centers their full catering costs and asked to hire us instead.

Increased competition also prompted Alicia's team to focus more on differentiating her business from others. This effort translated into more menu choices and increased quality of service.

> For instance, whenever clients from agribusiness come to me, I offer them the choice of using only their produce in every course of the meal. In this way, we have prepared courses featuring crops like eggplants or tomatoes from their best harvest in most or all of the dishes, and clients love it.

Moreover, Alicia was careful not to repeat the same course arrangement twice, always changing and switching menus and recipes to keep the dishes new and fresh. Weddings, the company's main focus, were planned as far as a year in advance, so that couples and families would receive all the attention and preparation necessary. Over the course of the months leading up to the wedding, couples enjoyed complimentary tastings to discover their options and fine-tune their preferences.

Before Alicia's expansion, her customer base largely comprised her relatives and close friends, but as word spread more people approached her. Companies and the state government began to hire "Alicia Escobosa Banquetes" for their important events and conferences. "I now have informal agreements with a number of companies, to whom I cater for their annual meetings and largest events year after year," she says. While all the events catered were in the same state, some customers were people or companies from out of state visiting Culiacán for a specific function. As Alicia specialized in high-quality service with a high mark-up and targeted high-end customers, payment rates remained high every year, with a collection rate typically over 98 percent of earned revenues.

Over the years, Alicia managed to turn a spare-time hobby into a professional catering business considered to be tops in the region. Along the way, she always found moral and economic support from her close relatives. "When my husband passed away," she said,

> many family members put together enough money to pay down my mortgage, so as to reduce the financial burden I had to carry. When

one of my cars broke down in 2003, a cousin presented me with a pickup truck to replace the broken car. And, all this time, my close relatives have always provided me with insight on how to improve the ways I do business.

Looking back at how it all started, it is evident that Alicia's business had a deep impact on the catering industry. When she was getting started, the entire industry seemed also to be in its nascent stage, with very few large conferences, weddings, or events being catered with full, multiple-course meals. Events larger than 500 guests were rare in the 1990s, and most of those were fairs, conventions, and other types of event that either had multiple vendors or offered a selection of hors d'oeuvres at most. Alicia's team usually catered multiple events week after week, many of which boasted over 1,000 guests. As competitors joined in, customer choice greatly expanded, with a full range of caterers offering options spanning from low-budget food preparation to gourmet offerings like Alicia's. Throughout the journey, Alicia's leadership also helped shape specific aspects of the business, such as constantly renovating the necessary equipment with higher-grade, more functional, or more aesthetic components, or maintaining an ever-expanding array of menu choices, extending over multiple world cuisines, to create the ideal blend for each customer.

Alicia took a unique path but always relied on examples along the way. As she saw it, the company's success was possible because, "in every event, I strive to give my best and exceed the customer's expectations, and I don't mind sacrificing profits to ensure the best quality possible." Alicia regarded the practices of a local businessman who had founded and grown a retail company to over 600 stores around Mexico, and those of a late uncle, who was a generous banker and businessman with a great social impact, as models to follow. Like her, these people always cared about their employees and looked for ways to improve the quality of their lives, providing them with high wages and education for their children. Looking back, Alicia said that "over time, I started realizing the great potential this catering business had, but I never really imagined just how much it did." She expanded to deliver for top companies, the media industry and national celebrities, renowned speakers and special conferences, distinguished weddings, and high-ranking politicians, including each president of Mexico to visit Culiacán since 1982. During the high season, the company usually catered for 6–8 events in a single weekend, serving over 4,000 people, with a unique menu for each event. Always aware of her competition, Alicia never stopped innovating and searching for new recipes, seeking great taste and radiant aesthetics, to deliver the finest gourmet food. The company's equipment was constantly updated, meeting the highest quality and hygiene standards. All the staff had to uphold the most rigorous health and safety standards to ensure that the food was free of harmful agents. When referring to Alicia's catering, people commonly said that "Alicia's is a guarantee."

Despite these achievements, the company still had room to grow and improve. Alicia's greatest challenge was securing a ballroom where the company would cater exclusively. A number of existing event centers would only use their own caterers, and Alicia would gain a much greater share with her own location. The size of the investment necessary to build a new event center kept Alicia from starting her own ballroom. Although demand for her services outside the state of Sinaloa was strong, high logistical costs and the fact that not enough employees could leave their families for extended periods of time limited the company's ability to cater in areas outside the base city, with a range of a little over 130 miles to nearby Mazatlán, about the same as a Philadelphia caterer serving in Washington, D.C. The cooks and staff could also further improve their skills, as some had not completed higher education. And while the staff had some degree of independence, being able to carry out small events on planned occasions, tasks such as handling the payroll, keeping records, and other management- and accounting-related activities still fell heavily to Alicia and a handful of employees, thus creating a heavy burden that reduced the time spent at the core of the business.

> As the business expands, the time I spend going through paperwork, running numbers and on the phone or computer has always been increasing, creating a burden that takes my time away from my customers and the kitchen. Finding skilled, hardworking and trustworthy people for the right wages to perform these tasks has proved very difficult.

Over time, however, Alicia was able to find ways to give her employees more responsibilities. One of the assistant chefs, who was an accountant by profession, also started keeping track of all the invoices and expenses. When Alicia went out of town, this assistant chef was able to take charge of the catering team for ever-larger events, eventually turning into the right hand of the business. Another cook became the purchasing manager, spending most of her time procuring materials and ingredients rather than preparing them. But on this, Alicia noted that, "still, these jobs have been defined rather informally and they still don't cover enough overhead functions to allow me to spend more time at the kitchen and with the customers." The marked seasonality of the industry was another challenge that hindered the company's opportunities, with the summer months seeing as little as one or even no orders in a given week.

Recent Developments

> Looking ahead, my goal is to keep being the best catering business, and to finally expand the business into other regions. For this, I am also aiming to start a high profile ballroom, which would require either

loans or an external investor. Taking courses at the Culinary Institute in Hyde Park, NY or the Cordon Bleu in Paris is another one of my goals, and possibly to later write a cookbook as well.

In September 2009 Alicia achieved one of those goals, finally taking two courses at the Culinary Institute, one of which focused solely on catering costs and managerial controls. "More than ever, I now realize the importance of preparation and innovation, and I will surely be taking more courses on catering and the food service business." Alicia also considered producing popular and easy-to-preserve products, such as dressings or jams, and marketing them nationally or internationally.

More recent events tested Alicia's hard-earned business in novel ways. The number of orders had comfortably expanded by more than 25 percent on average over 5 years. In the second half of 2008, however, the ongoing financial crisis cut families' discretionary spending and drove them back home and away from Culiacán, where the events were to be held. Even though the initial months of the year brought customary sales expansions, the business grossed a total of 5.7 million pesos in 2008, (roughly US$500,000 at 2008 rates), 10 percent lower than sales in 2007. For the first half of 2009, sales declined 10 percent when compared to the same period the year before. Alicia, with her business focused on event catering, suffered directly from the sudden decrease in the number of events being hosted in the city and the concurrent decrease in willingness to spend at those events, resulting in a decline in sales for the first time in the history of her business. Thinking of how to weather the current and future economic conditions, Alicia began to assess her options.

QUESTIONS

1 Is entrepreneurship a good option when women with children have few opportunities for employment?
2 Who were Alicia's role models?
3 Given the effects of the economic and financial crisis, should Alicia scale back her operations, cater to segments other than premium, or diversify into new businesses?

Note

1 Roberto Tolosa is one of Alicia Escobosa's children.

Part IV

Doing Good while Doing Well

Research indicates that many women engage in social entrepreneurship as a result of their experience in the community as mothers, daughters or organizers. While this tendency is also prevalent among men, previous experience in the household and in service-oriented occupations makes a large impact on women's entrepreneurship. In this section we will learn about the accomplishments of Rapanui, Chinese, and Peruvian entrepreneurs who saw an opportunity for doing good in their communities while doing well from a business point of view. We will also consider the case of a social entrepreneur in Thailand whose aims were purely not-for-profit.

16 Annette Zamora's
Naz y Rongo

A Scavenger Hunt in Search of the Culture of Rapa Nui

Leeatt Rothschild

Schoolteachers often take to entrepreneurship. They have organized schools, launched educational programs, started publishing houses, and sometimes joined their students in the pursuit of new ventures. Annette Zamora saw a need for classroom materials highlighting the local culture of the Rapa Nui, in the South Pacific. She launched a magazine and fashioned a scavenger hunt that proved popular with tourists as well as schoolchildren.

More than 3,000 nautical miles west of Chile is Rapa Nui, the "navel of the world," an enchanting volcanic island of 64 square miles that is home to one of the world's most distinctive cultures and famous for its monumental statues and ceremonial sites. Rapa Nui constitutes the easternmost point of this distinct Polynesian cultural triangle, with Hawaii to the north and New Zealand to the west. Preserving the fragile identity of Rapa Nui (also known as Easter Island) is the ultimate goal of Annette Zamora, a cultural entrepreneur who has enriched the lives of others by ensuring that her island's unique history and culture are preserved and cultivated by future generations.

Annette frames her dedication to promoting the diffusion of the Rapa Nui culture by saying, "when you believe in something, you will do anything for it"—a credo that has inspired her even in the toughest times. Trained as a teacher, she left the comforts and benefits of a classroom to start a comic book series and foundation to educate the young about the Rapa Nui culture. The daughter of a Rapanui mother and a mainland Chilean father, Annette was raised alone by her grandmother in Santiago. Her return to isolated Easter Island reflected her love for Rapa Nui—the indigenous culture and the people of the island. Her Foundation ECHO captures just a morsel of her passion and dedication to ensuring this culture continues.

Coming of Age in Santiago and the South Pacific

Annette's early years were filled with hardship, and she developed a striking maturity from those challenging experiences. She recounts memories of carrying heavy items, traveling across Santiago with her grandmother, and living a simple life. "I was raised like a bird: I ate the fruits around me, rose and slept with the sun; total liberty with no rules." But she always had a sense of uneasiness in not knowing who her father was. Through the difficulties of those years, she developed a precocious sense of appreciation. When her grandmother bought her a cookie, she recalls valuing the gesture more than the actual treat, an action she was quite young to appreciate as a child. "As a youngster I learned how to survive and from that I learned how to be happy despite the hardship of my life."

Annette's petite frame, high cheekbones, and charismatic eyes complement the passion and strength of her voice. She is direct in her speech and is aware of who she is. After all, she was pregnant as she pursued her master's in pedagogy at the Pontifical Catholic University of Chile—an institution known for helping women with children succeed academically. Annette promised herself that when she left Santiago to pursue her master's, she would not return to Easter Island without it. "I am persistent; and once I say I will do something, I do it." This explains how she successfully completed her degree, despite being a divorced mother of two in a foreign place with no family to support her. Her perseverance encourages her to push her ideas forward and allows her to continue developing Foundation ECHO despite the challenges.

Rapa Nui is unlike any other place in the world. It is an isolated, inhabited gem in the middle of the Pacific Ocean, dotted with over 360 massive *moai* statues that were built by the Rapanui people to serve as representative figures of sacred chiefs and gods.[1] It appears as if the original settlers first came from the Marquesas Islands around 800 CE; and genetic evidence supports a massive prehistoric settlement from Polynesia.[2] The first European visitors were the Dutch explorers who came upon the island on Easter Sunday, 1722. Rapa Nui had a turbulent history of conquests and foreign attacks and eventually became a Chilean colony in 1888, when twelve Rapanui chiefs ceded control to the Chilean captain, Policarpo Toro Hurtado.[3] Its history has intrigued archaeologists and historians alike, and today attracts over 46,000 tourists annually. Tourism fuels the island and represents 91 percent of its economy, generating over US$20 million annually. The Chilean government estimates that the island's population was 4,888 in 2010, the vast majority of whom are native Rapanui.[4] The island's three schools, spanning primary through high school, teach approximately 250 students.

The idea of starting Foundation ECHO to promote educational activities related to the Rapa Nui culture did not occur to Annette in one fell swoop. As a teacher, she was asked to travel to Hawaii to join the Annual

Polynesian Congress—a meeting involving Micronesian and other Pacific islands with the goal of sharing best practices to preserve the native cultures. This gathering marked a pivotal point in which Annette was introduced to a broader movement whose goal included the very issues she struggled with in the classroom.

In general, Rapa Nui was seen as purely folkloric. Apart from a dance or two, teachers did not feel an obligation to teach the island's history and culture to their students. Annette was different. She felt a keen obligation to educate her students about the Rapa Nui culture and to teach them the language. After all, she said,

> I had a tremendous responsibility—I was working with the future of the island; they are the new generation who will be responsible for the Rapa Nui culture. If they do not understand their own heritage, how will their ancient traditions continue?

This question plagued Annette. Preserving an indigenous culture is generally thought of as a community endeavor. Annette, however, was not content with sitting idle and waiting for others to take charge. She is not wired that way. This was an issue that concerned the future of her island and her people, and she wanted to do something about it. As a teacher, she was tasked with teaching her students the Rapa Nui alphabet and cultural values. She took this educational mandate personally; and the evolution of how she interpreted and internalized this task brings us to her comic book series and Foundation ECHO.

A Cultural Entrepreneur Is Born

What do you do when you find current didactic materials limiting, are passionate about teaching a rare topic, and do not want to wait for others to make things happen? Simple: you start a comic book series featuring two lovable indigenous cartoon characters, find the best artist in town, add a scavenger hunt, and watch your idea snowball into the island's most coveted monthly publication. At least that is what Annette Zamora did.

Annette should have known her comic book series, *Naz y Rongo*, would be a hit. When she began teaching the Rapa Nui alphabet to her first-grade students and felt that her teaching materials were lacking, she made an artistic alphabet banner for her classroom. It was such a success that letters disappeared on a daily basis—carried home in someone's bag for sure. Recounting the story, Annette smiles. Although the alphabet was supposed to stay in the classroom, she knows the banner educated her students as she had intended.

Naz y Rongo not only allows students to learn about their native culture, but also forces them to get out of the classroom and explore their island. Annette is aware of both the big picture and the finer details.

Figure 16.1 Annette Zamora with Drawings for the Comic *Naz y Rongo*
Source: Leeatt Rothschild, May 2009.

She understands her audience and her ultimate goal and creates the appropriate tools to combine both. She knows how children learn best, decided that fostering Rapa Nui education was critical, and determined that an experiential scavenger hunt was the best way to entwine the two. The result was a comic book that includes a scavenger hunt led by two indigenous characters who engage readers to use clues to seek answers physically.

Naz y Rongo takes readers on a real scavenger hunt. It requires people to explore the island to seek clues that guide them through a multi-episode scavenger hunt. The more you explore, the more clues you gather, and the closer you get to the final answer—revealed at the end of the school year, of course, for full suspense. Children have to interview the island's elders to learn customs and Rapa Nui phrases, and travel to *moai* sculptures or other archeological sites to find clues. This ensures that the children are fully captivated by and immersed in the learning process.

Thinking up the comic book series was already a huge feat. Bringing it to life from a mere germ of an idea was yet another. Doing so on an island 2,000 miles from any major city, with absolutely no cash to invest, where photocopying class material was a struggle, added a few more complications. But this was business as usual for Annette; and when she plans to do something, she makes it happen.

With the help of a mother at her school, Annette started the educational magazine/comic book strip. They decided to create two protagonist cartoon characters: Rongo, a messenger in Rapa Nui who is also found on a petroglyph on the northern part of the island, and Naz, who represents the ancient Nazca lines. Consistent with her philosophy of getting students involved in the learning process, Annette organized a contest to have the children select the final figures and colors of the characters. She enlisted a friend, an extraordinary artist on the island, to draw the comic strips and help design the magazine.

In 2005 the collaborators created the first eight pages of the comic book. In 2006 they published the first full *Naz y Rongo* series: ten monthly magazines. With the help of her American partner, John, Annette was able to raise funds to have enough copies of the series for 1,500 students printed in Kingston, New York, and shipped back to Rapa Nui.

What distinguishes Annette is not only her passion for the Rapa Nui culture, but also her sincere belief that she has a responsibility to educate the future Rapa Nui generations and her drive to make the most fantastic ideas come to life.

Although the magazine targets children and teens between the ages of 5 and 18, Annette soon saw the sweeping success of her work. "Adults would all stop me and say, I went to 'X' cultural site to try to figure out the clue." The idea was to integrate the entire island community into education about its collective heritage. "Kids had to look for clues and ask their siblings, parents and grandparents. . . . [T]he idea behind this was to have people discover the island." Despite the first edition's success, Annette has never forgotten the struggles of her efforts; nor does she pretend everyone was behind her work. "It was beautiful [the collective efforts], interesting, but also hard. Hard because people say they support you but then you see that that isn't so. They wonder where the economic value lies for them." And if they do not see how they will benefit from supporting her efforts, they ask, "Why should I help you?"

For this reason, all the funding and a tremendous amount of support came from the United States:

> Because I had an issue showing my emotions in front of my people, knowing their rejection of my efforts, the [low] level of awareness and interest they had, I sought funding from New York. There was more awareness in New York than from here. And there was much more bureaucracy, ways in which the island just made fun of me.

At the same time she and her colleagues were compiling the first edition of *Naz y Rongo*, Annette was working on a television program focused on social issues. She interviewed doctors, nurses, and hospital workers for a program designed to teach the people of Easter Island about modern hospital care. She translated all the material into the Rapa Nui language, which was a key element for the show. She also started an exhibition of contemporary Rapa Nui art by local artists. Here she worked with the older generation and imparted to them why she felt the necessity to better understand their culture from within. "Because we are so few, it's that much more important to know who everyone is—what we do, how we work."

Building Support

As much as people loved the magazine, they were unwilling to pay for it. Annette could not sell it on the island because people would not buy it. And yet she felt an innate calling to continue the beloved publication, for four years, as a not-for-profit endeavor. The first year each issue was 8 pages; the second year, 12 pages; and the third year, 16 pages. For the fourth year, each issue should have been 20 pages; but Annette and her collaborators lacked the funds and kept it at 16 pages. By the second year, they were able to convince LAN Chile, the country's national airline, to sponsor the shipment of the magazines.

On Rapa Nui, Annette met with government agencies and the mayor to solicit funding. Upon discovering that the magazine was written in both the Rapa Nui language and Spanish, no one was willing to provide any financial support. Annette's desire to teach the young generation their native language stems from the fact that every year the population that speaks this language shrinks even more. To her, the need to educate the children was obvious. The government, mayor, and other agencies were stuck on imagining the bilingual nature of the island's people—"they didn't understand the linguistic reality of the island." This is why Annette has been so fervent about teaching the young generation its own heritage's native language.

Annette saw her connection to Rapa Nui as one of many individuals who connect past to present to future. And although she recognizes she is merely one person, she takes her role in that lineage very seriously.

> What I am about to say might sound discriminating, but my work was focused on stimulating the Rapanui to wake up, to sense the importance that we need to leave our mark. We have the *moai* from our ancestors. What are we going to leave behind?
>
> Sometimes we were up until three or four in the morning. Everyone says it's good that I am doing this but no one is ready to give me money. Everyone is happy I am doing it . . . but nothing more. It was very hard, a challenge to even find money for printing. Sometimes it's not that easy to believe in your own dream because you can think that you are crazy.

Up until the third year, all the funding came from the United States— approximately $12,000 from generous philanthropic donations and people's desires to help. "Not that any of this money came to me. I only paid the painter . . . [W]hen you have a dream you sacrifice more than you imagine." In 2009, the fourth year of publication, Annette noted,

> this year will be the first one within the last four where I will actually earn some money. It is through a project I am doing with UNICEF. I am happy because someone is paying me so I can continue investigating something that I love.

Annette, her assistant Ulla, and painter Po worked in a small office off the main entrance to the town's most centrally located hotel. Annette was able to guarantee this work space, and they have a small storefront that leads to their office, as well as a back room that serves as the painter's studio. The studio has colorful drawings of *Naz y Rongo* pinned all over the wall, as well as various UNICEF project pieces propped up on a table. A large easel stands in the middle of the room, beside a desk that has dozens of paints, oils and crayons—a Mecca of tools for any artist.

Although the front-room office space is equipped with a computer and printer, the remainder of the room is reserved for showcasing items for sale: mugs and t-shirts with the *Naz y Rongo* theme, other Easter Island paraphernalia, CD-ROMs, batteries, and the like. Annette explains that she spent countless hours running around various agencies, meeting with officials in Santiago just to solicit grants of $1,000 or $5,000. She complained:

> So many documents . . . more papers, filling out more papers. You waste more of your time trying to get these funds. We said we had to invent more ways [to raise money], so we made mugs, t-shirts, stickers, which all serve as sources of funding.

By selling some of these items Annette and her colleagues could offset the basic costs of maintaining the office: "I have many dreams but I am a realist." Annette is a dreamer in that the challenges of launching *Naz y Rongo* would have prevented most individuals from even attempting such an undertaking. At the same time, she is a realist—once she puts into practice what she has ingeniously imagined, she takes action to make it a successful reality, for example by selling works of art for profit and persuading LAN Chile to sponsor printing shipments. After all, "The mom, my assistant, doesn't get paid. I can't ask her to always help me, work with me, if I do not pay her." Faced with this reality, Annette creatively seeks other ways to generate revenue. Moreover, given the challenges of setting *Naz y Rongo* into motion, she knows that, in order for Foundation ECHO to survive, she needs to seek self-funded projects. One result of this is her current project with the government group CONADI (the National Corporation of Indigenous Development)—a guidebook in Spanish and the Rapa Nui language about the process of pregnancy and delivery.

The magazine went far beyond what I imagined as a teacher. People wanted to participate. But it was hard because many people don't read. So it was harder for them to [follow the scavenger hunt]. I go against a concept here that assumes that one needn't make a magazine or newspaper because people don't read. But I say, well, at a certain point we'll need to teach them to read. So I go against that thought. I believe it's a role I'm assuming—the role of educating everyone, for everyone. Without waiting for anything. Give something for your own culture.

As Annette explains,

the goal of *Naz y Rongo*, in addition to teaching and stimulating children, is to invite the students to be the next painters, to do the interviews with the elderly to gain information, to contribute pieces to the magazine, etc. . . . under the supervision of the Foundation.

Annette is a big thinker, but she also considers how to make the Foundation sustainable. Given that the children have written back with comments and responses over the past few years, her ultimate goal is not too far-fetched. At the same time, Annette discloses that she has often considered stopping *Naz y Rongo*, "because I didn't have any more energy. More than that, it was because I left my own children aside because I was immersed in all this. But I can never leave this aside because I love it." She describes this vicious cycle by saying simply, "Mother's guilt."

Moving Forward

Annette never stops dreaming. When asked about where she sees the Foundation in 5–10 years, she says, "developing new lines of educational activities. New areas such as agriculture, social work. . . . I want to affect even more people." As a child, Annette loved studying and developing herself intellectually.

I never thought I would start a Foundation, but I recall being a kid and thinking about creating new books. I remember a book that I used in the fourth grade and thinking, "I wonder how they created this," and wanting to know how I could make it. I looked at each page, drawing.

Pensively, Annette adds, "I thought I would be doing something big, even bigger perhaps, than what I am doing now; the Foundation keeps me awake—it is an intellectual challenge."

Annette is humble. Her work ethic shows in her actions and the way she views the Foundation. When asked why she thinks she has been successful, she responds,

I don't know if I have been successful. I have received recognition but I don't know that I have a clear concept of what successful means. The Foundation—I see it as yet another thing that I should have done; I see it as an accomplishment only in that I achieved something I hoped to do.

Officially, Annette is president of the Foundation. But if you ask her what her role is, she will tell you, "I think. I generate. I seek. I establish. [A]nd when the first steps are made, I develop, stimulate, push at the end, and I deliver. Then I continue all over again." Annette's perseverance and dedication will be tested in the coming years. Given that the Foundation's initiatives require significant support from others, Annette will not enjoy any respite from seeking partnerships to develop her ideas, soliciting funding, or generating support from dissident opinions on the island. These obstacles have not stopped her from realizing her dreams to date. She hopes they never keep her from reaching her goals, because her creativity and passion allow her to go against all the odds to serve and educate her people and preserve her native Rapa Nui culture.

QUESTIONS

1   What are the critical resources a cultural entrepreneur must secure in order to succeed?
2   Which specific aspects of Rapa Nui helped Annette launch her venture?
3   Should Annette expand her partnership in order to augment her impact?

Notes

1   Shawn McLaughlin, *The Complete Guide to Easter Island* (Los Osos, CA: Easter Island Foundation, 2007), pp. 6–19.
2   Ibid., p. 15.
3   Ibid., p. 24.
4   Instituto Nacional de Estadísticas de Chile, *Población y Sociedad Aspectos Demográficos* (Santiago de Chile: Departamento de Estadísticas Demográficas y Vitales, 2008), p. 40.

17 Shokay

Luxury with a Story, Style with a Touch of Humanity

Emily Di Capua

Herders in remote mountain areas wishing to bring their goods to market face many challenges. Carol Chyau thought that she could use her skills and connections to help establish a worldwide distribution and sales network for yarn from yak, a bovine that lives in Tibet and southwestern China. She came up with a series of witty ways of positioning the product and the brand in a way that herders could benefit from higher sale prices.

Carol Chyau wants to use her education and training to help those less fortunate than she is.

During her junior year at the University of Pennsylvania's Huntsman Program in International Studies and Business, Carol spent a semester abroad in Peru. In meeting poor farmers there, she became aware of what life could be without opportunities, without the means to make one's dreams come true. As she notes,

> [The fact that] I could easily get on a plane and leave the poverty around me, but that the farmers not have that freedom or that choice really struck me. It's almost impossible for them to change their situation. They can't freely choose the way they want to live."[1]

During that trip Carol decided she wanted to work on a social venture and help change the fate of people with fewer opportunities than she had. Deciding just how to make this happen took a few more years.

After graduating from the University of Pennsylvania with bachelor's degrees in Spanish and business, Carol headed to Harvard's Kennedy School of Government, where she studied social entrepreneurship and public policy. Two important milestones during her time at Harvard led her to found Shokay.

First, Carol learned about Muhammed Yunas, the Nobel Peace laureate and founder of Grameen Bank, largely credited as the world's microfinance and community development bank. She had the opportunity to hear Mr. Yunas speak at Harvard and became fascinated with the for-profit social enterprise model, which uses a traditional business structure to solve a specific problem within society. With her undergraduate focus in business and her dedication to solving social problems, Carol decided this was the model for her.

Second, while Carol was at Harvard, she had the opportunity to travel to mainland China with a classmate from Hong Kong, Marie Liou. The two had become close friends and visited the country of their ancestors together during summer break. Marie was also interested in starting a social venture, but had not yet determined the specifics. As the two traveled in southern China, they discussed potential social venture opportunities and quickly decided to work together on an idea. From the very beginning, they knew they wanted to focus on the social enterprise model. As Carol notes, "We read a lot of [business] cases in school but we never saw a case on social enterprises in China. So we thought, could we come to China and promote the social enterprise model in China?"

Marie shares Carol's convictions: "I am from Hong Kong and I am surrounded by wealth everywhere, but that's not the case for so many people, especially in mainland China. So why not use our education to contribute to change this?"[2]

The new business partners first went to Yunnan province in China's southern basin. Yunnan borders Laos, Vietnam, and Myanmar and is rich both ecologically and demographically. It boasts the largest diversity of plant life in China and is home to twenty-five of China's fifty-six ethnic minorities. Every time Carol and Marie saw something interesting, they made a note of it, musing, "Could this be a potential business plan or idea?" Carol explains, "We saw big local peaches and we thought, could we mash the peaches into a powder and perhaps make a make-up? Or do the juices inside the seeds have some sort of use in industry?"

Carol and Marie were open to everything. But when they first saw yaks and yak herders in the Yunnan highlands, close to the border with Qinghai province, they paid them little attention. As Carol puts it, "We didn't know about all the treasures a yak provides for its herders."

Eventually Carol and Marie were introduced to the yaks' special characteristics and were amazed at all the riches they provide. One herder referred to every part of the yak as a treasure because the herders, for years, have been able to make a living solely from these animals. Thick yak hair is used to make tents and bedding; yak down makes warm clothing that protects against the winds on the Qinghai plateau; yak milk provides nutritious milk and cheese; and yak dung is used for fuel.

Carol and Marie learned about the Tibetan-speaking Zang minority, who herd most of Yunnan and Qinghai's yaks. Most of this group's capital is tied up in yaks, which are their main source of income. But that income usually hovers around 650RMB (US$100) per month. Carol wondered whether she and Marie could help the herders generate more income from the yaks so they would not be forced to leave their traditional way of life to get factory jobs in one of China's sprawling cities. "I remember thinking, how can I help create more economic value for these herders' traditions?"

As Carol reflected on all the "treasures" yaks supply to their herders, she was captivated by the soft yak down, under the coarse yak hair.

With yak down being just as soft as Mongolian and Chinese cashmere, Carol thought she might be able to market yak down products to the same market—foreign knitters looking for luxury yarn—while funneling most of the profits back to the herders. Thus was born "Shokay: Luxury with a Story, Style with a Touch of Humanity." (Shokay means yak in Tibetan.)

Shokay now sells and distributes yak down yarn and hand-knit and machine-woven yak down fashion accessories, children's clothes, household goods, and toys in Shanghai and around the world. The company distributes primarily to retail operations in Japan and the U.S. It also operates two stores in Shanghai—one in the historic Taikang Lu neighborhood and one in the Hong Qiao Sheraton. Both Shanghai retailers cater primarily to expatriates and wealthy Chinese customers.

Yaks 101: an Introduction

Yaks are long-haired bovines that typically reside in Tibet and southwestern China. As 95 percent of the world's yaks live in the remote Tibetan and Qinghai plateau, these gentle, grass-grazing animals are unknown to much of the world. References to yaks in Chinese literature point to the belief that they were domesticated in China over 3,000 years ago. They are valued by herders for their milk, meat, dung, and fiber. They are also used as beasts of burden.

Yaks produce two types of hair: a coarse, thick hair often used for bags, belts, and ropes, and a softer under hair called yak down. Like cashmere, yak down is smooth and long. Thus, when woven, it is as soft as cashmere, as Carol discovered. (One can contrast this with wool, which is short and "crinkled" and so causes an itchy sensation against the skin.) Unlike cashmere, yak down's natural color is a chocolate brown. Products of this color are the softest. The fiber must be "depigmented" to create other colors, a process that often reduces the softness.

Before Shokay was established, yak down was virtually unknown in the international knitting market. Given that cashmere is so wildly successful around the world, Chinese textile companies did not see a need to develop a market for this alternative product. In addition, not only are the yaks hard to access, but the low annual yield of their down (each yak produces only 2–3 pounds of fiber over the course of its 20-year lifespan, making shearing and collection a labor-intensive process) does not make it attractive to Chinese textile companies.

Shokay: the Business

Through trade shows and store trunk sales, Carol and Marie have developed their European, Japanese, and U.S. markets. Currently, Shokay sells to more than 130 stores around the world, most of them knitting yarn stores. Shokay opened in the Chinese market in late 2007 and directly manages only two stores in Shanghai. In addition to the yarn and product sales in China, Shokay's merchandise is sold to customers around the world as corporate gifts, to other fashion brands for co-branded projects, and to wholesale boutiques and distributors.

Carol's goal for Shokay was to create a social enterprise to improve the lives of the impoverished yak herders in the remote Yunnan and Qinghai provinces and the women knitters in rural Shanghai by directly sourcing the yak fiber and then selling the finished products to the Chinese and international markets. According to Carol, "A social enterprise is an innovative, profit-making but not profit-maximizing solution to a social problem." She looks at metrics that reflect the progress of this goal to assess Shokay's success. These metrics include how many employment opportunities have been generated and how much income growth has been created.

Currently, Carol has a staff of thirteen in Shanghai. There are also two employees in Xi Ning (the capital of Qinghai province in western China), local Tibetans who manage the fiber sourcing once a year. Shokay works with over thirty yak herders; and the knitting cooperative employs fifty women on Chongming Island, Shanghai.

The People of Shokay

Shokay employs a wide range of people. From knitting (*ayis* or aunties) in the knitting cooperative with grown children to expat summer interns interested in China and social ventures to local Chinese college graduates and a Parson's Fashion Institute of Technology fabric and fashion expert; part of the beauty of the Shokay stores and the Shokay head office is the warmth of a multicultural, engaged, and productive family.

Knitting Ayis

As of October 2009, Shokay employed fifty knitting *ayis* both in Shanghai and on Chongming Island, China's third largest island, situated on the Yangtze river estuary about 60 miles from central Shanghai. This area has been plagued by flooding for years, despite protective dykes built in the early twentieth century. Chongming's population currently hovers around 600,000, most of whom fish and farm. Over the last 20 years Chongming has faced a new problem: As labor and residential laws in China have been eased, there has been a mass exodus of youth, who look to the Chinese urban centers for opportunities. Families and parents are left behind to face dwindling farming opportunities.

Shokay approached the Chongming islanders in mid-2008 with an idea: to start a knitting cooperative on the island to harness skills the residents already possessed while also giving them the opportunity to supplement their incomes. The idea took off, and the Chongming knitting cooperative now employs forty knitting *ayis* who produce all of Shokay's handmade goods, from little stuffed yaks and baby booties to throw pillows and scarves.

Just like the herders, the *ayis* have found tremendous value in their partnership with Shokay. The company provides value for something the women of Chongming have done all their lives: knitting. Some women use this income to supplement their farming income, while others rely on Shokay as their full-time employer. Here are some of their stories:

Yuan Mei Ping raises fish for a living and supplements her income by knitting for Shokay. Lu Ping worked at a cotton factory and also knitted sweaters for export; working full time with Shokay now allows her a more flexible schedule to take care of her 14-year-old son.

Viola Zhang is one of Shokay's new product designers. She sits with the team in Shanghai bringing to life products like the stuffed baby yaks, key chains, and other accessories. Among her many other projects last summer, she worked on a "Twitter" stuffed bird to commemorate Shokay's presence on Twitter and a bride-and-groom yak pair for the top of a customer's wedding cake. No bigger than a postcard, the bride yak's intricate crocheted veil took weeks to design. Discouraged from knitting at a young age by her father, Viola secretly continued to knit presents for her family and friends. Her Shokay work gives her a sense of accomplishment, pride, and legitimacy.

Shokay also employs recent Chinese graduates with an interest in changing the world around them. Jocelyn Chu graduated in 2009 with a B.A. in economics from Shanghai Jiao Tong University. She had interned with a Chinese consulting company and was all set to return in June 2009. In spring 2009, however, she met Sam, a Shokay employee at the Taikang Lu store who introduced her to Shokay's concept and Carol's project. Intrigued by the story of the herders and Carol's dedication to keeping their traditions alive, Jocelyn decided to learn more. By graduation she had declined her consulting offer, and by July she was working full time for Shokay.

As Jocelyn says, Shokay allows her to "help people through what she does every day."[3] Thrilled to have found a job that holds meaning for her, she has thrown herself into her work. She manages the Shokay Sheraton store and guides the company's marketing and communications data management. While turning down the lucrative pay of a consulting job was very difficult, Jocelyn says she was unusually lucky to have her family's support in her decision.

Jocelyn's favorite part about working at Shokay is sharing the company's message and story with her peer group and customers. She finds herself repeating a few key messages again and again. She continually reminds her friends from college that Shokay is not a charity: "A charity is a one-time thing that might not guarantee any sort of long-term sustainability. You help someone once, but you're not helping them help themselves." Socially minded for-profit enterprises are relatively unheard of in China; and Jocelyn likes to share Shokay's unique business model with her friends, hoping they will be inspired to look into ways they can help their communities. With customers, it is sharing the Shokay mission and story that energizes Jocelyn. She makes sure everyone who walks through the door of the Sheraton store leaves knowing a little bit about yak down and the Tibetan yak herders Shokay is helping.

Jocelyn is convinced that Shokay plays a unique role on the Shanghai retail scene.

> Shokay is well-positioned to introduce the idea of the socially minded enterprise to Shanghai. Carol and Marie's background from the Kennedy School, as well as their dedication to the environmental impact of their products and alleviating the poverty and the modern social struggles of a sometimes-forgotten remote subset of the Chinese population, bolsters the company's clout in the minds of the Chinese consumers.

Jocelyn believes that "as long as consumers know about Shokay, they will support us."

Shokay in Shanghai

In just three years, Shokay has grown from one to three locations in Shanghai. Originally, Carol and Marie had not conceived of Shokay as a retail outlet, and Shanghai served only as Shokay's nerve center for inventory storage and order taking. In early 2008 Carol learned that a retail space in a charming historic shopping district was available and decided to open the next chapter in Shokay's story.

Taikang Lu, as it is now referred to by throngs of Chinese and expats, is a maze of tiny alleys behind the one block of Taikang Street in south central Shanghai. The alleys are exceptional, as they feature traditional Shanghai urban architecture—*shiku men* or stone archways—that have largely been bulldozed in Shanghai in favor of gleaming skyscrapers. Five years ago, Chinese artists took up residence in the warren of little alleys behind Taikang Street. Since then the area has been a Shanghai mecca to the laid-back, artistic crowd. The retail and restaurant outlets are tiny and squeezed right next to each other; and the alleys are often only four feet wide, resulting in a cozy, labyrinth-like atmosphere.

Figure 17.1 The Shokay Flagship Store
Source: Emily Di Capua, August 2009.

Taikang Lu is home to galleries, coffee shops, wine bars, dumpling stands, clothing stores, and, since 2008, Shokay's flagship store.

The Shokay store at 66 Taikang Lu is large for a Taikang Lu establishment. The store takes up what used to be the center room and two side rooms of a traditional *shiku men*-style home. Shokay's household goods, adult accessories, and children's clothing line the well-lit walls and shelves. Antique Chinese furniture and rugs harken back to the days when this *shiku men* was a home (see Figure 17.1).

Hongqiao is a wealthy, expatriate neighborhood to the west of central Shanghai with broad, tree-lined streets and many parks and shopping malls. Shokay's Sheraton Hongqiao store has a completely different look and feel from the Taikang Lu store. Walking into the hotel's marble foyer, one immediately notices a huge sign inviting guests to head up the sweeping staircase to visit the Shokay store. This store is like a little treasure chest of color. A plethora of baby yaks in rainbow colors is piled together in a corner, while accessories like ear muffs and scarves fill the glass display cases. The store, tucked next to the hotel's gourmet delicatessen and food shop, caters to tourists and business people visiting Shanghai.

Shokay's partnership with the Sheraton is exclusive. The hotel approached Carol in winter 2009 after a Sheraton representative met her and learned about Shokay at an International School Christmas fair. Shokay pays a subsidized rent for the Sheraton space, in return for which it enjoys exclusive retail rights, selling Shokay goods and basic toiletries. The Sheraton markets Shokay throughout its operations, from providing a flier introducing Shokay to guests at check-in, to inviting Shokay to participate in Sheraton promotional events. According to Sheraton, Shokay provides guests with a memorable and unique shopping experience and the Sheraton provides a steady stream of customers to Shokay.

Shokay's Shanghai headquarters is in a tall Chinese commercial and residential building situated in an upscale neighborhood. The Shokay team's lunch options range from a nearby noodle stall to an upscale food court complete with a Starbucks and sushi. The Shokay office occupies a small, jam-packed two-story space. Walking in, one is immediately aware of the buzz of a start-up. The first floor is overrun by desks; and everyone is on the phone, with customers, distributors, factory managers, the knitting *ayis*, one of the stores, or perhaps a CCTV press representative. (The Chinese press has gotten wind of Shokay and is interested in promoting its work. In early summer 2009, CCTV completed a video segment on the company.) On the second floor of the cramped Shokay headquarters, a large rectangular work table sits surrounded by shelves, one side bulging with brightly colored Shokay inventory and rainbow-like stacks of Shokay sample swatches, and the other side prepared for customers around the world. At the table Danielle is on the phone back and forth with distributors and the Tibetan connections all day long, while Rema, from Parsons, darts to and from her computer and the wall of Shokay products as she dreams up new designs for Shokay products. By the window sit two *ayis* who knit the prototypes. They are islands of calm in the busy office, surrounded by colorful yarns and some of their newest designs. Every now and then a funny story emerges in Chinese, English, or Chinglish, and within seconds everyone on the second floor is laughing.

The Marketing Challenge: Marketing on a Shoestring Budget

As a newly minted entrepreneur in Shanghai, Carol faces a growing number of expenses. There are new employees to hire, more storage space to rent for inventory, and more travel expenses as she and Marie travel to promote Shokay at trade fairs and meet with distributors around the world. With a slim operating budget and little beyond the proceeds of two business case competitions in terms of investment, a marketing budget for Shokay is out of the question. How, then, does Carol manage to spread the message about Shokay's products—"Luxury with a Story, Style with a Touch of Humanity"—around Shanghai and around the world? As Carol puts it bluntly, "We need to market our products to grow the business, with a marketing budget of zero."

Over the course of 18 months, Carol has come up with some imaginative marketing ideas that cost little or nothing and have established Shokay as a fixture on the Shanghai expat scene and in the world of social ventures.

Taikang Lu History Tour

When Shokay moved into its Taikang Lu store, little did Carol know that it would quickly become a retail landmark in the artsy neighborhood. With one of the largest retail spaces and one of the longest-running enterprises (in general, store turnover is extremely high), Shokay has become a "must-stop" on Taikang Lu visits. In spring 2009 Carol decided to capitalize on this and on the unique history of the neighborhood. One of her store employees, Sam, a recent Chinese college graduate, had grown up on Taikang Lu long before it was a tourist destination. He and his extended family have lived in one of the *shiku men* for generations, and he is well-versed in the twentieth-century history of the area. Seeing an opportunity, Carol helped Sam design a 45-minute "History of Taikang Lu" walking tour that starts and ends at the Shokay store. The tour takes visitors down Taikang Lu's meandering alleys as Sam points out architectural details and describes the neighborhood's relationship with the burgeoning construction springing up around it. Visitors can peek into a peaceful courtyard in front of the last remaining fully residential *shiku men*, which so many tourists simply miss as their trip turns into a shopping and eating frenzy.

One stop on the tour is the studio of He Zhang, a retired art professor from Zhe Jiang University who now photographs disappearing traditional neighborhoods in Shanghai. His simple studio, which doubles as his living room, is lined with black and white photos of Shanghai street scenes and *shiku men*. Professor Zhang shares the history and specific architectural details of *shiku men* with the tour group and holds a question-and-answer session. Shortly afterwards the tour arrives back at Shokay, where a knitting lesson with complimentary needles and Shokay yarn, accompanied by tea and yak cheese (from the Shokay yaks!), is provided for all the attendees.

Carol markets this new "Shokay: Taikang Lu Tour and Knitting Lesson" in free expatriate newsletters and embassy bulletins. Her primary target audience is expatriate wives who do not speak Chinese and perhaps would not venture out to Taikang Lu on their own. The tour package is priced at 350 RMB (US$50). It is too soon to gauge the success of the tour, but creativity like this helps circumvent the problem of no marketing budget.

Expatriate Publications/Consulate Newsletters

Carol makes use of every free expatriate publication in Shanghai, of which there are many. She and her team also promote Shokay in many Shanghai publications, such as the weekly *City Weekend* and the monthly *That's Shanghai*. Shokay does this not through paid advertisements, but rather through publicizing promotions and events at Shokay. These magazines have calendar sections in which local events can be listed for free. Shokay's events range from the Taikang Lu tour to brooch-knitting lessons in honor of International Women's Day, and from holiday specials (spend x amount, get a Christmas tree ornament) to frequent "readers-only" discounts. Carol also promotes Shokay through various consulate newsletters. All these forums are great ways to reach Shokay's target expatriate clients.

Marketing and Shanghai's International Schools

In the last 10 years the number of international elementary, middle, and high schools in Shanghai has grown exponentially. There are schools that offer curricula from anywhere in the world, in addition to religious schools, bilingual schools, and schools with unique foci, such as sports or the arts. The social events sponsored and hosted by these schools provide Shokay with many free or low-cost marketing opportunities: holiday fairs, gala raffles, special deals for school community members, and gift package ideas.

Carol notes that from November through the Chinese New Year (usually in mid-February), Shokay's schedule is packed with school fair bookings. The schools host holiday fairs during which local retailers will set up tables and display a selection of goods for sale, often with a holiday theme. The students, teachers, staff, and parents select holiday presents while being introduced to Shanghai retailers. Carol finds these fairs, which serve to increase Shokay's market awareness, also provide a lot of promotional material, and the sales staff can invite community members to visit the Shokay store. That Shokay also gets to sell goods is, according to Carol, the icing on the cake

The Tweeting Yak: Shokay on Twitter

Carol uses Twitter as a low-cost tool to spread Shokay news to customers, community members, social entrepreneurs, and knitting enthusiasts around the world. Shokay tweets fall into four categories: events and promotions, websites of interest and retweets, yak tracking, and opportunities with Shokay.

Primarily, Shokay will tweet about upcoming events at one of the stores, such as a yak-cheese tasting at the Sheraton store, a feature piece on Shokay in Chinese *Vogue*, or an upcoming 25 percent off sale. The Shokay family also tweets on topics of interest to its community. Recently Carol passed on a Fast Company study on social media in China. She also retweeted two articles: "7 Tools for Running a Startup Social Enterprise" and "How Knitters Can Create Positive Social Change."

When the Shokay family began tweeting, they thought it would be fun to strengthen the association of the Shokay name with the yak. Jocelyn and Carol started "yak tracking," tweeting photos and references to yaks that they found online or that customers had given them. An "I ♥ Yaks" tee shirt, spotted in NYC, was sent to Shokay and immediately tweeted about. This creates a fun and interactive game for those following Shokay and also serves to raise awareness of the company. Finally, Carol uses Twitter to announce employment opportunities that followers can learn more about on the Shokay website or in the stores.

To keep up with all this Twitter activity, Shokay uses mainly Twitpic and Tweetdeck. Twitpic allows Twitter users to easily upload photos and images for all followers to see. Shokay does this with the yak tracking and to post images of the many trade shows that Carol and Marie attend. Tweetdeck is a browser that allows users to manage their online social media updates in real time. Its users can manage more than one Twitter account (Shokay has two), retweet (Shokay uses this feature often), create Twitter follower lists, follow topics in real time, and easily see who is following them. During summer 2009, Danielle, an intern from the University of Pennsylvania, was in charge of setting up Shokay's Tweetdeck. To an outsider, the complexity of her main browser page with its constant Twitter follow updates and live streams from Facebook seems to rival the display of an airplane cockpit.

One neat feature of Tweetdeck is the ability to search all tweets for keywords and retweet them. Shokay uses this feature often. Any time anyone around the world tweets about coming to the Shokay store, using Shokay yarn, or wearing a Shokay piece and tweets about it, using "Shokay" in the tweet, Danielle finds it and retweets it to Shokay's other Twitter followers.

Carol's Imaginative "Yaks Around the World Campaign"

Carol recently began an inexpensive campaign that ties Shokay marketing to spreading the company's message of improving one's community and making the world a better place. Carol decided to use one of her best-selling products—the hand-knit, colorful, stuffed baby yaks—to create a network of people doing social good around the world.

The campaign, called "Yaks Around the World," was launched in Shanghai in summer 2009. Carol prepared twenty-five different baby stuffed yaks, each in a separate color with a different name and identity card. She then used her expanding network of friends and colleagues around the world who are involved in similar social ventures to identify twenty-five "change makers," people who are striving to make the world a better place. Each "change maker" receives a baby yak with instructions to photograph the yak in the "change maker's" community before sending it along to another "change maker." Ideally, the little yaks will travel around the world, connecting "change makers" from all different areas and thereby creating a global community of "change makers" who can share experiences and learn from each other. This campaign will also serve to generate interest in Shokay as people track the baby yaks on the company's website and members of the various "change makers'" communities learn about Shokay upon introduction to the baby yaks. So far, the little yaks have gone out to "change makers" who lead organizations as diverse as Circle of Women, the World Toilet Organization, Rubicon National Social Innovations, and Givology. These "change makers" have in turn passed the yaks onto others who share their values and thus the little animals are slowly making their way around the world.

As Carol looks towards Shokay's future she wants to continue engaging with her community—both locally through an expansion of events like the Taikang Lu tours and globally through social media like Twitter and creative engagements like her "Around the World Campaign."

> Marketing our brand is the most effective way we can improve the lives of the herders and *ayis*. Once people are introduced to Shokay through our marketing, they experience our products and hear about our mission and then they themselves spread the word.[4]

Besides running the day-to-day business of Shokay, how to expand current marketing efforts is a question that occupies Carol. How can she and the Shokay team continue to build brand recognition in both China and abroad?

QUESTIONS

1   What should be the revenue-sharing model between the herders and Shokay?
2   What new customer groups should Carol target?
3   What new marketing efforts should Shokay undertake?

Notes

1   Interview, August 1, 2009.
2   July 28, 2009.
3   August 1, 2009.
4   Interview, August 4, 2009.

18 Jessica Rodríguez's Art Atlas

Fair Fashion from Peru to the World

Dalila Boclin

Poverty is rampant in the highlands of Peru. This culturally rich area, however, is known for its original and world-renowned crafts. Jessica Rodríguez launched a venture to help local textile workers design and make products for export. She has demonstrated that communities in some of the most isolated parts of the world can be empowered to benefit from globalization and trade.

At a coffee shop in Boston or in a Parisian boutique, a "Fair Trade" sticker may signify little more than a label or a distant ideal. But at Art Atlas, fair trade is not a corporate strategy or a means to a mark-up; it is a way of life—a brand of human sympathy that cannot be understood in terms of products or currency. Jessica Rodríguez, founder of Art Atlas, knows this feeling well and has built a business based on fairness that has enriched the lives of hundreds of impoverished villagers across Peru.

Peru's history has been marked with political instability. Since its independence from Spain in 1821, military coups and authoritarian regimes have disrupted the official constitutional republic.[1] Persistent government turmoil and various political turnovers have undermined the economy's ability to achieve sustained growth. The national economy was struck yet again in 1982 with the occurrence of El Niño, which produced extreme weather patterns across the nation and caused international commodity prices to plummet lower than those of the Great Depression. The ensuing crisis worsened living conditions for Peru's poor, as did the political unrest that provoked the emergence of various terrorist groups and a destructive drug trade.[2] It was not until 2001, when the Toledo administration came to power, that Peru recovered its democracy and began to experience economic growth.[3] The economy began to expand rapidly in 2002. From 2002 to 2006 it grew by over 4 percent per year, and jumped to 9 percent per year during 2007 and 2008.[4] This boom has helped to lower the national poverty rate by about 15 percent since 2002, although the percentage of those living below the poverty line still hovers at around 36 percent.[5] The percentage of individuals who fail to earn income above the poverty index bears greater significance when considering the unemployment rate, which at 9 percent demonstrates a tremendous need for significantly gainful employment.[6]

Since 1999, Art Atlas has been producing sweaters, scarves, shirts, and other garments that have been exported all over the world, but whose value is still rooted in their origin in Arequipa, Peru. Launched as a socially driven enterprise, Art Atlas has created a production model that creates opportunity not only for its workers, but also for all those involved along every step of its process, from the collaborators and clients to the final consumers.

The Origins of a Social Enterprise

It is possible to identify the beginnings of Art Atlas decades before the company came into being. From her childhood onward, Jessica Rodríguez has always been acutely aware of the disparate conditions of people in Arequipa, and has cared about giving to those who have less. Every year as her birthday approached, Jessica would beg her mother to invite all the poor children from the province to her party. She could not understand why she, one of a working-class family, had more, while so many others around her lived in poverty. Then, she could only wish to share what she had. Today Art Atlas is a wish come true, both for those living in poverty and for Jessica.

The real groundwork for Art Atlas was laid when Jessica was working as the administrative secretary to the vice president at Michell, one of Peru's top producers of premium alpaca fabrics and yarns. Alpaca are native to the Andean region of South America, where, at its highest point, 4,500 meters above sea level, temperatures can range from plus or minus 20 degrees Celsius and both icy winds and solar radiation are uniquely intense.[7] Alpaca fiber is recognized not only for its warmth and durability, but also for its softness and elegance, akin to cashmere and angora. Peru, among the world's leading producers of alpaca fabrics and products, is home to many businesses that take advantage of the quality and distinctiveness of this product.

In 1999, a husband and wife team from France, hoping to learn more about Peruvian natural fabrics and refining processes, visited Michell, creating an opportunity to meet Jessica and begin a long relationship. Together, the three found that their mutual goals and philosophy could mesh to produce something far greater than any of them had anticipated. The couple had come to Peru hoping to partner with a producer of natural and organic clothing that they could sell in France. Their main concerns were health and environmental consciousness. They needed to guarantee that their garments would be produced only by ecologically sound processes and using only safe, natural, and organic materials. Jessica recognized that their concerns mirrored her own discomfort with social inequality and found a way to weave her own ambitions into the couple's plans. Her window of opportunity began exactly where Michell's ended: while Michell itself focuses on spinning, dyeing, and other processes leading up to final production, the French couple also needed a manufacturer to design and sew their clothing; the moment she heard this, Jessica imagined the hands of the artisans producing ecological garments. By framing her idea for a fair-wage venture according to the same tenets of responsible-living consumption, Jessica successfully entered into the first contract for what would become Art Atlas.

Social entrepreneurship has recently become a convenient term for describing businesses that generate profits but whose ultimate goal is social impact.[8] For social entrepreneurs,

> Earned income is only a means to a social end . . . Profits should not be treated with equal importance to social results. No amount of profit makes up for failure on the social impact side of the equation . . . Social entrepreneurs have only one ultimate bottom line by which to measure their success. It is their intended social impact, whether that is housing for the homeless, a cleaner environment, improved access to health care, more effective education, reduced poverty, protection of abused children, deeper appreciation of the arts, or some other social improvement.[9]

Thus, markets are not always the best platforms for social entrepreneurs:

> Markets do not do a good job of valuing social improvements, public goods and harms, and benefits for people who cannot afford to pay. These elements are often essential to social entrepreneurship. That is what makes it social entrepreneurship. As a result, it is much harder to determine whether a social entrepreneur is creating sufficient social value to justify the resources used in creating that value.[10]

When Jessica describes Peru's problem in alleviating poverty, she explains how the education and literacy qualifications required by most jobs preclude virtually all those living in rural areas, where schools are sparse and lack resources, from finding employment. When she was conceptualizing her enterprise, she was aware that skill or literacy training alone is insufficient: "You have to provide an outlet," she says, as she details how the first of Art Atlas' tailors and artisans came to be.

To recruit employees, Jessica did not have to travel very far from her home in the city of Arequipa. Just a few miles into the countryside of Pampa Cañahuas, impoverished families live on far less than basic provisions. There Jessica found countless women with little, if any, education or craft skills, anxious to feed and clothe their children and more than eager to learn about the jobs she had to offer. Thus, Jessica launched

Figure 18.1 Jessica Rodríguez with Two of Her Employees
Source: Dalila Boclin.

the first of many training sessions: for the initial groups she enlisted
professional seamstresses to conduct a series of lessons outlining the basic
styles and techniques for making sweaters. As her enterprise grew, her
veteran seamstresses would later work as instructors and helpers for
artisans-in-training (see Figure 18.1).

With the first orders under way, Jessica and her family worked diligently
to ensure the project would succeed. While still working full-time, Jessica
would return from work to her living room-turned-workshop, inspecting
and packing sweaters and ensuring their exceptional quality. Where today
dozens of workers contribute to a precisely enumerated process, in its early
days Art Atlas was a family affair, with Jessica's own family and her
husband's family coordinating production.

Pleased with the quality and care that they saw in the garments, the
French couple began to distribute catalogues and samples of Jessica's
products to organic markets throughout France. Little by little, Art Atlas
developed a loyal customer base and a steady stream of orders. Just a year
later, in 2000, Art Atlas was officially founded, although it would be
another 7 years before its operations moved out of Jessica's home. Jessica
expanded the enterprise as the number of orders increased. She was able
to run the business from her apartment for the first few years, but then
transferred her work (and personal life) to her first home. Later she added
a second floor to house the business and ultimately rented the two houses
next door to accommodate production. "Little by little, as we could afford
it," she reflects. Finally, in 2007, Art Atlas moved to its current location,

a warehouse in Arequipa, where all the administrative and some production tasks take place.

Today, both Jessica and her husband dedicate all their time to Art Atlas, Jessica focusing primarily on expanding sales and the production of high quality sweaters and her husband managing the company's finances to ensure the sustainability of its social mission. Although Jessica ultimately left her job at Michell to pursue her own goals, she was always candid about her desire to expand Art Atlas. Because she had been transparent all along about her plans, she was able to turn to her mentor, Mr. Bedoya, vice president of Michell, for support and guidance even after she branched out.

A Winning Formula

Art Atlas' distinguishing value rests in both the quality of its garments and its socially oriented employment practices. Meeting the French couple connected Jessica with the key to her success. She learned that there is a growing population concerned with the implications of their consumption beyond the transaction. She also gained insight into environmentally and socially conscious consumers and understood how the term "quality" could be applied to more than just a final product. With this in mind, she soon realized that there is a market for sound humanitarian practices, where fair prices are justified by their added social value. Just as the French couple were willing to pay a premium to ensure their own healthy and natural living, other buyers might be willing to ensure fair employment.

These two defining characteristics—exceptional quality and fair employment—are inextricably linked at Art Atlas. All of the company's products use premium fabrics and dyes, such as fine alpaca thread or organic cotton, and nearly all are handmade to ensure quality. Although many of Jessica's clients have some preference for buying from Art Atlas for its social mission, some care foremost about the garments themselves—whether for organic or fashion purposes. Nevertheless, Jessica has been able to offer such distinguished quality clothing because of the labor and care that her production process demands. Thus, ensuring that her product stands up to her clients' expectations is essential to justifying Art Atlas' premium prices and maintaining fair-wage labor.

Jessica's business has grown at a rapid pace, enabling her to offer generous training and employment opportunities across the province. She provides work for her artisans on an as-needed basis. Over the last 10 years she has incorporated over 700 individuals under Art Atlas' employment model, producing an average of 12,000 garments per month and generating about US$2 million annually in sales (as of 2009). However, even the socially conscious economy has slowed since the recession of 2008, but not without some moral cushion. While most Peruvian industries experienced an average decline of 30–40 percent in sales, Art Atlas was less affected, managing to maintain sales but not growing. Jessica chose to scale back on all her costs except for labor, and all Art Atlas employees received the same remuneration in 2009 as the year before.

Art Atlas' production relies on orders from highly developed nations, where a stable upper and middle class can afford to make up the difference for fair wages. This market has tremendous potential as well as limitations: there is the potential to expand the market for social consciousness in areas such as Europe, North America, Scandinavia, and Japan; however, it must be a well-known brand that combines the quality, the organic and the know-how. For example, Jessica has yet to put any effort into domestic sales because she understands that the conditions under which many people live in Peru cannot currently afford to accommodate her employment practices and fair wages. But Jessica continues to monitor the economic climate, and hopes to launch a unique Peruvian boutique when the time is right.

Jessica laments over the various obstacles she has faced in trying to employ people. She notes that today there is a waiting list of those who want to be trained as Art Atlas tailors. Unfortunately, there is not enough work to ensure that every pair of hands can be kept busy; and although she trains the friends and families of her workers, she cannot offer the same "express" employment to everyone. She recounts the experience of one of her employees' daughters who, at age 16, found herself pregnant out of wedlock. The seamstress turned to Jessica to help her daughter find meaningful employment. The legal age of employment in Peru is 18, and no minors may be employed in any way before they reach legal adulthood. Thus, regardless of her need, all the daughter could do was wait.

Because of this, guaranteeing a minimum amount of sales has been Jessica's priority for Art Atlas. She tries to communicate the importance of sustainable work to her clients abroad and to explain how there are no stores of food or savings in the Peruvian communities to cushion against hard times. She does not ask her clients to commit to enormous orders, but rather to small, monthly orders that can keep her artisans busy. The problems Jessica faces now are not time crunches, like those of her days working in the apartment, but rather lulls—days and months with too little work for so many needy workers.

Jessica has had to learn how to position her social endeavor within the fashion industry. Art Atlas' double bottom line is unique compared to other textile and garment producers, the majority of whom exploit cheap labor in developing nations. Jessica is keenly aware of her higher prices and narrower clientele. Thus, she has made incredible efforts to ensure she can continue to offer equal, if not greater, quality and value. For example, she assures her clients that Art Atlas can produce any garment in any stitch and has trained seamstresses in a variety of techniques. She also promises that she can produce any machine-made garment: because some of the tighter, more complicated stitches can be made only by machine, she does not want to run the risk of turning down orders that cannot be made by hand and has invested in several modern, industrial machines that can knit any difficult stitch. While she prefers orders for handmade goods, she recognizes the importance of having a diverse catalogue of services that match her clients' needs rather than her own. Because she can meet their demands, Jessica is able to negotiate sales, requesting that her clients commit to at least some handmade pieces for every order of machine-made garments.

Promoting handmade goods has been quite a challenge for the most labor-demanding also more time-intensive (and thus more costly) of products. However, it requires very little investment in either hardware (knitting needles) or training (it is among the easiest skills to teach) and is not physically strenuous. Thus, some of Jessica's neediest workers—older women who are better suited for simple tasks—usually bear the brunt of these compounded factors.

Jessica has been able to tackle this challenge and enfranchise the artisans in other ways as well. She has provided some of them with small loans to help them purchase their own manual machines. With this money, many of the tailors have been able to establish workshops in their own homes, working as "group leaders" for orders from Art Atlas, also employing as many as thirty people, and some selling directly to retailers themselves. Thus, Jessica is not only an entrepreneur herself, but has also enabled many impoverished villagers to sustain their livelihoods independently through micro-enterprises.

Training, Employment, and Production

Although work is tight, Art Atlas' training and employment program has improved over the years and is now a smooth operation. The first hand knitting classes were held in communal spaces that were accessible to anyone living in the surrounding area who expressed interest in Art Atlas. For example, Jessica located some of her first programs in a school building in Pampa Cañahuas and a communal kitchen in one of Arequipa's unofficial settlements. She also hired a professional seamstress to teach the trainees the processes and skills to make and assemble hand knitted garments.

Apart from providing group training sessions, Jessica also provides each group of artisans with a handbook of step-by-step instructions and details of how to knit each stitch and assemble each garment. However, some of these artisans come from extremely limited backgrounds—many have suffered from malnutrition and have not received a formal education. Consequently, some of her artisans are illiterate and limited in the skills they can acquire. These workers struggle more with the training process and require more initial investment, personal guidance, and tutelage to reach an acceptable skill level. Many are provided with hand drawings in place of written guidebooks to help them through each order.

Although most of the garments are hand made by the artisans, a tremendous amount of work is required on-site at Art Atlas—both pre- and post-production—to ensure that the village seamstresses create garments that meet the fashion and quality standards of Art Atlas' diverse clientele. Art Atlas created a defined process through which all orders must be handled. As the sales manager, Jessica is the first point of contact and is responsible for delivering each client's specific requirements. For example, the American brands that entrust their production to Art Atlas distinguish themselves as organic, fair-trade and high-end fashion. Once an order is received, Jessica records its details—organic threads and tints, color, and design—to create a unique description card that will accompany the order through the entire production cycle. This strict labeling system facilitates coherent control over each order by various quality control managers. As the order advances through the cycle—knitting, initial control, washing, pressing, linking, final control, labeling and packaging—the card is updated accordingly. Jessica has recently converted this labeling into a computerized bar-code system under the guidance of operations consultants.

Before production can begin, Jessica and the Art Atlas designers must have a prototype of each garment approved by the client. Then the 45-day production process begins with an initial training session for a group of artisans on how to produce the garment. Art Atlas orders most of its fabrics from Jessica's former employer, Michell, and supplies the artisans with the appropriate material for each order. Art Atlas never takes a back seat during production. Not only are the garments under constant surveillance while they are being made, but they are re-evaluated by at least two other quality control managers before they are packed and shipped. Quality control visits take place routinely while production is off-site, checking for any major errors in the design of the piece or the production of the stitch.

After the knitting is complete, trained employees thoroughly inspect each piece, looking for small snags and correcting any blemishes by hand before the knit is washed or assembled. Assembling the garments—e.g. connecting the sleeves, body, and hood of a sweater—is the next step and is usually done by special machines on-site, although some tailors may use the off-site machines they have purchased. Jessica does not allow the washing and treating processes to occur off-site for two main reasons: first, to ensure the quality, the softness of the garment is achieved during the washing process and must follow a very precise process that varies depending on both the quality of yarn and whether it is organic; second, the methods also require a great deal of attention; if done poorly, they can jeopardize the integrity of and investment in an entire batch of garments.

Sustainability

Jessica has expanded Art Atlas' services in an attempt to retain clients and try to ensure her employees have work throughout the year. She constantly tries to identify how she can incorporate her clients' many needs into her business. Although her company sells to some well-known brand labels, that provide their own designs, Art Atlas has its own designers for buyers who may be interested in selling high-quality, organic, or fair-trade items but do not wish to invest time or resources in producing their own designs. The company also has clients who occupy different positions along the spectrum, who bring some of their own ideas but also look to the Art Atlas team for inspiration. Jessica also offers her clients the option to outsource photography and catalogue production. Since 2011 she has also offered an Art Atlas collection called "Anntarah," available from an online store as well as boutiques in Peru. She hopes this will smooth the seasonal ordering trends and also provide an opportunity to build a customer base of end-consumers who will be loyal to her brand and mission.

As the sales manager and lifeblood of Art Atlas, Jessica works primarily to ensure and expand sales, particularly for handmade pieces. She is constantly negotiating on behalf of her workers and often has to make major concessions in order to preserve her social goals. Because Art Atlas is a fair-trade enterprise, the commitment is to pay always salaries of at least 200 soles (US$75) above the legal minimum of 750 soles (US$280) per month. Moreover, the employees' total yearly remuneration must amount to at least 14 months' salary.

Jessica always discusses wages with her artisans to be sure that each project appropriately rewards the labor it demands. Fair wages mean higher prices, especially when compared to the cost of production in East and Southeast Asia. This usually does not pose a problem for Jessica's French clients, nor for some of her American clients, who are conscious of fair-employment practices and are thus willing to pay a premium to promote workers' rights. Nonetheless, for some, mostly American companies, high prices pose an obstacle; and Jessica often reduces or eliminates Art Atlas profit margins, forwarding all the earnings as workers' wages. Jessica cannot jeopardize her relationship with her American clients, who make up an important percentage of her business; and although their price demands threaten Art Atlas' well-being, their orders are ultimately responsible for more than half of the workers' time.

Although Art Atlas' profits seem secondary, the company must take care of the administrative, accounting, and other on-site personnel it employs in addition to the seamstresses. Moreover, savings enable exactly the kind of small lending and advances that help facilitate economic advancement and flexibility for the workers. Jessica has never had a problem with loan repayment or untrustworthy staff. Rather, she and her employees have a shared faith in one another. What stands out about Jessica's model is the diverse investment she makes in her people. First, because she both funds their training and "recycles" their skills into her business, she has personally invested in their ability to perform and will shepherd their productive capacity because it benefits her business as well. This is a fundamental difference between an organization that trains but places its program graduates in external companies: In such an employment assistance model, the partner firm absorbing new labor has no true incentive to help the new employee adjust to and succeed in his or her new position.

Second, Jessica's interest and involvement in her workers' lives creates personal relationships that are not factored in to the accounting and the invoices. Jessica offers loans, advances, flexible work hours, and parental leave, not for the sake of profits but because she genuinely cares about her employees' well-being. She personally knows each individual tailor she employs and takes active responsibility for his or her happiness. Jessica has never had a problem with workers defaulting on loans or carelessly producing garments. Because she recruits from communities where previous employment history is sparse, she relies on her workers to evaluate people in the community for inclusion in the Art Atlas family. Art Atlas' employees value their relationships with the firm. Thus, they recommend good workers and treat their jobs with the utmost respect. This investment in social capital is unique to social enterprises. Whereas traditional for-profit ventures can rely on résumés and swift employee turnover to mitigate the risk of uncertainty with new hires, Jessica does not want to jeopardize the quality of her production or the empowerment she provides along with the paycheck.

Beyond Business

Not surprisingly, Jessica has tried to innovate to share Art Atlas' benefits with as many people as possible. It quickly came to her attention that knitting sweaters produces a great deal of scrap fabric. She saw the scraps as an opportunity and found a new way to keep her seamstresses' needles busy: From the leftover fabric they began sewing, stuffing, and selling small dolls whose profits would be used entirely for charitable causes. Because one of Jessica's priorities is advancing the quality and universality of education in Peru, she put the extra profits generated from the doll project toward supplying five underfunded schools in Pampa Cañahuas with basic school supplies, such as notebooks, pens, and crayons.

This is just the first of many charitable projects to come from Art Atlas. Once the business was firmly established, Jessica launched its sister, non-profit organization. Founded in 2003, the Art Atlas Foundation is independent of the business and provides Jessica with an avenue to donate Art Atlas' profits to charitable causes. Although Art Atlas is a social enterprise, Jessica realizes that while skills training and employment can jump-start social mobility, some communities live in dire conditions and need immediate relief. She cites one specific experience that changed her life and confirmed her belief in charity. It was a bitter cold day when she traveled with her family to Pampa Cañahuas to recruit workers. She was shocked by the disparity in living conditions: While she and her children were bundled from head to toe, she saw children running around without jackets or shoes and facing the biting wind so unprotected that their cheeks were dry and bleeding. Jessica and her husband still hold the face of one particular boy in their memory and retain this image as her and her foundation's motivation. Since its inception in 2003, the foundation has carried out various campaigns, from providing medical services to building barns for small farmers to protect their alpaca during the bitterly cold winters.

Jessica has managed to bring about more than isolated change: Recently, the Art Atlas Foundation secured a partnership with the municipality of Arequipa, with the government sharing in funding the foundation and creating awareness of this community's need. Ideally, Jessica would like to devote more of her time to the foundation. However, the demands of running her own business occupy most of her time. In 2009 she had to abandon her 5-year plan to establish a nursery or daycare center for working mothers because she simply did not have the time to dedicate to the fundraising and development necessary to get the project off the ground. Because she draws a clear distinction between Art Atlas' clients and the foundation's funders—she does not try to involve her clients in the foundation's non-profit work, regardless of whether they espouse the same social vision as Art Atlas—this compounds the problem of limited resources and demands that she devote time and energy to two distinct groups.

Jessica also serves as an advocate for women and small business owners in the political sphere. While she finds it frustrating that larger firms, with greater leverage, do not provide the same sort of political or social initiatives, she has worked enthusiastically to help those involved in every step of garment production, from the alpaca farmers to the seamstresses. She currently serves as director of the Chamber of Commerce in Arequipa and was president of the Small Business Owners Association, and is actually president of the AMEP Arequipa (Asociation of Women Entrepreneurs). Jessica would like to see more access to finance for women entrepreneurs, social enterprises, and social services in Peru, and believes the government should encourage and incentivize these activities.

In the meantime, Jessica organizes programs and services to connect unemployed women with some of the resources they need to empower their lives. For example, she sponsors a psychologist to visit Art Atlas three times each year to conduct motivational lectures focusing on the emotional challenges of rising out of poverty. She notes that many lower-class Peruvian families are trapped by unjust power relations between men and women: although it is mostly the women who labor and earn wages, many husbands snatch up their money and spend the family's financial resources on alcohol. What is more, Jessica sees many women who have been abused and abandoned by their husbands and are complacent about this treatment, covering their physical and emotional bruises with stories and excuses. Thus, this access to a professional counselor can be a tremendous resource for working women. Like Jessica, this psychologist recognizes the importance of providing aid to those in need and offers an extra service at no cost to the women who attend her talks by making herself available by telephone or e-mail in the event that any of the women need guidance or support.

Jessica has effectively created a business around programs for economic and social advancement. However, Art Atlas' social bottom line has at times taken a toll on its business operations. How do Jessica's social and profit goals interact with and inhibit each other? The challenges of a double bottom line are not limited simply to Jessica's business model: As we have seen, she relies on expensive foreign markets to finance fair wages. What might this strategy imply for future business development? How can Art Atlas and other social enterprises create a demand for social value? What types of practices should social enterprises consider when trying to maximize their social impact? Art Atlas is clearly unique in its investment in and dedication to its employees. This care and consideration have, in essence, been reinvested—through loan repayments, productivity, and referrals—thus increasing Art Atlas' efficiency. Consider how Art Atlas might be different if it had more than one person in Jessica's role: would it be possible for the company to serve an even greater community if there were two or three sales managers equally as devoted to employee well-being? Is this model expandable or replicable?

QUESTIONS

1 Do the accomplishments of Art Atlas demonstrate that "fair trade" is possible?
2 What should Jessica do in order to extend her model to other Peruvian areas?
3 Should Jessica consider launching a similar venture in industries other than textiles?

Notes

1 U.S. Department of State, *Background Note: Peru,* January 2010, www.state.gov/r/pa/ei/bgn/2962.htm (accessed April 14, 2010).
2 Ibid.
3 Ibid.
4 Ibid.
5 The World Bank, *Peru Country Brief: Development Highlights,* May 18, 2009, http://web.worldbank.org/WBSITE/EXTERNAL/COUNTRIES/LACEXT/PERU

EXTN/0,,menuPK:343633~pagePK:141132~piPK:141107~theSitePK:343623, 00.html (accessed September 26, 2010).

6 Central Intelligence Agency, *CIA World Factbook: South America: Peru*, April 7, 2010, https://www.cia.gov/library/publications/the-world-factbook/geos/pe.html (accessed April 14, 2010).

7 International Alpaca Association, *About Alpaca*, March 2000, www.aia.org.pe/aia.html?32 (accessed February 25, 2010).

8 J. Gregory Dees, "The Meaning of 'Social Entrepreneurship,'" working paper, 2001, Duke University, Fuqua School of Business, Center for the Advancement of Social Entrepreneurship, http://www.caseatduke.org/documents/dees_sedef.pdf (accessed September 26, 2010).

9 J. Gregory Dees, "Social Entrepreneurship Is About Innovation and Impact, Not Income," *Social Edge* (September 2003), www.caseatduke.org/articles/1004/corner.htm (accessed September 26, 2010).

10 Ibid.

19 Pianporn Deetes

Social Entrepreneurship to Protect the Environment and Empower Citizens

Victoria Johnson

Pianporn Deetes took on the challenge of helping protect the environment in her native Thailand and beyond. She joined Living River Siam in order to protect the rights of villagers along the Mekong River. She knew water is one of the most politically sensitive topics. Using her organizational skills, she has empowered villagers, giving them arguments and tools to uphold their interests. She stands as an example of how social entrepreneurship can help improve the lot of the poor while preserving the environment.

On March 6, 2010, Pianporn ("Pai") Deetes, a Thai social entrepreneur, flew from Bangkok with a group of twenty-eight journalists and Thai senators to the border between Thailand and Laos. Pai, who leads the nonprofit organization Living River Siam, wanted them to see the drought-stricken Mekong River with their own eyes. For more than a month, the Mekong had been so low that economic and agricultural activity dependent on the river was severely affected. Villagers who earned their livelihoods from fishing had seen their catch size decline; farmers no longer had enough water to irrigate their crops and care for their livestock; and ferry boat operators had had to suspend their services, badly affecting tourism and trade. While some blamed a long spell of dry weather for the drought, Pai was convinced that there was an additional and possibly more significant cause: several massive dams that had been built upstream on the Mekong in China.

The Mekong is one of Asia's longest rivers, flowing from its source in Tibet through China, Burma, Laos, Thailand, Cambodia, and Vietnam. Like many other major rivers around the world, the Mekong has seen the construction of hydroelectric dams designed to provide power to millions of people. While such infrastructure projects offer significant economic and social benefits, they also create environmental, economic, and social problems of their own. Dammed rivers can flood farmlands and villages, disrupt fish spawning cycles, and—as Pai believed was the case for the Mekong in northern Thailand—lead to severe drought conditions.

Among the members of the group Pai had brought from Bangkok to tour the region were members of the Thai Senate's Subcommittee on Mekong Development. If these key politicians learned about the damage to Thai ecosystems and livelihoods firsthand, might they be persuaded that dams on the Mekong were the source of the problem?

A Social Entrepreneur Is Born

Poised, articulate, and politically savvy, Pai had been working on behalf of the rivers of Southeast Asia—and the people who lived along their banks —for nearly a decade. But her personal connection with environmental issues went back to her earliest years. Pai had spent her childhood in a village in northern Thailand, where her parents had moved in the 1970s to help identify and promote sustainable agricultural practices among hill tribes such as the Lisu, the Karen, and the Hmong. In 1997, after two decades of work on behalf of these tribes and the ecosystems in which they live, Pai's mother, Tuenjai Deetes, was named one of twenty-five "Women Leaders in Action" on global environmental issues by the United Nations Environment Programme. Growing up in such a family meant that Pai was fluent in both the Lisu and Thai languages, was equally at home in the very different worlds of urban and rural Thailand, and was deeply attuned to the tensions between economic development and environmental protection. It also meant that she had, in her mother, a role model of a very dedicated and accomplished female social entrepreneur.

Successful social entrepreneurs have much in common with successful "classic" entrepreneurs: both kinds of entrepreneur seek to innovate— whether they are creating a new organization, a new service, or a new product —by turning a personal vision into a concrete reality through single-minded hard work. Social entrepreneurs differ, however, from classic entrepreneurs in that their *primary* goal is neither profit nor the production of a product or service, but instead the amelioration of social problems. Of course, profits, products, and services are sometimes the means to this goal. Indeed, one of the most famous social entrepreneurs in the world today, Nobel Prize winner Muhammad Yunus, has fostered commercial enterprise among the poor through the establishment of microlending institutions. Yet while some social entrepreneurs create for-profit businesses (sometimes called social enterprises or social businesses), many others work within the framework of not-for-profit organizations.

The term "social entrepreneur" was coined in the early 1980s by Bill Drayton, the founder of Ashoka, an organization dedicated to supporting citizens who seek to effect social change around the world. Drayton, whose organization awards prestigious Ashoka Fellowships to a small group of social entrepreneurs each year, defines the term with reference to large-scale social change:

Ashoka is only interested in ideas that it believes will change the field significantly and that will trigger nationwide impact or, for smaller countries, broader regional change. For example, Ashoka will not support the launch of a new school or clinic unless it is part of a broader strategy to reform the education or health system at the national level and beyond.[1]

Pai's mother, Tuenjai Deetes, was named an Ashoka Fellow in 1990. The funding, increased visibility, and new contacts that accompanied her appointment as a Fellow supported her efforts to help tribal villages on the Thai/Burmese border abandon slash-and-burn agriculture in favor of sustainable farming practices. In 2006, Pai herself was named an Ashoka Fellow for her work with Living River Siam. Ashoka selected Pai because her approach to the problem of the ecological devastation created by hydroelectric projects unfolds on three different social levels:

At the community level she engages the people in researching and documenting the ecosystem, natural resources, and livelihoods in the river basin. Nationally, she brings the issue into the national discourse regarding cross-border livelihoods and human rights. At the policy level, she advocates for legislation that protects the rights of affected communities.[2] Pai works toward these goals both individually and through her organization, Living River Siam.

Protecting the Environment, Empowering Citizens

Pai came to Living River Siam after earning her degree in English at Bangkok's Chulalongkorn University and working at several NGOs. In 2002 she joined the Southeast Asia Rivers Network (SEARIN), a precursor organization to Living River Siam. Founded on March 14, 1999, the International Day of Action Against Dams and for Rivers, Water and Life, this Thai not-for-profit organization was created by academics and activists concerned about the potential impact of dam construction on the riverine ecosystems of Southeast Asia. In 2005, SEARIN's name was changed to Living River Siam and the organization was restructured, with Pai taking a leadership role. Although Pai calls herself a "coordinator," her colleagues at Living River Siam consider her in many ways to be the organization's unofficial leader. One reason for this is her skill and experience in grant-writing; another is her comfort in interacting with a variety of constituencies, including villagers, academics, journalists, politicians, and activists, both locally and internationally.

Like its predecessor, SEARIN, Living River Siam is a campaign-based organization, working to support local communities' rights to their water resources, promote local knowledge-based sustainable water resource management, and oppose threats to rivers and riverine ecosystems in

Thailand and neighbor countries in the Mekong and Salween river basins, such as large-scale dams and water diversion projects.[3]

Living River Siam occupies a spacious two-story house on the outskirts of Chiang Mai, the second largest city in Thailand (Figure 19.1). Although Chiang Mai, located in the hilly northwestern region of the country, suffers from severe air pollution, the suburban neighborhood from which Living River Siam operates is leafy and green, and the air is fresh. In the warm Thai climate, staff members work on the porch and in rooms open to the outdoors. Hanging on the walls and spread out across tables are maps tracing the courses of the Mekong and the Salween rivers, key sites in Living River Siam's efforts to protect villagers and ecosystems. In the kitchen, an apron hanging on a hook bears the image of a beaming Nelson Mandela.

Pai divides her time between Bangkok, where her husband is employed, and Chiang Mai, where she meets and works with the Living River Siam staff. No matter which city she is in, however, she is working on behalf of her organization. During a conversation in the Chiang Mai headquarters, her infant daughter sits on her lap as Pai discusses the mission, structure, and strategy of Living River Siam. The first step in protecting the rivers, Pai and her team believe, is collecting accurate information on their ecosystems, so that any proposed dam projects can be thoroughly evaluated in advance for the potential impact on the river in question—and in the

Figure 19.1 Living River Siam Headquarters, Chiang Mai, Thailand
Source: Victoria Johnson, March 2010.

event that a dam is constructed, its actual impact on ecosystems can be measured. Living River Siam employs a novel strategy for collecting this information. Instead of relying on academic or government experts, the organization's members work closely with the villagers who make their living from the rivers and know the cycles of its flora and fauna more intimately than anyone else. As Pai points out, this obviates the need for a large organization. Instead, the seven full- and part-time staff members strive above all to support the villagers in gathering, organizing, and disseminating data about the river ecosystems in which they live, farm, and fish. As she explains,

> [t]he nature of our organization is that we are not taking the campaign or the work by ourselves. The way we work is that we support the local villagers; we try to help them strengthen local networks and community organizations, linking them with information we get from a higher level, linking them with the media . . . and helping them use their local wisdom, because we believe that every single community living in the river basin knows best about natural resources and how to manage these resources in a sustainable way, because otherwise they wouldn't have survived, right? . . . Most of the time we see that the studies done by experts or academics depend only on scientific information; they ignore local knowledge, they ignore local use of the natural resources.[4]

In order to gather and disseminate local knowledge, Living River Siam employs a method called *Thai Baan* ("Thai villager") research that is designed to maximize villager involvement in the process. In each village that agrees to participate, several Living River Siam staff members and/or volunteers guide the participants through a set of key steps. First, representatives of the organization visit the village in question to introduce the Thai Baan method and to discuss which research topics are most important for that particular village. "The topics of the research," Pai says, "are chosen by the villagers themselves," according to what concerns they have about the impact of dams on their river and their livelihoods.

The next task is to decide with the villagers on a group of about five to ten researchers selected from among their number. Any villager is considered eligible for participation; researchers might include, for example, an eighty-year-old fisherman who has known the river and its cycles for decades, or a ten-year-old boy who has fished with his father since he was a toddler. Most villagers are very receptive to Living River Siam's research initiatives. As one villager involved in a Thai Baan study on the Mun River put it:

> We are the receiver of the problem, we are [the] directly affected people, our lives have been destroyed by the dam. When fish and nature [are]

restored to the river, our lives are restored, too. We try to make other people to see and understand the impacts of what is going on after the dam gates are opened. And so we think of documenting the impact of the opening of [the] gates by doing our own research. If outsiders conduct research, we are afraid that they will not see and collect all aspects of impacts from the dam because they are outsiders who live in cities and do not understand our lives. They do not know about fish, ecosystem[s], and the Mun River like us. If they conduct research, they have to come to observe and interview us. Therefore, we decide to do research of our own.[5]

Next, Living River Siam staff work with the villagers to collect basic information on the selected research topics, such as the local names of relevant fish species, types of native plants, the medicinal uses of those plants, and so on. A timetable for the research is also agreed upon, and the villagers begin the fieldwork. In this phase of the project, the researchers collect data and take relevant pictures—for example, of fish they have caught, of water levels, or of local plant species—in the course of their routine daily activities. Because, according to Pai, the villagers "do not read or write; they just verbally explain," staff members from Living River Siam gather the information collected by the village researchers into a written report. This report is discussed with the researchers, who are invited to suggest changes or additions. If additional information is needed, the village researchers collect and submit it to the Living River Siam staff, who revise the report accordingly. Also, in order to further strengthen the data, staff members conduct in-depth interviews with key informants in the community as well as focus group discussions with sets of villagers. The draft is revised on the basis of these conversations and the final draft is presented to and discussed with the community.

The next phase of the process takes place outside the village, as Pai and her colleagues work to bring the information generated by the villagers' research to bear on national and international policy-making concerning the construction and operation of dams along the rivers of Southeast Asia. Given the number of governments, corporations, and communities involved in these projects—and all the competing interests they represent— this is by far the most challenging stage of the Thai Baan method. Yet for Pai and her colleagues, having a positive impact on the fate of Southeast Asian rivers is the single most important outcome of their work.

The Challenges of International Water Politics

Humans have been constructing dams for centuries, but in recent decades the pace and scale of dam projects has increased dramatically. From Egypt's Aswan High Dam, constructed in the 1950s, to the current Three Gorges Dam project in China, hundreds of dams have been built through the collaboration of governments, developers, and international funding organizations to harness the power of flowing water to bring electricity and a higher standard of living to millions of people around the world. And while supporters point to hydroelectricity as a renewable and relatively clean source of power and to the control of the river's flow as a source of transportation, opponents point to side-effects such as the flooding of farmlands and villages, the disruption of natural land-fertilization cycles, and the destruction of the ecosystems crucial to fish and other wildlife. As Pai put it:

> For the engineer, for the developer, when they want to clear the rapids and sand dunes to make the river a superhighway for large ships to navigate, they just see them as obstacles, but for the villagers, they see, for example, this is where this fish spawns in these rapids . . . so we try to explain the importance of the subecosystem and the flow and the seasonal circle of the ecosystem of the river, that provides food security, and well-being, and the livelihood of the people.[6]

In Thailand, one of the earliest major dam projects was the Pak Mun dam, constructed on the Mun River in 1994. This project, partially funded by the World Bank, displaced approximately 5,000 people and led to intense, ongoing protests over the negative impact on locals' livelihoods. In January of 2000, more than 800 villagers from the affected region traveled to Bangkok by train and camped out in a city park for over a week in order to bring their plight to the attention of the urban public and the government. In response to their protests, the government eventually announced a policy of opening the gates for several months a year in order to permit fish to migrate and spawn. In 2007, however, the gates were closed permanently. While the Pak Mun protests have thus far been largely unsuccessful in keeping the river flowing free, the movement against the dam gave rise to the Southeast Asian Rivers Networks (SEARIN) and, in turn, to Living River Siam. And in addition to ongoing work on behalf of those affected by the Pak Mun dam, Pai and her colleagues have expanded their focus to include villagers on the Salween and Mekong rivers.

The Salween River begins in Tibet, travels through China and Burma, and forms the Thai/Burmese border for over one hundred kilometers. According to Living River Siam, "over 10 million people from at least thirteen different ethnic groups including Nu, Lisu, Shan, Wa, Kayah, and Arakan rely on the rich natural resources of the river for their livelihoods."[7] And while the Salween is currently undammed, the governments of Thailand, China, and Burma have been discussing a number of new hydroelectric projects in recent years. Thailand's energy authority, the Electricity Generating Authority of Thailand (EGAT), is a strong supporter of these dams, which would generate electricity for it to sell in Thailand. On April 5, 2006, the Thai and Burmese governments signed an agreement to build a dam on the Salween in Burma's Shan state, and discussions continue over the Hatgyi dam in Burma's Karen state. China has also proposed building a series of thirteen dams on the river in its territory.

Deeply concerned about the impact of these projects on Southeast Asia's longest undammed river, Pai has spearheaded a multi-pronged effort to protect the Salween. Her unusual childhood, her formal education, and her persistence and dedication all play important roles in this work. First, she has helped coordinate Thai Baan research among the residents along the river in the Thai section of the river basin. This research is conducted mainly in the Karen language, although the Burmese political situation does not permit the conduct of this research among the Karen who live across the border.

The reports generated by this research are compiled and translated into Thai under Pai's supervision and disseminated widely to university and government representatives involved in the study of and policy on dam projects. Pai's large network of contacts, built up through her work and expanded further by her appointment as an Ashoka Fellow, facilitates the distribution of this research. She also writes many opinion pieces for the *Bangkok Post* and other regional newspapers and sees to it that these are circulated widely on the web and to relevant organizations, government officials, and university representatives and researchers. For example, in June 2008, regarding proposed dams on the Salween and Mekong rivers, she wrote in the *Bangkok Post*:

> Perhaps Prime Minister Samak Sundaravej thinks it is still the 1960s. As new prime minister, he autocratically announced water diversion projects for the Mekong and Salween rivers, callously calling these international rivers "public waters" in the faulty belief that anyone can utilise them without repercussions. In power for only four months, he has already revived almost all the historically rejected water infra-structure schemes, including the infamous Pa Mong dam—the Mekong's Hoover, proposed by the US some four decades back—along with other multi-gigawatt dams and poorly planned water diversions . . . Mr Samak's logic is tragically wrong, and we will all pay the price for his folly.[8]

In addition to writing for newspapers and blogs, Pai also works with the Prime Minister's Office as an advisor on the Salween River. In this capacity, she was able to draw attention to research conducted by Living River Siam showing that an earlier environmental impact assessment on the Salween project, a legally required stage of the dam construction process, had addressed only the Burmese stretch of the river, neglecting cross-border impacts of the proposed dam. In part due to her efforts, EGAT signed an order in late 2009 for a new environmental impact assess-ment that would investigate the potential social and environmental consequences of the project for Thailand. In order to celebrate and draw attention to this important gain, Pai worked with other environmental organizations and villagers to plan an event on the banks of the Salween River. On March 14, the annual International Day of Action for Rivers, 600 villagers came together in a Buddhist ceremony to bless the river and register their opposition to the dam projects.

While working on the Salween campaign, Pai and her colleagues continued to monitor developments on the Mekong River, which flows through Thailand, Burma, Cambodia, Vietnam, and Laos. Recognizing the complicated cross-border issues raised by hydroelectric projects on this important river, four of the countries through which it flows—Thailand, Laos, Cambodia, and Vietnam—came together in 1995 to form the Mekong River Commission. Currently, the four main goals of this organization are:

Goal 1 To promote and support coordinated, sustainable, and pro-poor development;

Goal 2 To enhance effective regional cooperation;

Goal 3 To strengthen basin-wide environmental monitoring and impact assessment;

Goal 4 To strengthen the Integrated Water Resources Management capacity and knowledge base of the MRC bodies, National Mekong committees, line agencies, and other stakeholders.[9]

In 1996, Burma and China became "dialogue partners" of the Mekong River Commission. Given that most of the extant and planned dams on the Mekong are located within Chinese borders (where the river is known as the Lancang), China's lack of full membership is alarming to opponents of the dam projects. A major problem, according to Pai, is that China releases very little data about its operation of the dams, which makes it impossible to determine the impact they are having downstream in Thailand. In order to draw attention to the plight of villagers living along the Mekong, and of the river itself, Pai decided she needed to take senators and journalists to view the drought conditions themselves.

The brief trip had an impact on diplomatic relations almost immediately. Within a few days, journalists who had been on the trip asked the prime minister of Thailand whether China should be held responsible for the drought on the Mekong. In turn, according to the *Bangkok Post*, "China's Assistant Foreign Minister Hu Zhengyue told Prime Minister Abhisit Vejjajiva . . . [that] China's dams were not a major cause of problems along the river."[10] A counselor at the Chinese embassy in Bangkok pointed out that "only 64 billion cubic metres of water—about 13% of the water that feeds the Mekong—comes from China. The other 86.5% comes from the downstream countries."[11] Members of the Mekong River Commission offered support for China's stance. Undaunted, Pai began countering China's response right away, arguing that while only 13 percent of the entire Mekong (Lancang) is indeed in China, 95 percent of the waters *upstream* from the drought-stricken area are in China.

The Continuing Work of Social Entrepreneurship

The fate of the Mekong, and the livelihoods of millions of people, will continue to hang in the balance while Pai and those who share her concerns struggle to make the case for an alternative future. Social entrepreneurs rarely enjoy straightforward "success" in their efforts. Instead, they work in difficult conditions to try to make a dent in daunting and persistent social problems. In the face of the powerful vested interests involved in international water policy, Pai displays a quiet but intense determination. And although the organization she works with is very small—she doesn't pursue government or industry grants because of possible conflicts of interest—the potential impact of her brand of social entrepreneurship is exponentially bigger. When Pai and her colleagues lead villagers through the steps of Thai Baan research, they aren't merely collecting information on river ecosystems. They are also teaching villagers how to articulate and defend their way of life, which depends on healthy rivers. Impoverished Thai citizens who had never before considered communicating with, let alone standing up to, more powerful members of their society now have research experience and public-speaking skills that are enabling them to contribute to national debates. As Pai put it:

> Our final goal is that the villagers work for themselves and protect their rights by themselves, that the media cover the issues, that the public is aware of the impact of the environmental impact of water infrastructure projects, and that the policymakers allow public participation without us . . . We want to strengthen each section of society.[12]

QUESTIONS

1 In what ways does social entrepreneurship differ from mainstream, for-profit entrepreneurship?
2 How can one measure the success of a social enterprise?
3 Would you characterize Pai as a transformational leader or as a charismatic one?

Notes

1 www.ashoka.org/support/criteria
2 www.ashoka.org/fellow/3864
3 www.livingriversiam.org/about_e.htm
4 Pianporn Deetes, personal interview, Chiang Mai, Thailand, March 10, 2010.
5 Thongdham Chatapan, quoted at www.livingriversiam.org/work/tb_research_en.htm
6 Pianporn Deetes, personal interview, Chiang Mai, Thailand, March 10, 2010.
7 www.livingriversiam.org
8 Pianporn Deetes, "Plans for some old dams unfortunately never die," *Bangkok Post*, June 23, 2008.
9 www.mrc.org
10 Apinya Wipatayotin, "China denies hogging Mekong River water," *Bangkok Post*, March 12, 2010.
11 Ibid.
12 Pianporn Deetes, personal interview, Chiang Mai, Thailand, March 10, 2010.

Part V

Leveraging Resources across Borders

Entrepreneurship is all about combining resources of an economic, financial, cultural, and social kind. Most entrepreneurs launch a business that leverages local resources, but an increasing number of them draw on resources located in different parts of the world. This section offers the experiences of a Japanese-Brazilian hotelier, an Algerian beauty expert in Paris, and a Korean-Chinese maker of traditional clothing as examples of cross-border entrepreneurship, of women who found a way to combine resources from various countries and cultures in order to pursue their dream businesses.

20 Chieko Aoki and Blue Tree Hotels

Blending Japanese Culture with Brazilian Warmth

Lilian Wouters

After gaining considerable managerial experience in the hotel business, Chieko Aoki found her true calling: launching her own brand of hotels. She chose to exploit her Japanese-Brazilian background to create a new hospitality concept. She quickly found that training employees was the biggest challenge facing her.

"Knowing Japanese culture is really helping the Blue Tree Hotel business," explains Chieko Aoki, the Japan-born, naturalized Brazilian, multitalented woman entrepreneur. "My vision of the world's best hotel has a touch of European luxury, Brazilian warmth and generosity, and, very importantly, reliable service like that of Japan." Chieko grew up in a Japanese family, and her upbringing has affected the way she approaches the hotel business. "I have uniquely incorporated 'Japanese-ness' in my hotel business." She believes in Japan there are many unspoken words or concepts that do not need to be taught, as they are instilled in the Japanese culture. She teaches these concepts and ideas to her employees at the Blue Tree hotels. In addition to being the first president of LIDEM, the group of Leading Businesswomen in Brazil, she is also the founder and chairman of Blue Tree Hotels—a company that currently operates in Brazil, Argentina, and Chile—and manages hotels for business travelers as well as resorts for leisure.

Chieko Aoki's Early Professional Career

Chieko Aoki (née Nishimura) was born in Japan and raised in São Paulo. She grew up speaking Japanese at home and Portuguese at school, and studied law at the University of São Paulo. After graduation, she lived in Tokyo and attended Sofia University, a branch of the very prestigious Jyochi University, where she studied administration and culture. She later married her Japanese husband, who still resides in Tokyo.

Chieko's interests in hotel management grew from her early career. Her husband's construction company, Aoki Construction, bought a stake in Caesar Park Hotels in Brazil, partnering with a local company. Chieko initially helped her husband's business by managing the Caesar Park hotels. As she notes, "the more I worked in the hotel business, the more I enjoyed every aspect of hotel management." At that time, she and her husband also traveled to many parts of the world and had the opportunity to stay in very nice hotels. "During this time, I also observed and learned what customers value in their hotel experience." She developed a passion for understanding customer service at premium hotels and decided to pursue this interest through a summer course at Cornell University in the United States, where she studied hotel administration.[1]

In 1982 Chieko returned to São Paulo and rejoined her husband's construction company. She first worked at the Caesar Park São Paulo Hotel as the director of marketing and sales. At that time there were few women in the hotel business, and she was slowly earning respect from other women and from female entrepreneurs. The Caesar Park Hotel business was very successful in the 1980s, due in large part to Chieko's initiatives to improve its occupancy levels and profitability. Chieko eventually became president of Caesar Park Hotels and developed a remarkable reputation for high-quality service. In 1988, Aoki Corporation acquired the Westin Hotels and Resorts chain. Chieko became the vice chairwoman of Westin Global and later the president of Westin South America. In 1994 Starwood Hotels acquired the Westin chain; and a Mexican group, Posadas, bought Caesar Park Hotels. Both hotel brands were then able to expand internationally to include management contracts for ninety-two hotels around the world. As Chieko notes, "It is interesting how people in Brazil still identify me as the owner of Caesar Park Hotels . . . it is interesting how branding is something very strong.[2]

Beginnings of the Blue Tree Hotel Business

By 1992, before the Caesar Park and Westin Hotels were sold, Chieko founded a subsidiary of Caesar Park—Caesar Towers Hotels and Resorts—as she envisioned that the market would need a chain with premium four-star-level hotels, slightly below the rating of Caesar Park Hotels. In 1996 and following the sale of the Caesar and Westin chains, she began to dedicate her energies fully to Caesar Towers—which, in 1997, became Blue Tree Hotels and Resorts—with the objective of operating five-star deluxe hotels and four-star business hotels.

Blue Tree Hotels came from her husband's name. *Aoki* in Japanese means "blue tree" or "blue leaf." When Chieko was considering a name for the hotel, she sought input from many professionals; however, she did not like any of their suggestions. She did not want to use *Aoki* because she thought the name would sound too Japanese to a Brazilian ear. At first, she was not fond of the name "Blue Tree" either. In 1997 Brazilians did not speak English very well, so it was also hard for them to recognize the meaning of Blue Tree. Eventually, the name Blue Tree Hotel became synonymous with prestige and high quality. Over the years, the Blue Tree Hotels expanded rapidly in Latin America. There were twenty-seven as of 2009, and Chieko planned to open seven more hotels by the end of the following year. In São Paulo alone, there are seven Blue Tree Hotels.

Impact of the Economic Crisis on the Hotel Industry

Because of the economic crisis, the number of international guests traveling and staying at premium hotels plummeted. Compared to other hotels in Brazil, the Blue Tree Hotels are doing very well. However, five-star hotels are facing the toughest times. The hotels that are expanding the fastest are the budget/cheaper hotels. In addition, rather than traveling, many people are conducting meetings through video conferences. Chieko also noticed that "fewer people travel on business trips, but may stay for a longer time period."

To overcome this challenge, Chieko is planning to launch a new three-star budget hotel concept under the name Spotlight Hotels. She notes that

> this hotel will be similar to a traditional Japanese hotel like the *ryokan*, where there are fewer employees working at the hotel. Instead, there are one or two head receptionists who manage the hotel front desk and other logistical operations of the house.

In Japan, the head receptionist at a *ryokan* is usually a woman, similar to a "mother," who takes care of the hotel guests. This budget hotel will also be much smaller, and the rooms will measure only 18 square meters.

In naming this budget hotel, Chieko argues that "we will not call it the Blue Tree Hotel because customers will expect four- or five-star service with the Blue Tree name." Previously, Blue Tree had opened a three-star hotel with the Blue Tree name. But guests were disappointed when they realized the service was not the same as the four- and five-star Blue Tree hotels they knew. Therefore, Blue Tree had to upgrade this site to a four-star hotel.

Japanese Immigrants in Brazil

Before introducing some of the astonishing aspects of the Japanese concepts instilled in the Blue Tree Hotel's service, it is important to understand the history of the Japanese Brazilians. The first immigrant ship, *Kasato Maru*, landed in Santos port on June 18, 1908, with the Brazilian government subsidizing the trip from Japan. Campaigns advertised abundant employment opportunities in Brazil on the coffee plantations and elsewhere. Most of the immigrants intended to work for a few years, save money, and return to Japan. However, they soon found that the promises fell far short of the realities. Living and working standards in Brazil were much harsher than expected, and the immigrants faced harsh realities on the coffee plantations, with very low salaries, inadequate living conditions, exhausting working hours, and contracts that bound the workers to unfair conditions. For example, they had to purchase supplies (and daily necessities) from the plantation owners at outrageous prices. Instead of saving money, many went deeply into debt. The most frugal of them became small- and medium-sized rural landowners.[3]

Most Japanese immigrants were concentrated in the state of São Paulo. Between 1932 and 1935 around 30 percent of the immigrants who entered Brazil were of Japanese origin. Many of the Japanese children born in Brazil were educated in schools for Japanese communities in rural areas, thus preserving their culture and language. However, the third generation heralded a change in the characteristics of this population, with many moving to urban areas. In addition, during World War II Brazil closed all the Japanese schools, forcing the Japanese to integrate and attend Brazilian schools, where they learned Portuguese. There are currently 1.95 million Japanese Brazilians living in Brazil, about 90 percent of whom live in São Paulo and Plana. Roughly 4 percent of São Paulo's population is Japanese-Brazilian.[4] Chieko's family immigrated to Brazil in 1957.

Bringing the Japanese Side into the Hotel Business

Chieko's key innovation was to incorporate "Japanese-ness" into the hotel business. Many subtle Japanese concepts are utilized in training the staff. "These words or concepts do not exist anywhere else in the world other than Japan, so it is difficult to explain to the staff," Chieko notes. "I believe in *sarigenai service* [subtle service]. This is a very difficult concept for Brazilians to understand." One example is preparing a special gift that is specific to each guest before the guest arrives. Chieko tries to explain these subtle concepts by first teaching her employees about *chado*, the tea ceremony. The Brazilian staff are very surprised by all the minute details involved in the ritual of drinking tea. But Chieko then discusses *Sennorikyu*, a very intellectual Japanese tea-ceremony "teacher" from the Ando Momoyama period (1568–1615), who taught the essence of the tea ceremony to the Japanese people. According to Sennorikyu, every single motion and act of pouring and drinking tea is vitally important.

In the same manner, Chieko wants to convey to her employees the importance of *sarigenai service* and the meaning behind these subtle concepts—that every single motion or act by a hotel employee is very important. She notes that "in any different country, people will agree to anything if they understand the meaning and process behind the act." Even the manager of one of the Blue Tree hotels at Faria Lima knows about the Japanese concept of *atarimae,* which means unquestionable common sense.

Another important Japanese concept in Chieko's Blue Tree Hotel business is *ki*, which means feeling. "I believe it is extremely important to develop the human side of the staff. Having a warm heart is vital in the best hotel service, which is again related to the character *ki*." *Ki* is used in many different words and phrases—for example, *ki wo tsukau, kizukau, ki ga tsuku,* and *kikubari.*

These words all mean doing something for somebody else. If you don't have the feeling of wanting to give or do something for someone, there is no real service. If I feel the need to warn or scold an employee, I must have the *ki*, feeling,

she says. "It is very interesting that all the employees at the Blue Tree know what *ki* means. Brazilians don't know what these ideas mean in the beginning, so they really try to understand." But because it is the norm for Japanese people, they will not think or reflect too deeply.

In addition, the rooms and amenities at the Blue Tree hotels display Japanese characters, such as *ai*, which means love, and *zen*, which means good. These characters are all related to feeling and human emotion.

"Service in Japan is the best in the world," observes Chieko. "But I question whether the staff and employees in Japanese hotels really have 'true warmth.'" People in Brazil are not as well-educated as those in Japan. What Chieko really values in Brazilian culture are the warmth and generosity of the people. "When there is a sick guest in the hotel, the staff in the Blue Tree Hotel will go to the customer's room and take care of them 24 hours," she explains. "This is the type of kindness that Brazilians have that cannot be taught, in countries such as Japan and the U.S." She always trains the staff to smile, be happy, and treat guests as if they were your family. Historically, Brazilians have been used to helping each other in times of crisis, and Chieko believes Brazilians have a lot of volunteer spirit. (Brazil is probably ranked number two or three in the world for hospitality/warmth.) "I believe warmth and generosity are one of the most important assets of the service at the Blue Tree hotels," she notes.

Another interesting concept Chieko has brought to the Blue Tree Hotels business is using the *obi*, or sash/belt, for the bed instead of a bed cover. Instead of a bed cover, the hotel chain employs a Japanese visual effect. This gimmick also reduces costs. Normally, a bed cover is about 1.8 meters long. But by using an *obi,* the chain uses only a strip of bed cover.

In fact, the appearance of the bed improves with the *obi* because it is delicate yet very simple. It is also easier for the cleaning lady to wash and make the bed with an *obi* than a long, heavy bed cover. This new type of bed with an *obi* is becoming prevalent around the world.

Chieko thinks that when standards or concepts are copied elsewhere, the standards of all hotels increase, which is good for the overall hotel industry.

Challenges of Managing a Hotel Business

Chieko asserts that "one of the most difficult challenges in managing a hotel business is the human relations involved in managing investors' property and assets." Since institutional investors own the hotels, while Chieko manages them, she needs to be able to talk to them efficiently. For example, if she wants to refurbish one of the hotels (for a long-term investment), it is difficult to persuade the investors since they often look at the short-term results. "I want to build trust among customers and want to have as many returning customers that want to stay at the Blue Tree hotels when they return to Brazil, Argentina, and Chile for a business or personal trip." Therefore, the infrastructure, service, appearance, amenities, and hotel atmosphere are very important. These are some of the challenges she faces.

The other challenge that Chieko faces is training and educating the employees in the best way possible. "I believe the training of employees is crucial in building a successful hotel." Chieko has always been involved in training her staff and employees since the start of her hotel business career. "Without good employees, it is difficult to sustain a good hotel." She personally interviews all candidates for director and managing director positions, even if they are located in Argentina or Chile. She takes the employees' training very seriously.

When selecting people to work at the Blue Tree hotels, Chieko always looks for people who have some particular value that she or the other hotel staff lack. For example, "I want to hire staff [who are] superior to me." Chieko can manage the hotel but wants to be surrounded by employees who excel at their tasks so she can concentrate on other activities. "The hotel cannot just be healthy. Just like a woman, it needs to always want to be pretty." She takes the hiring process very seriously, noting that "the most important features I look at when choosing the candidates is the employees' personalities and whether they are hard working. Most importantly, I look for kind and caring employee candidates."

Chieko says that many people have influenced her to become a better entrepreneur. She tries to learn from other people's leadership styles and has incorporated many of their values. For example, she observes managers who excel at marketing, human relations, and leadership skills. "Almost everyone has a good value to share and look up to. So I spend as much time [as possible] meeting with wonderful entrepreneurs or managers outside of the hotel business, because I am inspired by all of them" (see Figure 20.1).

Chieko's Role as a Female Entrepreneur in Brazil

Chieko has taken on many leadership roles as a female entrepreneur. She participates in many private and governmental organizations, such as the

Figure 20.1 Chieko Aoki
Source: Chieko Aoki.

Business Leaders Group (LIDE), the Business Council of Latin America (CEAL), and the Association for the Centennial of Japanese Immigration. In addition, until 2008 she was president of LIDEM and the Leading Businesswomen in Brazil and took on a position in the Brazilian Events Academy, an entity that brings together the best Brazilian professional events. She is also a member of Academia de Marketing, formed by the best marketing professionals in Brazil. In addition, she was recently elected president of the Consulting Council of ADVB-Japan (Associacao dos Dirigentes de Vendas e Marketing do Brasil). "The significance of the women in LIDEM is that they are lady-like. . . . The similarities I see in the successful female entrepreneurs are that women respect what it means to be a true woman." Successful female entrepreneurs are very team-oriented and are good at delegating tasks to others. Women excel at training their employees. They are also great at knowing the atmosphere in an organization. "If there is an issue or obstacle that needs to be analyzed, women, more than men, like to talk to the staff and understand the situation, and try to improve the situation."

The number of women entrepreneurs in Brazil and Latin American is increasing. In addition, the number of women traveling on their own is rising. Chieko created a new concept she called WTA, "women traveling alone." She wanted to provide services and facilities especially for women. Since she used to travel alone in her early career days and felt that she was not safe or secure at some of the hotels, she hopes that women feel safe staying alone at the Blue Tree hotels. One of the featured concepts of these rooms is to provide women with rest through color therapy. Chieko has chosen a light shade of green to suggest relaxation and peacefulness. For example, the bed has white covers coupled with light green cushions. The cushions, amenities, food menus, and toiletry boxes are all light green and have the Japanese character *bi* (_) , for beauty, written on them. In addition, all the printed materials feature phrases by influential women leaders such as Coco Chanel, Audrey Hepburn, Anita Malfatti (a Brazilian painter), and Clarice Lispector (a Brazilian writer).

Some of the special services that women receive at the Blue Tree hotels are assistance for scheduling hairdressers, manicures, massages, and restaurant reservations; use of deposits; and late check-out until 4:00 p.m. The hotels also offer special surprise gifts, such as fresh fruits, aromatic pillows, therapeutic and relaxing footbaths, and powerful hair dryers. As Chieko points out, "I want to create a room that is peaceful and serene, and a room that most women want to come home to." In addition, guests have the option of purchasing some items from a custom kit of cosmetics, such as nail polish and pantyhose. The female guests can also receive discounts and benefits at the hotel laundry and restaurants.

Many of the Blue Tree Hotel staff describe Chieko Aoki as a renowned global woman entrepreneur. In fact, many institutions, schools, and companies in Brazil contact her to help them create luxurious, comfortable stays for their clients. For example, hospitals have asked her to help with new ideas or concepts to create more efficient and comfortable hospital rooms. Galleries and exhibitions also ask her to speak about her hotel concepts to large audiences.

Chieko is determined to always strive for the best. Even when faced with challenges, she works hard to find solutions. She instills the concept of *kaizen*, which means improvement, in her employees as well. Japan and Brazil are 18,500 kilometers apart, but it is still astonishing that so many Japanese concepts are found in the Blue Tree Hotels' services and employees' training. However, can Blue Tree Hotels expand its business across all of Latin American and on a truly global scale? Can Chieko's vision of having both Brazilian concepts and Japanese-ness in her hotel service be transferred around the world? Will the launch of the budget and women-centric hotels and rooms work in Latin America? Can Chieko also convince Blue Tree Hotels' investors that the chain can expand internationally in this downturned economy? As Chieko thinks of answers to these questions, she is certain about one thing. "Success can be attained by hard work and the passion to want to create the best hotel with warm and friendly staff." After all, she has successfully built prestige and luxury into the Blue Tree Hotel name.

QUESTIONS

1 How well could the combination of Japanese taste and Brazilian warmth in the hospitality industry be replicated in other countries?
2 Is the "women traveling alone" concept one that should be implemented through a different brand of hotel?
3 What do you see as Aoki's best strategy for further international expansion?

Notes

1 Gilbert, Gregory. "Chieko Aoki and Brazil's Blue Tree Hotels." *Knowledge at Wharton* 6, July 2010.
2 Ibid.
3 "History of Immigration in Brazil," *Advocacia Dias Marques*, last modified 2010, www.diasmarques.adv.br/pt/historico_imigracao_brasil.htm#Japonese
4 Ibid.

21 Yasmina Zerroug

Arabian Beauty, from Algeria to Paris

Swita Charanasomboon

Divorced and new to Paris, Yasmina Zerroug decided to launch a beauty salon drawing on her Arabic roots in her native Algeria. Her son, a business graduate, and a nephew provided her with the administrative skills.

It is a sunny spring morning in Paris' residential 12th arrondissement. Yasmina Zerroug is putting on a CD of soft Arabic music, getting her beauty salon ready for its daily opening at noon. Yasmina, the entrepreneurial owner of Charme d'Orient, is an Algerian-born French resident. Expressive, dynamic, warm, and maternal, she stares directly into people's eyes and is unapologetically proud in describing the history of her business. At 60, she looks 45, with smooth skin and dancing eyes, befitting the owner of a beauty salon.

Yasmina grew her Charme d'Orient empire from a one-salon location to a €2 million tri-fold operation: the flagship salon in Paris, a branded and patented comprehensive range of beauty products sold retail and online, and a training institute for oriental beauty treatments. Despite not having had a formal business education (her degree in Algeria was in Spanish literature), she learned by doing and later enlisted her son's help after he received his business degree from ESSEC, one of France's prestigious *grande école* programs. She is driven by a true passion for bringing Algerian beauty rituals to France and by economic necessity stemming from her divorce.

> When you have nothing, when you've fallen to the bottom, you have the choice to either crumble or fight. I got up and didn't allow myself to crumble. I believe that women will find themselves getting up and fighting. That's what led me here today,

says Yasmina in her typical warm and inspirational manner. She embraces the opportunity to discuss topics dear to her heart: getting up after falling, how beauty links women globally across educational and racial boundaries, looking out for her clients' best interests, putting her son's education first, and passing on her experience to other underprivileged/minority women in France. One uniting theme emanates from everything Yasmina touches: empathy and beauty.

From Algeria to France

Yasmina enjoyed an upper-middle-class, liberal upbringing in her native Algeria, but left for France in 1979 with her husband and two young children. In Algeria her husband owned a successful cardboard/carton-manufacturing business. However, Yasmina's beliefs did not fit in with those of her home country at that time: "[The Algerian government] stopped French school; there was no good schooling. It was dictatorial, there were no women's rights, I didn't speak Arabic very well and I couldn't teach my children their lessons." So they moved to France. In elaborating on her Algerian roots, Yasmina notes that she is Muslim "and proud of it." But she adds that she does not agree with fundamentalists "who restrict everything." Her schooling was in Catholic schools. Her father prayed every day and showed her "the Muslim side that was not fundamentalist." Yasmina earned her B.A. in Spanish literature and wrote her thesis on Cervantes. Among her strongest values are learning through reading and her children's education.

Yasmina's "rock-bottom" situation was her divorce in her 40s. She describes its devastating effects: "I am of a higher class standing, but once one divorces, one has nothing! But instead of crying, I took action." This was by necessity as her legal bills were very high. Yasmina had her jewels back in Algeria sold—a huge loss for an Algerian woman, whose jewelry is passed down from generation to generation. She also obtained a loan from a cousin.

Her son Sofiane, then a teenager, gave her the idea of opening a tanning salon. She did not feel any passion for this endeavor, but pursued it anyway, "in the same way I would have pursued owning a fruit stand—out of necessity, rather than interest. I needed to pay the bills." She describes her nervousness about embarking on this entrepreneurial venture: "I didn't know where I was going; I was in a black hole." Since her degree in Spanish literature did not translate into anything practical in the job market and because she could not type quickly, she agreed to the tanning-salon plan.

The Start of Her Entrepreneurial Adventure

Yasmina spent an entire year walking all over Paris looking for the perfect location for her tanning salon: "every day, from morning to nightfall, I would walk, to find a location." At that time she was staying with a friend, with whom she left her two sons while she scoured Paris. "It was a difficult situation . . . very complicated." Her origin did not help. As soon as prospective landlords saw her Arab name on the application, they rejected her. This continued for an entire year. Fortunately, the owner of the space she now rents in the 12th is a doctor, "and thus a humanitarian." The doctor empathized with her situation of being a newly divorced and determined single mother and allowed her to rent the little corner in the 12th. Yasmina did not like the location at first (even now, it is difficult for some of her clients to find, she admits)—the boulevard, with its little grocery store and a bank, does not attract much foot traffic. But the situation was pressing. She could not afford to wait and needed the income right away—so she quickly signed the lease.

Her tanning salon, Top Soleil (Top Sun), was immediately a huge success due to Yasmina's ability to stand apart from her competitors. The salon had an oriental ambience—everything was colorful and in wood, and oriental music played in the background—a vast difference from the other UV places, which were white and sterile. Also important was the spirit of her service. "It's all in the manner in which I greet and treat my clients." She describes it as warmth and "it comes naturally to Algerians." She is alluding to the minimal level of customer service France is known for. Most of all, her clients came to trust her advice. "I think being ethical really differentiated me." Yasmina recalls the teenage girls who wanted to tan three times a day. She told them about the dangers of too much UV exposure and would not let them stay for more than an hour. Being extremely hands-on, she timed all her clients on the tanning beds for their safety. "I wasn't business-business even though I did want to make money; but being ethical was important." Her clients immediately appreciated her genuine concern and brought their entire families.

Yasmina found that owning a UV salon was not intellectually stimulating—she was just running the business to pay for her sons' studies. The salon's success enabled her and her sons to move into a wonderful apartment, with lots of space for quiet study. Yasmina put all her earnings toward the rent. "I didn't go to restaurants, the movies, or take vacations. I knew I had to have priorities, and that was the apartment and my sons' education." Yasmina emphasizes again that she had always placed her children's education first. Before the divorce, as a housewife in Paris, she dedicated her time to helping them learn. It paid off handsomely. Her surviving son, Sofiane, graduated from the prestigious *grande école* ESSEC.

Yasmina takes a break from explaining her business model to discuss the importance of having an education and a well-informed view of the world. She recalls that, when she lived in Algeria, she spoke French better than Arabic and could not bear to see her children not speak fluent French, even if they had stayed in Algeria. Her father himself opened her up to the larger intellectual world by sending her to Catholic school even though they are a Muslim family. In discussing the Arab–French riots in Paris, Yasmina sits squarely in the middle: She does not buy into fundamentalism and opposes Arab women in France wearing veils. Genuine concern for women is also one of her core values. She feels strongly that the current French political group founded to support the rights of Muslim women, Ni Putes Ni Soumises ("neither prostitutes nor submissive"), is going too far to be political rather than to really help women. This will be a recurring theme across the entire interview: Yasmina wants things to serve their original purpose and not become too grandiose, too proud, or too politicized—all of which ruin their original meanings. This sense of integrity drives all of her business—and life—decisions.

The Birth of France's First Oriental Beauty Salon

The turning point in Yasmina's entrepreneurship began when her regular clients suggested she add aesthetic services to her tanning services so they could choose from a full range of options. Yasmina is not an aesthetician, so she hired one; but that employee came and went as she pleased "because it's France," laughs Yasmina, leading her to close this new component of her business. She was sad about this. The aesthetician provided hair removal that reminded her of her youth in Algeria when she went to the *hamams* (Turkish baths) with her mother; and that made her feel nostalgic. She knew, however, that the hair removal process done by aestheticians in France was "superficial" compared to what women in Algeria did in the *hamams*. One night while she was at home conducting this beauty ritual the Algerian way—in the kitchen preparing the removal paste with sugar in the pan—it dawned on her that her clients would like that process. Her son Sofiane explains that "hair removal is something that is communicated to every adolescent girl in Algeria, so it is something that Yasmina grew up with." Yasmina immediately called her cousins in Algeria to say, "Don't shave, I am flying to Algeria to practice on you for my clients."

This was the birth of the first oriental beauty institute in Paris, in 1994. Lines extended outside the door of Yasmina's salon. Her first formula for hair removal included sugar. Yasmina asked her clients for feedback. They said the sugar formula hurt a bit and created pimples in sensitive areas. Yasmina then recalled that the Algerian middle class use sugar but the upper class use honey, which is more calming for sensitive French skin. She patented her new formula 4 years later in 1998. Given its all-natural ingredients—honey and fruit mixtures—this formula has no adverse effects. Yasmina's popularity exploded, and she found herself working every day, including Sundays and holidays. But she did not mind. "I loved it. I didn't go out at all. I really invested myself," she explains, eyes shining at the memory. Her days were hectic. When she came home, she prepared her paste—in her kitchen and bathroom, the traditional way women prepared their pastes in Algeria, without a lab. Her son finished high school, and came up with the idea of offering training services for oriental hair removal to other beauty institutions. This training is now recognized by the Ministry of Labor (Le Ministre du Travail) in France. Yasmina soon expanded beyond hair removal pastes to black soap, using traditional Algerian ingredients, and now has 150 SKUs. Her clients are "Françaises de souche"—non-minority and non-immigrant French women—who have a love for the exotic looks of the Middle East and North Africa. (Yasmina's counterparts—immigrants from Arabic lands—are not clients since they already know how to do the beauty rituals on themselves.) It is worth noting that, historically and presently, the French refer to the Middle East and North Africa as "the Orient"—which includes the three Maghreb countries of Morocco, Tunisia, and Algeria. Thus, in France the name Charme d'Orient would produce associations with the exotic Arab region, a cultural conception that runs through French history, literature, and imagination. Yasmina, indeed, chose a name in line with her passion and motivation to share her beauty rituals with French women.

When Yasmina's son Sofiane finished his studies at ESSEC business school around 1998, Yasmina was earning €30,000 a year from selling a few products. Sofiane explains that there was no real organization, as Yasmina was not a business person. He saw that products were sent out but payments were not coming in. He had planned to move to the U.S. for work. Wanting to wait out the downturn after the dot.com bubble burst, he stayed in France to help his mother.

Yasmina's products include scented oils, body milk, body butters, facial care products, and ambiance setters including candles and incense. All her packaging bears the Charme d'Orient cursive logo reminiscent of Arabic script; and her patented honey hair-removal paste label prominently displays "*methode Yasmina.*" The paste is sold exclusively to professionals. All of Yasmina's products come in different sizes and many fragrances (jasmine, rose, fruit, orange flower, ylang-ylang, fig, and date, to name a few). Charme d'Orient imports raw materials, outsources the manufacturing, and brands its own products.

Under Sofiane's guidance, Charme d'Orient revolutionized its packaging and created a distribution center. Previously, Charme d'Orient products came in very rough packaging with no brand name, as it was sold B2B to other beauty institutions. Sofiane also created a distribution center as demand rose. At the same time, he actively decided not to expand aggressively. "We could have gone much faster, gotten loans from bankers, but we wanted to take it step by step." In its more-than-10-year history, the Charme d'Orient salon had grown from €30,000 to €2 million in revenue.

Charme d'Orient also offers hands-on training for beauty professionals, conducted at the client's site or at the Charme d'Orient salon. Groups are limited to four people, each of whom receives a certificate of completion. Sessions, conducted by Yasmina, cover hair removal using honey paste, *hamam* rituals (body and facial care), and henna tattoos.

Location, Location, Location

Charme d'Orient is sited in the 12th arrondissement (see Figure 21.1), a two-minute walk from popular métro station Daumesnil, on a peaceful tree-lined boulevard alongside a few cafes, a BNP bank, a real estate agency, and high-rise residences.

The salon includes several service rooms and a *hamam* with a shower. Bright and airy, it is decorated in warm tones with Arabic fabrics. Calming and soothing tracks of Arabic music and Jane Birkin play softly in the background.

The warehouse/offices are in Lognes, some 30 minutes outside Paris by RER commuter train. A partially industrial town, Lognes is also the home of Honda's training center. The warehouse/offices were originally in a small office in Paris but were moved to this suburban location 2 years ago due to space constraints. The office is a different world from the Charme d'Orient salon in the 12th. Here is the land of desks, phones, and a distribution center set in a utilitarian flat cement office park. Yasmina's son Sofiane and nephew Raouf occupy two unpretentious offices next to each other, with a simple Ikea table with four chairs outside Sofiane's office and a simple chaise longue covered with magazines. Behind a bright blue door, in the distribution center, two employees are selecting and packing shipments. Behind the door at the other end, there are more offices, housing the accountant (Sofiane's dad and Yasmina's ex-husband) and two clerical assistants. The entire place exudes a small, familial feel. Even here, where no clients come, there is evidence of oriental charm: The screen around a desk is made of carved oriental wood, for example.

The channels for Charme d'Orient's branded products cover beauty institutes, spas, and top French retailers, including BHV and Monoprix Beauté. Export sites account for 20 percent of the company's revenues and

Figure 21.1 Charme d'Orient Salon, Paris, France

Source: Swita Charanasomboon, May 2009.

include Italy, Russia, Canada, Eastern Europe, Germany, and the Gulf states (primarily to hotels that want to provide their international clientele with Arab products).

The €2 million annual operation is run by managers Sofiane and Raouf (Yasmina's son and nephew), a trainer, a quality control expert, two clerks/secretaries who take the telephone orders, an accountant (Yasmina's ex-husband), two warehouse workers, and, of course, Yasmina, whom Sofiane refers to as "the soul of the brand."

Giving Back to Women Immigrants

Yasmina presently has four aestheticians—three maghrebines (women like herself, of Arab heritage) and one French. She prefers to hire the former, she says, as a way of giving back. It is more difficult for these young maghrebine women to find jobs in France. Yasmina transmits her knowledge to them through training, but will also lend them books and talk to them about literature and philosophy, "so that they have a future." Some of her success stories include one maghrebine, a cleaning lady before Yasmina hired her, who is now an aesthetician at a prestigious spa in the posh 16th arrondissement frequented by Madame Chirac, wife of former president of the republic Jacques Chirac. Everyone calls Yasmina to poach her aestheticians, knowing how rigorously she trains them. Surprisingly, Yasmina is not worried about competition from her former trainees. "Everyone's touch is different," she says. She truly believes that every aesthetician and salon is original and that competition helps grow the oriental beauty industry in general. Given this frame of mind, one easily understands why Yasmina is so happy to train aestheticians and spread her knowledge of Arab beauty.

Learning from Yasmina and Sofiane

Mother and son have learned the importance of listening to their clients for product innovation. Yasmina is head of R&D but gets her inspiration from clients. "One must know how to listen to them," she says. Such is her organic approach to product development. She has no set goals for how many new products should be launched per year, nor does she believe that innovation is essential in the beauty sector. However, Charme d'Orient will always innovate with her roots in mind—keeping close to the oriental ingredients and not diversifying much beyond that.

Yasmina and Sofiane have also consciously chosen a similarly organic approach toward marketing and sales. "We are 10 years old, but we have no sales people," says Sofiane proudly. Sales are made by training—the people who are trained by Charme d'Orient feel a deep affinity for the products: "They become loyal and know our tradition and will push the products to their customers," Yasmina explains. Once again, she lets her products and tradition speak for themselves.

Sofiane explains that he has learned a lot about the importance of trustworthy suppliers from Algeria. "These are not big companies we are working with; these are small companies that mostly do not have experience with exporting." Sofiane often makes trips to Algeria to do his due diligence on the suppliers. He further explains that he has learned to be aware of cultural differences. Even though he is Arab, the notions of time and deadlines in Algeria and Arabic countries, in general, are different, so he has learned to manage his expectations. To diversify risk, he has several dozen suppliers with whom he has learned and grown together as a team.

Competition and Future Risks

Charme d'Orient's major competitor is Sultane de Saba, which has the exact same business model: oriental/Arabia-themed beauty salons, branded product distribution, and training. However, Sultane de Saba is larger, with three salons in France, one in Belgium, and one in Switzerland. The company also does a lot more marketing and less word-of-mouth training. It sells at higher prices at more distribution points (such as Sephora, the LVMH-owned cosmetics retailer) and is now diversifying beyond Arabia to Japanese- and Indonesian-inspired beauty solutions. Yasmina and Sofiane both agree that Charme d'Orient will never move beyond its core of Arabia-inspired products. They will not move beyond their roots and what they truly understand. After all, Charme d'Orient works more with professionals to train them, so credibility is extremely important. Yasmina and Sofiane would not feel comfortable training on Japanese products, for example. Indeed, the theme of true passion and authenticity plays into their business model once more.

Sofiane brings up one concern that he quickly dismisses: Charme d'Orient does "have all its eggs in one basket"—the Arabia basket. Will Arabia ever pass out of favor with the French and the world? No way, Sofiane affirms. France and the world have a long-standing fascination with the region. The love is *inepuissable* (inexhaustible), he adds.

Future View

Yasmina explains that she has no plans for expansion. After working every day, including holidays, for so many years, she would now like to travel and see the world. She is also planning to write a book about her life and career path and perhaps include some recipes. If she were younger, she muses, perhaps she would have considered expanding into New York City. There would certainly be demand: her guest book at the salon entrance shows an entry from a recent visitor who wrote, "I am moving to the U.S.

Where will I find a Charme d'Orient there? If you ever want to expand globally, I will be your very first client!" But then again, Yasmina admits, she never started with the idea of getting rich. She had always wanted to stay simple and make enough for her children's education. This sums up the success of Yasmina and Charme d'Orient. Yasmina knows what her drivers are, and she stays close to her core competencies and passion. "Every woman loves beauty. Beauty unites women all over the world, across cultures," she says in evidence of her passion. She ends the interview with these words of advice to future women entrepreneurs:

> When you have nothing, when you've fallen to the bottom, you have the choice to either crumble or fight. I got up and didn't allow myself to crumble. I believe that women will find themselves getting up and fighting. That's what led me here today.

QUESTIONS

1   How can Yasmina fend off competitors and imitators in Paris?
2   Should she consider expanding into other large, cosmopolitan cities?
3   Should she partner with a large distributor or cosmetics company to sell her products globally?

22 Songok Ryu

Traditional Korean Clothing in China

Johanna Kuhn-Osius

While working as a seamstress in the Korean Autonomous Prefecture of China, Songok Ryu realized that innovative design, premium branding, international sourcing, and modern selling techniques were not necessarily at odds with traditional clothing. She arbitrages cost and quality across borders, employing hand-embroiderers in North Korea, sourcing high-quality fabrics in South Korea, and producing in China for a local niche market. She is a borderless entrepreneur in the strictest sense of the term.

"Please wait a few minutes while I call Pyongyang. They are very particular about being called on time," says Songok Ryu, the premier *hanbok* (traditional Korean clothing) designer and manufacturer in China, as she dials Pyongyang on her iPhone. From here in her office in Yanji—the capital of China's Yanbian Korean Autonomous Prefecture—she conducts business in China, North Korea, and South Korea, without ever missing a beat in transition.

Ryu has always been ahead of the market. When everyone else in Yanji was still selling *hanbok* exclusively in outdoor markets, she opened a store—Yemi Hanbok.[1] And, although at first everyone told her it would be impossible to sell *hanbok* from a store, there are now thirty other *hanbok* stores in Yanji. Still, Ryu is at the top; and she does not mind that others have taken part of the market share because she has already thought of new ways to increase the market size. "The first mover doesn't earn more money. But who remembers the second mover later on?" she says. Ryu now has stores in three cities in China and more than fifty distributors across the country. She employs more than eighty people and produces about 18,000 sets of *hanbok* annually.

Moreover, Ryu is a celebrity in the Korean Autonomous Prefecture, and her work has been recognized nationally and internationally. Politicians from the Korean Autonomous Prefecture always wear her clothes on formal occasions (see Figure 22.1), and she appears frequently on television and radio. Her clothes have been worn by Jackie Chan, CCTV announcers, and other Chinese celebrities. She has met two South Korean presidents,

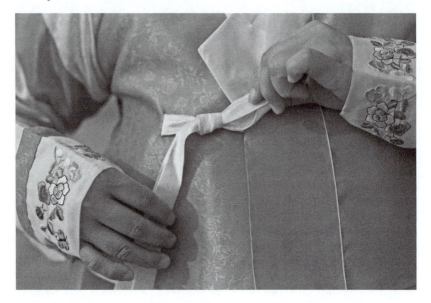

Figure 22.1 Tying the Traditional *Hanbok*
Source: Photo by Laura Elizabeth Pohl.

Noh Moo-Hyun (2006–2008) and Lee Myung-Bak (2008–2012), and has appeared on television in South Korea. She has also received awards in North Korea and was honored by the North Korean minister of culture. In 2003 Ryu was selected to represent ethnic Koreans at a juried Paris fashion show that showcased the traditional clothing of all fifty-five minority groups in China. She was placed first.

Ethnic Koreans in China

Songok Ryu is one of approximately 1.9 million ethnic Koreans living in China. Their population is concentrated in the Yanbian Korean Autonomous Prefecture, a self-governed region in northeastern China's Jilin Province. This is a territory of approximately 43,509 square kilometers, a bit larger than Belgium; and the capital, Yanji, where Ryu's business is located, is a city of about 133,000 inhabitants. It is important to understand that the Koreans in Yanbian, far from being recent immigrants trying to assimilate into the larger Han Chinese culture, have been living in this area for generations, carrying out traditional agrarian lifestyles indistinguishable from those found in Korea. At the same time, their current struggle is to find a new place in the world now that the agrarian era is clearly over.

Although parts of modern northeastern China—where the ethnic Koreans live today—belonged to early Korean kingdoms hundreds of years ago, those areas were populated by other ethnic groups or only sparsely populated until the late Choseon Dynasty. During the latter part of Korea's Joseon Dynasty (1392–1910), farmers from the northern provinces of the Korean peninsula began to migrate to Manchuria to engage in wet paddy rice cultivation. The earliest record of their arrival in the area is from the seventeenth century.[2] Repeated famines in the late 1800s in northern Korea spurred migration.[3] By 1910, when Japan annexed Korea, 250,000 Koreans were living in Yanbian.[4] This number grew to 1.3 million by the end of the Japanese colonial period as a result of Japanese resettlement policies.[5]

The People's Republic of China (PRC) officially recognizes fifty-five ethnic minority groups and accords members of these groups certain privileges—such as exemption from the one-child policy. In addition, the PRC has five minority autonomous regions at the provincial level and twenty-nine minority autonomous prefectures, of which the Yanbian Korean Autonomous Prefecture (Chinese: *Yanbian Chaoxianzu Zizhizhou,* Korean: *Yeonbeon Joseonjok Jachiju*) is one. Even though the autonomous regions and prefectures are, in reality, hardly "autonomous" from the central government, they provide certain benefits to the local minority group, such as an official bilingual policy—including minority-language education, in Yanbian's case all the way to the tertiary level. Among the ethnic minorities in the PRC, Koreans have enjoyed especially close relations with the Chinese Communist Party, and Koreans have been well-represented in the central government.

Since they were overwhelmingly engaged in the agrarian economy, reform and opening-up did not bring as many changes for the inhabitants of the Korean Autonomous Prefecture as they did for residents of other parts of China. The biggest changes for Yanbian came as a direct result of the commencement of diplomatic relations between the Republic of Korea (South Korea) and the People's Republic of China in 1992. For nearly 50 years South Koreans and Koreans in China had had almost no contact with each other. Throughout this period, each side was constantly told that the other was the enemy. Suddenly the floodgates opened, and Yanbian was dramatically affected by inflows of capital and outflows of people. South Korean investments and tourists flooded into Yanbian. At the same time, attracted by the much higher wage rate, ethnic Koreans from Yanbian went to work at menial jobs—such as restaurant work or construction—in South Korea, both legally and illegally, sending home their earnings. Also at the same time, as more people attained a tertiary education, young people went to study overseas and in other parts of China. In addition, many young women went to South Korea for marriage. As a result of a combination of these factors, the Korean population of Yanbian Korean Autonomous Prefecture is currently suffering from twin brain-drain and low birthrate problems. Most blue-collar jobs in the prefecture are now done by Han Chinese, who receive a lower wage since there is less opportunity for them to do equivalent work in South Korea. The decrease in the number of Koreans and the increase in the number of Han Chinese is causing the continuation of a long-term demographic shift in the Korean Autonomous Prefecture: the fall in the proportion of the Korean population from over 60 percent in 1952 to less than 40 percent in 2007.[6] As a result, the economic and social profiles of the prefecture are in the midst of a radical transformation.

Hanbok

Hanbok, literally meaning "Korean clothes," is a term that refers to all traditional Korean clothing. *Hanbok* was the exclusive clothing style for all Koreans until contact with the West began to gradually change tastes in the nineteenth century. Today, in both North and South Korea and in China's Korean Autonomous Prefecture, *hanbok* is reserved mostly for special occasions, although some people may wear it on a daily basis or as a uniform, especially in a culture-related workplace. Special occasions for which people usually wear *hanbok* include, but are not limited to, weddings, a baby's 100th day of life, a baby's first birthday, 60th birthdays, new year celebrations, and harvest festivals.

Hanbok for women consists of a slip, a floor-length full skirt with a high waist (*chima*), and a short, long-sleeved jacket with a long tie (*cheoggeori*). *Hanbok* for men consists of long pants tied at the ankles (*baji*) and a long-sleeved jacket (also called *cheoggeori*). The *hanbok* colors are typically bright, and different color combinations signify the wearer's position within his or her family. For example, a green jacket and red skirt signify a newly wed woman.

Hanbok can be divided into two principal style categories: traditional and simplified (*gaeryang*). "Traditional" refers to *hanbok* worn for special occasions that is made of silk or ramie and can be lavishly embroidered or embossed with gold or silver. "Simplified" refers to *hanbok* with a simplified design, typically a shorter, less full skirt with a lower waist and a longer jacket. Simplified *hanbok* is usually made of more durable and less delicate fabrics, such as cotton, and is used for uniforms and daily wear.

Becoming an Entrepreneur

Ryu grew up in Ryongjeong, a farming village near Yanji, and began her career as a seamstress there. "I couldn't study because of the cultural revolution," she explains.

> That is my regret. I am jealous of young people [who] have the opportunity to study and learn so much. I want to study now, and my daughter tells me, "Mom, what do you want to do that for?

In recent years Ryu has participated in and completed several executive business education courses in Yanji.

Before starting her *hanbok* business, Ryu made daily-wear clothing and blankets. She studied embroidery, cutting, and dressmaking from the best teachers she could find in Ryongjeong and Yanji. In 1984, at age 27, she decided to design her own outfit, consisting of matching pants and an embroidered shirt. "I was young and very self-confident, and I thought that my design was very beautiful," she says. With the help of five other women, she sewed 4,000 outfits. Her husband was a buyer for the government store, and she used this connection to persuade twelve other buyers to take 100 outfits each. She brought the rest to the market in Yanji and passed them to a trader there. Within 2 months all of the outfits were sold. As a result of this great success, her family became the first in the entire Korean Autonomous Prefecture to buy a television. Inspired by the success of her first original design, she made her next design in thirty-six different colors and five different sizes. She traveled to different cities and chose the most expensive price she saw anywhere as the price for her outfits. For a week not a single outfit was sold, and she became nervous. People told her her price was too high, but she would not lower it. Finally, someone from a village came and bought seven outfits, which he managed to sell in his village in just one day. After that, everyone wanted the outfit. Ryu says she realized early on that people want something that others do not have and that people with money are willing to pay a significant premium for this type of unique product. This insight guides her to this very day.

During this time, when most people in the Korean Autonomous Prefecture had never even left the area, Ryu traveled all over China, going as far afield as Guangdong and Shanghai, to learn about different techniques of clothing manufacture.

Ryu had to face competitors, imitators, and dishonesty early on. One day she found another trader in the market selling her clothes. She confronted the person, who insisted the clothes were not made by her. Ryu knew otherwise and eventually learned that one of the five women working for her had been stealing one outfit per day and giving them to that trader. Competition from copycats who charged lower prices was serious. Whenever Ryu came out with a new design, it would soon be imitated. After 3 years, in 1986, she decided she was tired of the business and turned to something new: blankets.

Koreans traditionally sleep on a heated floor and use a traditional blanket, called an *ibul*. Ryu's passion is embroidery, and she thought blankets would be a perfect canvas to showcase her skills. At first the business was very successful; but, again, imitators moved in. One competitor in particular, Han Okhee, began bribing traders to sell her goods, thereby completely spoiling the market for the other blanket makers. As a consequence, in 1988 Ryu decided to return to *hanbok*. Eventually, Han Okhee was found guilty of swindling investors of 107 million RMB, or approximately US$13.5 million, and publicly executed by firing squad in Yanji in 1997.[7]

Ryu went into *hanbok* with a friend who invested money in the business and managed sales while Ryu concentrated on the design and manufacture. She always loved her work and describes this time as both exciting and stimulating. At the same time, she faced family problems. As her relatives and her husband's relatives saw her financial success, they asked for her help. She also argued with her husband about work because he is more family-oriented while she is more extrovert. After a period of some struggle, she eventually became the chief decision-maker for both families. Numerous family members also joined the business. Seven extended family members currently work for Ryu.

A turning point for Ryu came in 1998. Her only child, a daughter, firmly told her mother that, although she was interested in the *hanbok* business, she would never manage the factory. As Ryu's business partner had been in charge of sales, her daughter's decision led Ryu to break up with her business partner of more than 10 years and to train her daughter in sales.

Around this time, Ryu also went on her first trip to South Korea. When she saw how well people lived there, she cried for two weeks. "I was so sad that we were living like animals in China, while South Koreans enjoyed such high standards of living." She thought hard about leaving China and moving to South Korea, as many Koreans from China were doing at the time. In the end, she decided to stay in Yanbian and ended her trip to South Korea by taking advantage of the 1997–1998 Asian financial crisis to buy a used German-made computerized embroidery machine at a fire-sale price. Initially, the machine caused Ryu a great deal of grief for two reasons—no one in the company could read the English-language instruction manuals and, because it was an old machine, it kept breaking down. Ryu had to fly a repair technician in from South Korea at great expense. Although the machine was a sinkhole for the first year, it was the first computerized embroidery machine in Yanbian, and Ryu's investment turned a profit in the second year.

In 2003, after several store and factory visits by government officials, Ryu was selected to represent Koreans at a juried fashion show in Paris that showcased the traditional clothing of all of China's fifty-five official minority groups. She was nervous. She recalls, "I felt that if I did not do a good job, I would shame my people [Koreans] and my country [China]." She spent months preparing a dozen *hanbok* outfits for the show, showcasing different patterns of lavish embroidery, *hanbok* worn in Korean drumming performances, and even *hanbok* in the style worn by the royal court during Korea's Joseon Dynasty. At the end of the show, Ryu's work was chosen as the most outstanding, and she was awarded first place.

Competitors and Advertising

As Ryu's fame increased after the Paris fashion show, so too did the jealousy of other *hanbok* makers in the Korean Autonomous Prefecture. In 2003 her store was broken into three times. The first time, photos from the Paris show were stolen; the second time, new samples were stolen from mannequins; and the third time, the one sample that had been left behind in the second break-in was also stolen. No cash was taken. Although Ryu suspected who the perpetrator might be, the police said they would not intervene unless the thief was caught red-handed. As a result, Ryu decided to keep her store exterior plain, so as not to fan her competitors' jealousy. She also never displays new samples in the store window.

Although Ryu was the first in the prefecture to sell *hanbok* from a storefront rather than at the market, thirty other stores now sell *hanbok* in Yanji, with some differentiation between competitors. For example, as the ethnic Koreans in China have become more oriented toward South Korea, South Korean goods are perceived as trendy and high-quality; and several of Ryu's competitors specialize in selling *hanbok* imported from South Korea. Ryu differentiates herself through her styles, which combine North and South Korean influences, the high-quality embroidery on her *hanbok*, and her very strong brand.

In the early years of her *hanbok* business, Ryu frequently advertised. At one time, she even paid for the exteriors of an entire fleet of Yanji city busses to be painted in bright yellow with a picture of her favorite model—her daughter—in *hanbok*. Because her brand has become so well-known, she no longer needs to spend as much on advertising. Instead, her personal appearances on local and even South Korean TV and media coverage of government officials and popular stars wearing her clothes serve as free publicity.

Organization and Workflow

Ryu's daughter, Aehwa Park, is the store manager; and her niece, Mihwa Ryu, is the factory manager. The Yemi Hanbok factory has seventy employees in four different manufacturing groups and an office group. The manufacturing groups are (1) computerized embroidery, (2) sewing for uniforms and simplified *hanbok*, (3) custom *hanbok*, and (4) crafts—for *norigae* (a type of *hanbok* accessory), wrappers for traditional wedding boxes, floor pillows, belts, and decorations, among other items. All the products are made to order. *Hanbok* fabrics are imported from South Korea because of the superior quality that can be found there. They are ordered in the necessary colors or else dyed in the factory. The variety of products made in the factory is staggering. On average, a new design is created every day.

Traditional *hanbok*, especially for weddings, is the most profitable business segment, as all the work is made to order. A customer comes into a Yemi Hanbok store, chooses a design and colors, and is measured. The fabric is then sent to Pyongyang in case it needs to be hand-embroidered, and is returned to the factory to be completed. Prices range from 1,400 to 2,800 RMB, representing a month's wages for the well-to-do inhabitants of the prefecture and two months' earnings for those less well-off. The *hanbok* uniforms are not as profitable as the traditional *hanbok*, but the orders are substantial.

Yemi Hanbok is in a unique position in that it can work with both North and South Korea. As Ryu explains, "The salary here in Yanji is 1,400 RMB per month. In Pyongyang it is 200 RMB per month. We simply can't afford to do the hand-embroidery here." At the same time, factory salaries in South Korea are seven times higher than those in Yanji. As a result, Yemi Hanbok can design an item, have the embroidery done in North Korea, cut the fabric in China, and sell either unfinished *hanbok* or crafts to South Korean customers. Currently, Ryu has a contract with Yedan, the largest *hanbok* company in South Korea for unfinished products.

The main store is in Yanji; and there are two branches, one in Dalian and one in Shanghai, that sell Yemi Hanbok clothes exclusively. In addition, more than fifty stores, spread throughout China, carry Ryu's designs.

The Yemi Hanbok factory workers enjoy above-average monthly salaries and every Sunday off. Although they were all ethnic Koreans in the past, today this group prefers not to do factory work in China and would rather go abroad, where they can earn much higher salaries. As a result, the proportion of ethnic Koreans has fallen to about one half. The other half are Han Chinese workers from as far afield as Hubei Province, in south-central China. When asked if she had been familiar with *hanbok* before coming to work in the factory, one Han Chinese worker from Heilongjiang Province answered, "No, I had never seen it before I came to work here, but now I think it is very beautiful!" Ryu has clearly become a cultural ambassador even beyond the ways she had originally intended.

Ryu's style and business model are unique in the global *hanbok* industry. As Mihwa Ryu, Ryu's niece and business manager, explains, since the Korean populations in China, North Korea, and South Korea were largely isolated from each other for about 50 years, *hanbok* styles had developed separately in these three countries. Ryu's designs are based on the Chinese style, but with inspiration and influence from both of the other two styles; and she also makes ample use of embroidery. In addition, she has developed a special style, wedding *hanbok*, based on traditional *hanbok* for festive occasions but in white, recalling the Western-style wedding dresses preferred by most modern brides for the wedding itself. She makes traditional *hanbok*, royal *hanbok*, *hanbok* for performances, simplified *hanbok*, *hanbok*-

inspired clothing colored with natural dyes, and various traditional accessories and bags.

Ryu's business model is also unique in its high level of vertical integration. In South Korea, where the market is larger and there are more competitors at every step of the value chain, one company would never engage in activities as diverse as dying fabric, doing embroidery and silk screening and making ornaments, Ryu explains. Because the Korean Autonomous Prefecture market is smaller and there are no competitors, she can fully express her creativity by experimenting with different methods at each stage of production.

Politics and Government Influence

Unlike many other business people in China, Ryu has not used membership of the Chinese Communist Party (CCP) to enhance her success. "I never was interested in that kind of thing," she says. "In politics, I would only do politics. I prefer studying and researching clothing." Nevertheless, she has shrewdly leveraged politics and politicians. For example, when she started Yemi Hanbok, she gave ethnic Korean politicians free outfits to wear for government occasions and events, and to this day she still lends politicians clothes for government occasions if they ask for them. She has also joined several government committees, such as the Yanbian Women in Business Committee, and gives free outfits for committee portraits and events. As a result of her fame, she also knows important local as well as national politicians, including the minister for minority affairs, who is an ethnic Korean.

Although many ethnic Koreans from the Korean Autonomous Prefecture have emigrated to South Korea, Ryu says she is glad she lives in China. She says that, particularly after the 2003 Paris show, she realized she enjoys certain advantages in China. The costs of the fashion show were covered for the most part by the Chinese government, for example. There are also funds earmarked specifically for minority-owned businesses. In her factory she shows off a brand-new computerized embroidery machine which she purchased with the help of 400,000 RMB (approximately US$50,000) in government support. Another new business she started in the last few years also relies on the prefectural government's support of Korean culture. Ryu has won contracts to supply simplified *hanbok* to the prefectural government for daily wear by all government employees, as well as uniforms for students and teachers in five schools in the prefecture.

Looking Forward

Ryu is a woman with many plans and visions for the future. After her daughter decided she wanted to be part of the design and marketing side of the business, Ryu sent her and her son-in-law to South Korea to study *hanbok* design and business. Now that the next generation will be ready to take over the business in the next few years, Ryu is thinking about the future.

Several years ago Ryu initiated a project to color fabrics using natural dyes. Although she has a great passion for natural dyes and fibers and had expended serious effort on this project, she finally concluded that she was ahead of her time. She may try to launch this venture again in a few years.

In the meantime, Ryu has purchased a plot of land in the countryside near her birthplace. She envisions building a traditional Korean farmhouse there and turning it into a *hanbok* museum. The land is situated perfectly according to the principles of *feng shui*, with a mountain in the back and a stream in front. In addition, the property is close to the route tourists must take to visit the birthplace of Dongju Yun, one of the most beloved poets in South Korea. Could a museum be her next undertaking?

QUESTIONS

1   What types of resources made it possible for Ryu to succeed as an entrepreneur?
2   What were the most formidable obstacles she faced along the way?
3   Is the organization of her business conducive to creativity, flexibility and efficiency?

Notes

1   *Yemi* translates roughly as "proper and beautiful," reflecting the fact that the *hanbok* is usually worn on formal family occasions, such as a marriage, a baby's first birthday, or a 60th birthday.
2   Chae-Jin Lee, *China's Korean Minority: The Politics of Ethnic Education* (Boulder, CO: Westview Press, 1986), p. 15.
3   Bernard Vincent Olivier, *The Implementation of China's Nationality Policy in the Northeastern Provinces* (San Francisco, CA: Mellen Research University Press, 1993), p. 19.
4   Lee, *China's Korean Minority*, p. 19.
5   Ibid., pp. 27–28.
6   Kwak Seung-Ji, "3. Sahoemunhwajeok cheukmyeon-ingu gamso munjae (20)," *Dongbuka Sinmun*, December 16, 2008.
7   This incident was widely reported in the Korean-language press in both China and South Korea. See, for example, Munhwa Ilbo, "Junggugpan Jang Yeongja' Han Okhee Ujeon Gongeopmuyeokchonggongsa Sajang Gonggaechongsalhyeong," February 4, 1997.

23 Economic Development, Women Entrepreneurs, and the Future

Mauro F. Guillén

The journey through the world of women entrepreneurs in the previous chapters illustrates the dynamics of venture initiation and growth that characterize all entrepreneurial activity. They also speak to the specific opportunities and challenges faced by women entrepreneurs when compared to men, and the impact of the institutional context in developing and emerging economies. In his 1911 book, *The Theory of Economic Development,* Joseph Schumpeter presented the entrepreneur as the hero of the market economy. Decades later, in his famous book, *Capitalism, Socialism and Democracy* ([1942] 1975: 82), he argued that

> Capitalism [. . .] is by nature a form or method of economic change and not only never is but never can be stationary. The fundamental impulse that sets *and keeps the capitalist engine in motion comes from the new consumers'* goods, the new methods of production or transportation, the new markets, the new forms of industrial organization that capitalist enterprise creates. [. . .] The opening up of new markets, foreign or domestic, and the organizational development from the craft shop and factory to such concerns as U.S. Steel illustrate the same process of industrial mutation [. . .] that incessantly revolutionizes the economic structure *from within,* incessantly destroying the old one, incessantly creating a new one. This process of Creative Destruction is the essential fact about capitalism.

Schumpeter also reminded us of another feature of entrepreneurs which characterizes many of the women analyzed in this book. The entrepreneur is not necessarily an investor who puts his or her own capital at risk, but rather someone who combines resources (including capital) to launch a venture. The women entrepreneurs featured in this book succeeded only to the extent that they managed to combine resources such as knowledge, social relationships, human labor and raw materials as well as capital.

The cases of women-launched ventures in this book also speak to the potential contribution of women to economic development. Prior to the 1980s, development theorists and practitioners focused their attention exclusively on the so-called "obstacles" to development, identifying and seeking to address hindrances such as the lack of physical infrastructure or the traditional values espoused by the population, which they saw as inimical to economic growth (Guillén 2001 and Naudé 2010 for a review). During the 1980s, in the wake of some of the worst economic and financial crises in the developing world, a new mode of thought emerged, focused on the institutional underpinnings of economic dynamism. It was quickly dubbed the Washington Consensus. While it placed the emphasis on a new set of variables that could foster entrepreneurship as the engine of growth, it inherited from its predecessors in economic development thinking an inclination to impose a one-size-fits-all recipe or "best practice" for success, and an inability to specify the processes of innovation that entrepreneurs and firms were supposed to spearhead.

The specific policy consensus that emerged during the 1980s and 1990s, especially at the International Monetary Fund and the World Bank, was that fiscal discipline, financial liberalization, openness to trade and investment, privatization, deregulation and protection of property rights were necessary to create the foundations for sustained economic growth. Lackluster results in Latin America led development theorists and practitioners to enlarge the agenda to include an even more sweeping list of necessary reforms, including corporate governance, labor market flexibility, independent central banks, and anti-corruption measures, among others. This "augmented" Washington Consensus, while theoretically on target, placed too much emphasis on eliminating inefficiencies and on the virtues of free financial flows without seriously considering dynamic innovation as the engine of growth. Moreover, the success of this model of economic growth requires wholesale institutional reform on several fronts, something that is likely to be opposed politically, and may not always be conducive to superior economic outcomes (Rodrik 2006).

The increasing attention paid to institutions also served to reignite interest in new firm formation, small firms, and their contribution to economic and employment growth (OECD 2004; Naudé 2010). In particular, micro and small enterprises (MSEs), those with fewer than fifty employees, were found to represent a greater share of employment in developing countries than in developed ones (Nichter and Goldmark 2009), thus presenting more opportunities to accelerate economic development.

Given the emphasis on institutions, much of the research effort into the potential for new firms to accelerate economic growth was placed on the conditions that enabled and hindered firm formation. Thus, in 2002 the World Bank launched the "Doing Business" project to assess the institutional rules and regulations affecting small and medium enterprises through their life cycle, i.e. those having to do with "starting a business, dealing with construction permits, employing workers, registering property, getting credit, protecting investors, paying taxes, trading across borders, enforcing contracts and closing a business" (World Bank 2010a). Over the years, comparative data on as many as 183 economies were compiled using teams of local experts. The underlying assumption was that "economic activity requires good rules," an idea that was first proposed by sociologist Max Weber (1978: 328–329) and the "old institutional" school in economics that Hernando de Soto, an influential Peruvian economist, helped popularize in policy circles during the 1990s, and that the law-and-finance economists at Chicago and Harvard pioneered in terms of formal modeling and cross-national data (La Porta et al. 1998). The focus was on the formal sector of the economy, under the assumption that informality tends to limit firm growth and the potential contribution to economic development (Nichter and Goldmark 2009).

The indicators included in the Doing Business database are highly correlated with other indices of the overall business environment and competitiveness, such as those compiled by the OECD, the World Economic Forum or IMD. The body of empirical research that uses these indicators seems to confirm that better institutional conditions reduce informality, facilitate new firm formation, encourage entrepreneurship, and increase employment (World Bank 2010a; Klapper et al. 2010). These findings make a great deal of sense given that the institutional indicators measure such egregious obstacles to doing business as the number and cost of bureaucratic procedures to start a firm, do construction, register property, resolve a commercial dispute, pay taxes or engage in international trade, although other indicators are more controversial, including those having to do with labor market rigidities and investor protections. Other research and documentation efforts have focused on the motivations and prevalence of entrepreneurship in different societies. The most comprehensive dataset is provided by the Global Entrepreneurship Monitor, an academic research consortium launched in 1999 that has conducted adult population surveys on entrepreneurial activity in fifty-four countries (GEM 2009).

The Contributions of Women to Economic Development

Development scholars and practitioners did not pay systematic attention to women until a Danish economist working for the United Nations, Ester Boserup, published her influential book, *Woman's Role in Economic Development* (1970). Boserup's analysis was so powerful because she showed the enormous extent to which women contribute to economic development. She forcefully argued that women play a key role in development, inside and outside the household. Her work inspired the United Nations Decade for Women (1975–1985) and laid the foundations for the wave of studies and programs arguing that promoting women's role in the economy could become a major contributor to development (OECD 2004; World Bank 2001; Browne 2001; see Jaquette and Staudt 2006 for a review). The concern by development scholars interested in gender was not only to advance gender equality as a goal in its own right, but also to explore ways in which women's economic activities could contribute to economic growth and to economic development, in the sense of a transformation of the economy through innovation.

These and other subsequent studies documented that development created a segregated labor market along gender lines, with women clustering in more labor-intensive activities in light manufacturing (e.g., textiles, food-processing) that paid lower wages, or being self-employed in the service sector (Boserup 1970; Browne 2001). Attempts were also made conceptually and statistically to distinguish among the prevalence and contributions to development of unpaid household labor, unpaid work at the family farm or business, self-employment, and entrepreneurship by women (UNIFEM 2005; International Labour Organization 2009). A related argument about women's role in economic growth and development was formulated by Gøsta Esping-Andersen (1999), a Danish sociologist, who argued that in advanced postindustrial societies the incorporation of women into the labor force triggered the growth of all manner of market-oriented service activities that women used to perform in the household without pay. By the beginning of the 1990s entrepreneurship by women was fully recognized as a dynamic contributor to economic development. The main argument in this new line of inquiry and policymaking became that countries that did not make it possible for women to participate fully as economic agents would be underutilizing half of the talent pool (OECD 2004; World Bank 2001).

Entrepreneurship by women, however, was not found to be unproblematic. Researchers reported that entrepreneurs, whether men or women, tended to initiate activities related to their previous job experience. Given the pre-existing gender segregation by type of sector, industry or activity, the effect of previous experience on entrepreneurial activity generated a segregated pattern of entrepreneurship by gender, with women overwhelmingly launching new ventures in the service sector in general, and in retail and personal services in particular, where capital requirements tend to be lower and their household and self-employment experience more relevant (Carter et al. 2001; Carter and Shaw 2006). It is important to note that this sector of the economy produces for the most part non-tradable services, thus reducing the potential for international growth. As we shall see in the next section, the self-selection of women entrepreneurs into specific industries and activities helps explain many of the observed gender differences. In addition, in many developing countries researchers found that more than half (and in some cases more than three-fourths) of the smallest firms, accounting for a large share of total employment, were owned by women, and that they were generally characterized by slower growth rates and informal practices (Nichter and Goldmark 2009). Lastly, there is virtually no research on whether better educated women from advantaged social backgrounds are more likely to benefit from entrepreneurial opportunities, new aid or government programs, and the like, thus perpetuating other sources of inequality.

The Impact of Gender on Patterns of Entrepreneurship

As is true of other related fields of inquiry, research on women and entrepreneurship is split between two seemingly irreconcilable models. First, there are researchers who propose that there is one unique and universal model of entrepreneurship, which is gender free. From this perspective, when studying entrepreneurship by women, the most important task for the researcher is to understand, explain, and provide solutions to the difficulties they may encounter, such as securing the necessary resources to launch a new venture. This type of analysis may be useful for educational and policymaking purposes, but it suffers from a serious theoretical and methodological shortcoming. Understanding differences in entrepreneurship between men and women by reference to a universal model of entrepreneurship can easily succumb to the temptation of an essentialist conception of how gender affects entrepreneurial processes and outcomes. Essentialism consists of characterizing a group of people or other entities by a small set of fixed properties, while ignoring the conditions under which such identities emerged, discounting any possibility of change or variation within the group (for a review of these arguments and the empirical evidence, see Mirchandani 1999; Lewis 2006).

A second group of researchers argues that there are many types of entrepreneurship, and that gender is not just one more variable that may help explain certain processes or outcomes. Rather, women entrepreneurs may have distinct preferences for choosing, organizing and managing a venture, and may define success in terms of goal achievement, a better work/family balance or community benefits, as opposed to growth, profits and fame. Ahl (2006) reported that the foundational texts in the field of entrepreneurship (including Schumpeter 1934) used words such as self-efficacious, strong willed, resolute, skilled at organizing, visionary, daring, courageous, detached, achievement oriented, and astute to describe the entrepreneur, terms that correlate very highly with index scales of what psychologists refer to as "masculinity." Ahl also found that the opposites of those traits correlated with index scales of "femininity." Other researchers observed that entrepreneurship is often defined by reference to masculine traits such as ambition, independence, individualism, competitiveness, self-reliance, and risk-taking. According to these scholars, entrepreneurship by women, however, draws on different resources and opportunities, resulting in a qualitatively different kind of economic activity based on women's distinctive characteristics (for reviews, see Ahl 2006; Bird and Brush 2002; Brush 1992; Brush et al. 2006b, 2010; Fielden and Davidson 2010a, 2010b; Mirchandani 1999; Lewis 2006).

These opposing ways of looking at entrepreneurship by women resonate with the two classic strands in feminist thought. Liberal feminist theory holds that men and women are similar and that any differences in opportunity or achievement are the result of discrimination or structural barriers. By contrast, social or radical feminist theory maintains that men and women are different, and that the latter's traits constitute resources that can be mobilized to pursue meaningful social or economic action in ways that are distinct from those observed in men.

Perhaps the most useful way to reconcile these two perspectives is to view gender not as a given, but as a socially constructed category, as we have seen in the previous chapters. Women are socially constructed individually and as a group in different ways depending on time and space. Thus, all gender research, including research on entrepreneurship by women, should start by unveiling the assumptions underlying such constructions in the specific context and time in which it is taking place (Ahl 2006). This preliminary step is very important in the case of studies of women entrepreneurs across time and/or space, when political, cultural, religious and other social variables are not constant.

The empirical evidence comparing men and women entrepreneurs does not offer a clear picture as to the presumed differences in terms of the motivations, processes and outcomes of entrepreneurship. The existing reviews of the massive literature on this topic conclude that overall there is little support for differences between men and women engaged in entrepreneurship, with only two exceptions: (1) men and women self-select into different kinds of entrepreneurial activities, sectors and industries, mostly based on their prior work experience; and (2) ventures founded, owned and/or managed by women tend to grow less over time, mostly as a result of structural constraints of various sorts. We have seen these dynamics illustrated by the cases of women entrepreneurs presented in the previous chapters. Virtually all of them launched a venture based on their previous experience in the household, in education, or in employment.

We have also seen illustrated in our cases the enormous range of variation in terms of the process of entrepreneurship, a feature that makes it hard to make generalizations about the experience of women entrepreneurs. Thus, it is very hard to point to a gender model of entrepreneurship whereby women think and do differently than men. This is consistent with the existing literature, which does not find systematic evidence of differences in terms of the motivations to become an entrepreneur, attitudes toward entrepreneurship, the social or psychological characteristics of entrepreneurs, the process of starting the business, the management or leadership style or even ongoing access to finance. While some studies find evidence of such differences, others do not (for reviews of the literature, see Brush 1992; Brush et al. 2006a, 2010; Carter et al. 2001; Ahl 2006; Nichter and Goldmark 2009).

Perhaps the most intensively studied aspect of entrepreneurship by women is access to finance. Several of our cases highlighted the difficulties faced by women in this area (e.g. Kisyombe, Sambo), while others did not (e.g. Debayle, al Ghunaim, Aoki). Our sample, of course, is biased towards women that did launch a venture and made at least some progress with it. Thus, it probably underestimates the funding difficulties faced by women entrepreneurs. The emerging consensus in the literature, based on more representative samples, is that access to startup capital is more limited for women than for men. Aspiring women entrepreneurs tend to be asked to provide guarantees that lie beyond their existing assets, relationships or track record. The evidence on discrimination when it comes to accessing capital on an ongoing basis, i.e. after the business is up and running, yields more ambiguous and inconsistent results, although most research indicates that the relationship between women entrepreneurs and bankers is mired by gender stereotyping. Still, much of the gap between men and women's access to finance can be explained by previous business experience, self-selection into specific activities, sectors and industries, or track record (Carter et al. 2001; Carter and Shaw 2006).

Another heavily researched area is networking. The women we studied relied on extensive personal and professional networks in order to launch and grow their ventures. The existing literature documents that women entrepreneurs often complain that they do not have access to the necessary resources for launching and growing their venture because their network connections are not the most appropriate for success. Those resources include not only material ones but also advice, mentorship, and role models. The existing body of research shows that women entrepreneurs, when compared to men, have fewer network ties in general, and weak (i.e. intermediary or brokerage) ties in particular. Both men and women entrepreneurs tend to have same-gendered ties, which makes it more difficult for women to find mentors and role models in fields in which there are few of them, as the cases of women like Ancharya in genomics outsourcing and al Ghunaim in investment banking. These differences are largely attributable to prior employment history and job experience. In fact, regardless of gender, salaried men and women tend to have more network contacts than the self-employed (Carter et al. 2001; World Bank 2011: 233). Although evidence for entrepreneurs is lacking, research on salaried men and women managers in the United States shows that women reap fewer benefits from weak ties and encounter more difficulties obtaining mentorship and advice. They also face different, and often more demanding, role expectations when they are "tokens," i.e. in the numerical minority in their fields of activity (for a review, see Rothbard and Brett 2000).

Yet another area of controversy concerns work/family balance. Women's role in the family is seen in the literature as both constraining and enabling entrepreneurship. On the one hand, research has shown that the family obligations shouldered by women can detract energy and time from other activities and make it harder for them to build the experience, reputation, and networks necessary for success. On the other, research also indicates that entrepreneurship can help women make more flexible arrangements to balance work and family than the typical 9-to-5 job, as we saw in the case of Kisyombe, and that family life can be an inspiration for certain entrepreneurial activities (Ahl 2006), as illustrated by Debayle and Escobosa. These arrangements, however, may imply that the venture is located in the household, which tends to be a major constraint on growth, at least in developing countries (Nichter and Goldmark 2009).

It is important to note that the most important explanations for the differences found between men and women entrepreneurs when it comes to accessing resources, including networking—lack of experience, limited track record, or self-selection into specific activities—in no way imply the absence of discrimination or the futility of public programs and policies geared at providing women with more opportunities. Analyzing the impact of experience and self-selection are precisely key to determining the best solutions to the obstacles that women experience when becoming entrepreneurs, which the literature has identified as having to do with a long list of interrelated factors: insufficient education or experience, barriers of access to various material resources (especially capital), lack of mentors and role models, competing demands on time, and so on (Carter et al. 2001; Carter and Shaw 2006; OECD 2004; Ahl 2006).

Previous research and the cases in this book clearly indicate that enabling women entrepreneurs to participate in all manner of activities, sectors and industries—not just in those in which they have prior experience—and to maximize the growth opportunities of their ventures will surely help them make an even greater contribution to economic development (Brush et al. 2006a, 2010; Carter et al. 2001). This is perhaps the most solid conclusion that can be reached from our efforts to understand the drives of women entrepreneurship, one that justifies the efforts at creating programs aimed at improving women's access to professional education and social activities.

While we have emphasized self-selection as a powerful force shaping the activities of women entrepreneurs, there is no denying that discrimination places limits on women's entrepreneurial opportunities. Perhaps the most blatant aspect of discrimination has to do with laws and regulations that place women at a disadvantage. A recent report by the World Bank covered 128 developed and developing economies. As of 2009, in forty-five countries women did not have the same legal capacity to act or engage in economic transactions, in forty-nine women were prevented from working in certain industries, and in thirty-two they did not have equal inheritance rights. Legal discrimination has an impact on entrepreneurship. Equal legal rights were found to result in a greater percentage of businesses owned or managed by women, and higher gender legal equality correlated with per capita income, although it was not clear what the direction of causality is (World Bank 2010b; see also World Economic Forum 2011).

Are There Enough Women Entrepreneurs around the World?

We illustrated in this book the positive impact that entrepreneurship by women can have on their families, communities, and countries, as well as on the women themselves. Assessing the prevalence and predicament of women entrepreneurs continues to be thwarted by the scarcity of systematic statistics and case-study evidence. Unfortunately, the World Bank's Doing Business databases on the institutional conditions for business and on new firm registrations do not consider gender as a variable (World Bank 2010a; Klapper et al. 2010), although it has recently launched a pilot program to document in which countries women are discriminated against in laws and regulations related to doing business, including aspects such as accessing government authorities, property, getting a job, dealing with taxes, building credit, and going to court (World Bank 2010b).

In general, the situation of women entrepreneurs is closely related to the overall status of women in the society and the economy (Brush et al. 2010; Carter et al. 2007; Fielden and Davidson 2010b). It is no surprise that, even after decades of effort, the socio-economic status of women around the world is not on a par with men, and that the progress that women have experienced towards gender equality is unevenly distributed by country. In 47 out of 192 countries and territories included in Table 23.1 (below), the average number of children per woman (i.e. the total fertility rate) is equal to or greater than 4. These are mostly poor countries in which women lag behind in terms of educational opportunity (see Table 23.2 below, with the correlations between pairs of variables). Having children triggers a number of complex effects on the chances that a woman will achieve high educational status, enter the labor market, pursue self-employment, or launch her own business, as the case studies in this book illustrate. In fact, the proportion of women who participate in the labor force, or the share of the total labor force that they represent, is not correlated with education, number of children or per capita income. A host of cultural, legal, and institutional variables also seem to intervene.

Global statistics on the prevalence of women entrepreneurs are of poor quality and coverage. The World Bank's World Development Indicators reports the proportion of incorporated businesses in which women participate as owners. This statistic is not available for the richest countries in the world. Within the developing and emerging economies for which data exist, the higher the per capita income, the labor market participation by women, and especially the ratio of female-to-male enrolled in university, the greater the proportion of women who are business owners. Higher fertility, by contrast, is associated with a lower proportion of women who are business owners. It should be noted that these last two variables could be driven by religious and legal practices that simultaneously promote large families and prevent women from being entrepreneurs or business owners (World Bank 2010b).

The survey data collected by the Global Entrepreneurship Monitor (GEM 2009) reveals other nuances. The proportion of adult men or women engaged in early-stage entrepreneurial activity (i.e. 42 months or less in duration) increases with the number of births and decreases with per capita income, whereas the proportion of men or women who are established business owners does not. This may be an indication that in many countries both men and women are driven to start a business out of necessity rather than in pursuit of a distinct, attractive opportunity. The GEM study corroborates this suspicion: the ratio of opportunity-to-necessity motivations, as reported by the respondents, is negatively correlated with early-stage entrepreneurial activity but not correlated at all with established business ownership, for either men or women. This ratio measures how frequent are women entrepreneurs who launched a business in response to an opportunity (e.g. Monteiro or Debayle) relative to those who started a business out of necessity (e.g. Kisyombe or Escobosa). Most importantly, the higher the per capita income of the country, the greater the opportunity-to-necessity ratio. This indicates that the poorer the country, the more men and women start a business out of necessity, i.e. for lack of other viable alternatives of employment or income. With the exceptions only of Japan and Thailand, in the other thirty-nine countries for which data are available, the ratio of opportunity-to-necessity was lower for women than for men. This piece of information, though, needs to be carefully examined before jumping to any conclusions, because the question of motivation to become an entrepreneur can be asked only of those who actually decided to become entrepreneurs (see also World Bank 2011: 207).

Intriguingly, countries with more women business owners, more women engaged in early-stage entrepreneurial activity or more women who are established business owners do not necessarily have a greater proportion of seats in parliament occupied by women. However, a higher opportunity-to-necessity ratio for female or male entrepreneurs is highly correlated with more women in parliament, perhaps indicating that opportunity-driven entrepreneurship is higher in countries in which women are politically more empowered, and that these variables are likely jointly determined by a set of other social, political, and cultural institutions.

This evidence underscores the main conclusions to be drawn from this book, which are all related to the context in which entrepreneurship takes place. First, the experiences of women entrepreneurs vary immensely from case to case as well as across industries and countries. Second, while it is difficult to generalize, there are distinct patterns of self-selection into

Table 23.1 Indicators of Women's Socio-Economic Status and Entrepreneurship

Country	A	B	C	D	E	F	G	H	I	J	K	L	M
Afghanistan	6.6	—	33.0	26.6	2.8	—	—	—	—	—	—	27.7	1,103
Albania	1.9	—	48.9	42.3	10.8	—	—	—	—	—	—	7.1	7,293
Algeria	2.4	140.1	36.6	31.2	15.0	—	—	—	—	—	—	7.7	8,036
Andorra	1.3	145.2	—	—	—	—	—	—	—	—	—	25.0	—
Angola	5.8	—	74.3	46.8	23.4	—	—	—	—	—	—	37.3	5,820
Argentina	2.2	152.3	51.1	41.1	30.3	17.5	11.3	15.8	4.2	2.0	1.2	40.0	14,313
Armenia	1.7	120.2	59.0	49.6	31.8	—	—	—	—	—	—	8.4	6,075
Australia	2.0	128.1	58.4	45.3	—	—	—	—	—	—	—	26.7	38,784
Austria	1.4	120.4	53.4	45.5	—	3.1	1.8	7.3	4.8	12.0	6.8	32.2	37,912
Azerbaijan	2.3	83.1	60.6	50.2	10.8	—	—	—	—	—	—	11.4	8,771
Bahamas, The	2.0	—	68.3	48.1	—	—	—	—	—	—	—	12.2	—
Bahrain	2.3	253.1	32.2	20.3	—	—	—	—	—	—	—	2.5	34,899
Bangladesh	2.3	55.4	58.3	40.9	16.1	—	—	—	—	—	—	15.1	1,335
Barbados	1.5	—	65.9	47.9	—	—	—	—	—	—	—	10.0	—
Belarus	1.4	143.2	54.5	49.5	52.9	—	—	—	—	—	—	29.1	12,278
Belgium	1.8	125.6	46.9	44.9	—	4.3	2.0	1.9	0.9	19.0	9.1	35.3	35,238
Belize	2.9	—	46.3	36.1	—	—	—	—	—	—	—	0.0	6,743
Benin	5.4	—	66.7	45.7	43.9	—	—	—	—	—	—	10.8	1,473
Bhutan	2.6	58.6	51.2	38.9	31.3	—	—	—	—	—	—	8.5	4,759
Bolivia	3.5	84.1	62.1	43.9	41.1	—	—	—	—	—	—	16.9	4,277
Bosnia and Herzegovina	1.2	—	54.8	47.1	32.8	—	—	—	—	—	—	11.9	8,095
Botswana	2.9	99.9	72.0	47.5	40.9	—	—	—	—	—	—	11.1	13,574
Brazil	1.9	128.9	59.9	43.5	59.3	12.7	12.7	12.7	7.2	2.0	1.5	9.0	10,304
Brunei Darussalam	2.1	198.7	59.9	43.0	—	—	—	—	—	—	—	—	50,822

Table 23.1 Continued

Country	A	B	C	D	E	F	G	H	I	J	K	L	M
Bulgaria	1.5	122.1	49.4	46.3	33.9	—	—	—	—	—	—	21.7	11,792
Burkina Faso	5.9	50.0	77.7	47.0	19.2	—	—	—	—	—	—	15.3	1,160
Burundi	4.6	43.3	91.0	52.7	34.8	—	—	—	—	—	—	30.5	383
Cambodia	2.9	53.6	73.3	48.8	—	—	—	—	—	—	—	16.3	1,951
Cameroon	4.6	79.3	53.0	39.8	15.7	—	—	—	—	—	—	13.9	2,195
Canada	1.6	.	62.1	46.9	—	—	—	—	—	—	—	21.3	39,078
Cape Verde	2.7	123.8	52.6	42.9	33.1	—	—	—	—	—	—	18.1	3,202
Central African Republic	4.8	32.6	71.4	46.6	—	—	—	—	—	—	—	10.5	741
Chad	6.2	14.6	63.2	45.3	40.1	—	—	—	—	—	—	5.2	1,337
Chile	1.9	100.8	43.8	37.5	27.8	16.5	10.4	11.9	5.6	5.1	2.3	15.0	14,436
China	1.8	99.7	67.5	44.6	—	19.3	13.4	9.7	7.0	1.6	1.1	21.3	5,971
Colombia	2.4	99.0	40.5	35.7	43.0	26.9	18.8	15.5	7.8	1.7	0.9	8.4	8,797
Comoros	4.0	.	73.1	46.3	—	—	—	—	—	—	—	3.0	1,170
Congo, Dem. Rep.	6.0	34.9	56.2	40.6	21.2	—	—	—	—	—	—	8.4	314
Congo, Rep.	4.4	.	62.5	43.5	31.8	—	—	—	—	—	—	7.3	3,949
Costa Rica	2.0	125.6	45.3	35.2	—	—	—	—	—	—	—	36.8	11,232
Côte d'Ivoire	4.6	—	50.5	36.7	61.9	—	—	—	—	—	—	8.9	1,652
Croatia	1.5	122.3	46.1	45.5	33.5	9.4	5.1	5.8	2.7	2.0	0.8	22.0	17,663
Cuba	1.5	168.7	42.0	38.0	—	—	—	—	—	—	—	43.2	—
Cyprus	1.5	99.4	54.5	45.6	—	—	—	—	—	—	—	14.3	26,919
Czech Republic	1.5	127.0	49.4	43.4	25.0	—	—	—	—	—	—	15.5	24,643
Denmark	1.9	140.7	61.0	46.9	—	6.2	4.6	8.5	3.4	28.0	17.7	38.0	36,845
Djibouti	3.9	68.8	61.1	43.9	—	—	—	—	—	—	—	13.8	2,138
Dominican Republic	2.6	—	50.7	38.9	—	18.9	14.5	9.0	6.1	2.9	1.8	19.7	8,125

Ecuador	2.6	122.3	46.8	37.9	32.7	—	—	—	—	—	—	25.0	8,014
Egypt, Arab Rep.	2.9	—	22.8	23.9	34.0	—	—	—	—	—	—	1.8	5,425
El Salvador	2.3	108.8	47.0	42.2	39.6	—	—	—	—	—	—	16.7	6,799
Equatorial Guinea	5.3	—	38.4	30.1	—	—	—	—	—	—	—	6.0	33,899
Eritrea	4.6	—	60.2	43.6	4.2	—	—	—	—	—	—	22.0	642
Estonia	1.7	163.8	55.2	49.2	36.3	—	—	—	—	—	—	20.8	20,651
Ethiopia	5.3	31.1	78.3	47.1	30.9	—	—	—	—	—	—	21.9	869
Euro area	1.6	—	49.2	43.7	—	—	—	—	—	—	—	25.2	33,452
Fiji	2.7	120.4	38.9	32.7	—	—	—	—	—	—	—	11.3	4,358
Finland	1.8	123.0	57.5	48.1	—	9.0	4.8	10.3	4.8	8.1	3.6	41.5	36,195
France	2.0	127.8	50.9	47.0	—	4.1	2.2	2.5	1.0	2.6	1.6	18.2	33,058
French Polynesia	2.2	—	47.7	40.7	—	—	—	—	—	—	—	16.7	14,575
Gabon	3.3	—	69.0	46.4	33.1	—	—	—	—	—	—	9.4	1,363
Gambia, The	5.1	—	70.6	46.2	21.3	—	—	—	—	—	—	6.0	4,966
Georgia	1.6	119.2	55.4	47.0	40.8	—	—	—	—	—	—	31.6	35,374
Germany	1.4	—	52.9	45.4	—	—	—	—	—	—	—	10.9	1,463
Ghana	4.0	54.0	73.7	49.2	44.0	—	—	—	—	—	—	14.7	29,356
Greece	1.5	110.3	43.0	40.4	—	8.0	3.5	14.6	12.0	12.8	5.4	—	—
Guam	2.5	—	51.8	39.8	—	—	—	—	—	—	—	12.0	4,760
Guatemala	4.1	99.7	48.1	37.8	28.4	—	—	—	—	—	—	19.3	1,056
Guinea	5.4	33.5	79.0	46.8	25.4	—	—	—	—	—	—	14.0	537
Guinea—Bissau	5.7	—	59.5	42.4	19.9	—	—	—	—	—	—	29.0	3,064
Guyana	2.3	141.9	45.7	34.6	—	—	—	—	—	—	—	4.1	1,124
Haiti	3.5	—	58.2	42.7	—	—	—	—	—	—	—	23.4	3,932
Honduras	3.3	151.5	41.6	34.0	39.9	14.3	5.8	7.5	3.8	2.6	0.9	11.1	43,957
Hong Kong SAR	1.0	101.8	52.5	45.8	—	9.3	4.5	5.9	3.8	3.1	1.6	33.3	19,789
Hungary	1.4	145.5	42.7	45.4	42.4	17.4	7.4	13.4	4.0	9.9	4.0	9.1	36,902
Iceland	2.1	186.9	73.1	45.8	—	9.5	7.5	8.7	2.2	2.1	1.8	11.6	2,946
India	2.7	69.9	33.1	27.8	9.1	—	—	—	—	—	—	—	3,994
Indonesia	2.2	99.9	52.0	38.4	—	—	—	—	—	—	—	—	—

Table 23.1 Continued

Country	A	B	C	D	E	F	G	H	I	J	K	L	M
Iran, Islamic Rep.	1.8	113.9	31.2	30.1	—	—	—	—	—	—	—	2.8	10,965
Iraq	4.1	59.5	13.3	16.1	—	—	—	—	—	—	—	25.5	—
Ireland	2.1	126.8	53.8	42.8	—	10.6	5.9	12.7	5.4	11.7	6.0	13.3	41,850
Israel	3.0	132.5	53.7	46.0	—	7.1	3.8	3.6	1.1	3.4	1.7	14.2	27,905
Italy	1.4	140.7	38.3	40.4	—	6.7	3.3	8.9	2.2	5.3	3.0	21.3	31,283
Jamaica	2.4	—	56.9	45.1	—	—	—	—	—	—	—	13.3	7,716
Japan	1.3	87.9	48.6	41.5	—	3.5	5.2	8.7	8.6	1.5	2.8	9.4	34,129
Jordan	3.5	111.4	23.4	22.8	13.1	—	—	—	—	—	—	6.4	5,474
Kazakhstan	2.6	144.2	66.2	50.0	34.4	11.2	7.6	6.8	4.8	3.0	1.8	15.9	11,323
Kenya	4.9	59.7	75.8	46.5	37.1	—	—	—	—	—	—	8.9	1,551
Korea, Dem. Rep.	1.9	—	54.7	42.6	—	—	—	—	—	—	—	20.1	—
Korea, Rep.	1.2	67.3	49.9	41.9	—	—	—	—	—	—	—	13.7	27,658
Kosovo	2.4	—	—	26.1	10.9	—	—	—	—	—	—	—	—
Kuwait	2.2	231.7	44.3	24.3	—	—	—	—	—	—	—	3.1	48,268
Kyrgyz Republic	2.7	136.1	56.0	42.6	60.4	—	—	—	—	—	—	25.6	2,193
Lao PDR	3.5	77.6	77.8	50.6	39.4	—	—	—	—	—	—	25.2	2,124
Latvia	1.5	184.8	55.5	48.9	46.3	7.7	1.4	4.9	2.0	5.6	1.0	20.0	16,357
Lebanon	1.8	123.6	21.8	24.9	27.9	—	—	—	—	—	—	4.7	11,777
Lesotho	3.3	118.7	70.3	52.4	18.4	—	—	—	—	—	—	25.0	1,564
Liberia	5.9	—	66.6	47.6	53.0	—	—	—	—	—	—	12.5	388
Libya	2.7	—	23.8	21.9	—	—	—	—	—	—	—	7.7	16,208
Liechtenstein	1.4	49.3	—	—	—	—	—	—	—	—	—	24.0	—
Lithuania	1.5	156.5	51.3	48.9	38.7	—	—	—	—	—	—	22.7	17,753
Luxembourg	1.6	111.9	46.9	43.3	—	—	—	—	—	—	—	23.3	78,922
Macao SAR	0.9	90.9	65.4	48.2	—	—	—	—	—	—	—	—	59,476

Macedonia, FYR	1.4	126.7	42.7	39.7	36.4	—	—	—	—	—	—	31.7	9,337
Madagascar	4.7	89.2	84.1	49.2	50.0	—	—	—	—	—	—	7.9	1,054
Malawi	5.5	50.6	75.1	49.9	23.9	—	—	—	—	—	—	13.0	805
Malaysia	2.6	123.6	44.1	35.2	13.1	—	—	—	—	—	—	10.8	14,215
Maldives	2.0	—	56.1	42.5	—	—	—	—	—	—	—	12.0	5,597
Mali	6.5	45.2	37.0	36.8	18.4	—	—	—	—	—	—	10.2	1,129
Malta	1.4	141.5	33.7	33.7	—	—	—	—	—	—	—	8.7	21,143
Mauritania	4.5	36.5	58.5	41.7	17.3	—	—	—	—	—	—	22.1	1,918
Mauritius	1.6	117.4	42.0	36.4	16.9	—	—	—	—	—	—	17.1	12,356
Mexico	2.1	98.0	43.4	36.0	24.8	—	—	—	—	—	—	23.2	14,570
Moldova	1.5	144.6	46.8	50.7	53.1	—	—	—	—	—	—	21.8	2,979
Mongolia	2.0	156.9	67.2	47.4	52.0	—	—	—	—	—	—	4.2	3,557
Montenegro	1.6	—	—	—	26.0	—	—	—	—	—	—	11.1	13,385
Morocco	2.4	88.7	26.5	26.1	13.1	—	—	—	—	—	—	10.5	4,263
Mozambique	5.1	49.4	84.9	52.1	24.4	—	—	—	—	—	—	34.8	838
Myanmar	2.3	137.1	63.9	44.5	—	—	—	—	—	—	—	—	—
Namibia	3.4	131.6	51.9	46.7	33.4	—	—	—	—	—	—	26.9	6,398
Nepal	2.9	—	63.2	45.4	27.4	—	—	—	—	—	—	33.2	1,104
Netherlands	1.8	109.6	59.2	45.5	—	6.6	3.7	8.6	4.1	6.3	3.9	39.3	40,961
Netherlands Antilles	2.0	—	56.0	49.6	—	—	—	—	—	—	—	—	—
New Caledonia	2.2	—	44.4	38.9	—	—	—	—	—	—	—	—	—
New Zealand	2.2	148.9	61.7	46.2	—	—	—	—	—	—	—	33.1	27,260
Nicaragua	2.7	—	46.2	37.8	41.4	—	—	—	—	—	—	18.5	2,689
Niger	7.1	34.4	37.5	30.8	17.6	—	—	—	—	—	—	12.4	683
Nigeria	5.7	69.5	38.9	34.9	20.0	—	—	—	—	—	—	7.0	2,099
Norway	2.0	157.6	64.2	47.6	—	8.6	4.3	8.2	3.5	29.0	12.9	36.1	58,714
Oman	3.0	128.7	24.8	18.3	—	—	—	—	—	—	—	0.0	22,695
Pakistan	4.0	85.2	21.2	19.2	6.7	—	—	—	—	—	—	22.5	2,538
Panama	2.5	159.3	49.4	36.9	37.1	—	—	—	—	—	—	16.7	12,498

Table 23.1 Continued

Country	A	B	C	D	E	F	G	H	I	J	K	L	M
Papua New Guinea	4.1	—	71.2	48.9	—	—	—	—	—	—	—	0.9	2,180
Paraguay	3.0	112.9	55.9	38.7	44.8	—	—	—	—	—	—	12.5	4,704
Peru	2.6	106.3	57.4	43.3	32.8	25.7	26.1	18.1	12.4	2.9	2.5	29.2	8,509
Philippines	3.1	124.1	48.7	38.2	—	—	—	—	—	—	—	20.5	3,513
Poland	1.4	139.6	46.8	44.8	47.9	—	—	—	—	—	—	20.2	17,275
Portugal	1.4	122.0	56.2	46.8	—	11.7	5.9	9.8	4.4	10.1	4.9	28.3	23,254
Puerto Rico	1.8	—	36.7	41.7	—	3.2	3.0	4.1	0.9	3.7	3.4	—	—
Qatar	2.4	605.0	48.2	11.6	—	—	—	—	—	—	—	0.0	65,182
Romania	1.4	133.1	46.9	44.5	47.9	5.0	3.1	3.3	1.7	5.0	2.6	9.4	13,449
Russian Federation	1.5	135.5	57.1	49.7	33.1	3.8	1.6	1.6	1.7	4.7	1.5	14.0	15,923
Rwanda	5.4	61.8	86.3	52.8	41.0	—	—	—	—	—	—	56.3	1,027
Samoa	4.0	—	38.0	31.4	—	—	—	—	—	—	—	8.2	4,555
São Tomé and Príncipe	3.8	—	44.2	37.9	—	—	—	—	—	—	—	1.8	1,748
Saudi Arabia	3.1	165.5	20.8	16.3	—	—	—	—	—	—	—	0.0	23,991
Senegal	4.8	54.4	64.5	43.1	26.3	—	—	—	—	—	—	22.0	1,793
Serbia	1.4	129.8	—	44.0	28.8	12.1	5.1	7.7	2.8	1.5	0.3	21.6	10,554
Seychelles	2.3	—	—	—	—	—	—	—	—	—	—	23.5	21,392
Sierra Leone	5.2	—	65.7	51.4	7.9	—	—	—	—	—	—	13.2	782
Singapore	1.3	—	54.2	41.7	—	—	—	—	—	—	—	24.5	49,321
Slovak Republic	1.3	149.5	51.0	44.7	30.9	—	—	—	—	—	—	19.3	22,138
Slovenia	1.5	146.9	53.5	46.5	42.2	6.8	2.7	6.8	2.3	10.4	3.8	13.3	27,866
Solomon Islands	3.9	—	23.6	31.5	—	—	—	—	—	—	—	0.0	2,613
Somalia	6.4	—	56.5	40.9	—	—	—	—	—	—	—	8.2	—
South Africa	2.5	—	47.2	43.7	22.6	—	—	—	—	—	—	33.0	10,116

Spain	1.5	123.4	49.3	43.0	—	9.8	5.5	8.2	4.6	5.3	3.0	36.3	31,674
Sri Lanka	2.3	—	34.6	32.7	—	—	—	—	—	—	—	5.8	4,564
St. Lucia	2.0	225.2	50.4	41.5	—	—	—	—	—	—	—	11.1	9,836
St. Vincent and the Grenadines	2.1	—	55.6	40.9	—	—	—	—	—	—	—	18.2	8,998
Sudan	4.2	—	30.9	29.5	—	—	—	—	—	—	—	18.1	2,155
Suriname	2.4	—	38.0	36.8	—	—	—	—	—	—	—	25.5	7,401
Swaziland	3.5	97.4	52.8	43.4	28.6	—	—	—	—	—	—	—	4,927
Sweden	1.9	156.7	60.8	47.4	—	5.8	2.5	6.9	2.5	6.0	2.9	47.0	36,961
Switzerland	1.5	93.1	61.2	46.5	—	7.6	4.9	8.6	4.6	5.3	3.3	28.5	42,415
Syrian Arab Republic	3.2	—	21.0	20.7	—	—	—	—	—	—	—	12.4	4,583
Tajikistan	3.4	39.5	55.6	43.6	34.4	—	—	—	—	—	—	17.5	1,907
Tanzania	5.6	47.7	86.3	49.4	30.9	—	—	—	—	—	—	30.4	1,301
Thailand	1.8	—	65.9	46.2	—	27.8	26.0	23.2	19.5	2.3	2.5	11.7	8,086
Timor—Leste	6.5	—	58.8	40.9	—	—	—	—	—	—	—	29.2	802
Togo	4.3	—	63.2	43.3	31.8	—	—	—	—	—	—	11.1	830
Tonga	4.0	—	53.4	41.7	—	—	—	—	—	—	—	3.1	3837
Trinidad and Tobago	1.6	127.9	54.0	43.0	—	—	—	—	—	—	—	26.8	25,173
Tunisia	2.1	149.9	25.5	26.6	—	—	—	—	—	—	—	22.8	7,956
Turkey	2.1	76.5	25.1	26.2	40.7	8.7	2.4	9.5	1.3	1.4	0.5	9.1	13,417
Turkmenistan	2.5	—	61.0	46.7	—	—	—	—	—	—	—	16.0	6,625
Uganda	6.3	80.0	78.4	46.6	34.7	—	—	—	—	—	—	30.7	1,166
Ukraine	1.4	124.8	51.8	48.9	47.1	—	—	—	—	—	—	8.2	7,277
United Arab Emirates	1.9	205.4	41.8	15.5	—	—	—	—	—	—	—	22.5	—
United Kingdom	1.9	139.9	55.2	45.7	—	7.4	3.6	7.6	2.6	6.1	2.9	19.5	35,468
United States	2.1	141.1	58.9	46.1	—	12.0	7.3	6.5	3.5	4.8	3.0	16.8	46,350
Uruguay	2.0	175.2	53.1	43.7	41.6	17.3	7.2	8.6	4.5	2.5	0.8	12.1	12,744

Table 23.1 Continued

Country	A	B	C	D	E	F	G	H	I	J	K	L	M
Uzbekistan	2.6	71.1	58.0	45.9	39.8	—	—	—	—	—	—	17.5	2,658
Vanuatu	4.0	—	79.0	46.6	—	—	—	—	—	—	—	3.8	3,935
Venezuela, RB	2.5	169.5	50.8	39.1	—	23.5	16.8	5.9	4.9	2.6	1.6	18.6	12,818
Vietnam	2.1	—	68.2	48.7	—	—	—	—	—	—	—	25.8	2,787
Virgin Islands (U.S.)	1.9	—	48.8	43.5	—	—	—	—	—	—	—	—	—
West Bank and Gaza	5.0	123.0	16.0	18.0	—	—	—	—	—	—	—	—	—
World	2.5	108.4	51.9	40.4	—	—	—	—	—	—	—	18.5	10,394
Yemen, Rep.	5.2	42.1	19.5	20.8	—	—	—	—	—	—	—	0.3	2,416
Zambia	5.8	—	59.9	43.8	37.2	—	—	—	—	—	—	15.2	1,357
Zimbabwe	3.4	—	59.9	47.8	—	—	—	—	—	—	—	15.2	185

Key:
A: Fertility rate, total (births per woman)
B: Ratio of female to male tertiary enrollment (%)
C: Labor participation rate, female (% of female population aged 15+)
D: Labor force, female (% of total labor force)
E: Firms with female participation in ownership (% of firms)
F: Early stage entrepreneurial activity (≤42 months), males (% of adult male population)
G: Early stage entrepreneurial activity (≤42 months), females (% of adult female population)
H: Established business owner, males (% of adult male population)
I: Established business owners, females (% of adult female population)
J: Opportunity-to-necessity ratio as motivation for entrepreneurship, males
K: Opportunity-to-necessity ratio as motivation for entrepreneurship, females
L: Proportion of seats held by women in national parliaments (%)
M: Per capita income, GDP per capita, PPP (current international $).

Sources: Columns A–E and L–M: World Bank (2010c), data are for 2008 or most recently available year starting in 2005. Columns F–K: GEM (2009), data are for 2007.

Table 23.2 Pairwise Correlations between Indicators of Women's Socio-Economic Status and Entrepreneurship

	A	B	C	D	E	F	G	H	I	J	K	L
A	—											
B	-.47											
C	.22	-.22										
D	-.07	-.30	.82									
E	-.26	.39	.21	.38								
F	.41	.03	.19	-.22	-.06							
G	.44	-.13	.20	-.20	-.06	.92						
H	.18	-.21	.17	-.24	-.07	.70	.73					
I	.05	-.28	.26	-.03	.11	.63	.76	.83				
J	-.10	.23	.26	.28	.18	-.32	-.31	-.08	-.12			
K	-.06	.13	.24	.24	.02	-.30	-.22	-.03	-.04	.96		
L	-.14	-.05	.27	.34	-.02	-.15	-.16	-.00	-.15	.47	.46	
M	-.55	.52	-.10	-.02	.17	-.51	-.52	-.23	-.26	.60	.56	.23

Note: Correlations .22 or greater in absolute value are significant at the p < .05 level.

Key:

A: Fertility rate, total (births per woman)
B: Ratio of female to male tertiary enrollment (%)
C: Labor participation rate, female (% of female population aged 15+)
D: Labor force, female (% of total labor force)
E: Firms with female participation in ownership (% of firms)
F: Early stage entrepreneurial activity (≤42 months), males (% of adult male population)
G: Early stage entrepreneurial activity (≤42 months), females (% of adult female population)
H: Established business owner, males (% of adult male population)
I: Established business owners, females (% of adult female population)
J: Opportunity-to-necessity ratio as motivation for entrepreneurship, males
K: Opportunity-to-necessity ratio as motivation for entrepreneurship, females
L: Proportion of seats held by women in national parliaments (%)
M: Per capita income, GDP per capita, PPP (current international $).

specific entrepreneurial activities based on previous household and non-household experience. Third, while gender discrimination does not account for all of the difficulties experienced by women entrepreneurs, there are many legal, cultural and political barriers that policymaking could address. Fourth, women find the resources to pursue entrepreneurial ventures in a variety of spheres, including the family, social networks, and various programs and initiatives available to them. The difference with male entrepreneurs lies not in the nature of the resources or in how they are combined, but in the degree to which women have access to them. And fifth, women's entrepreneurial ventures have the potential to raise communities and countries up economically. More of them will surely help reduce poverty and develop better communities, as the cases in this book amply demonstrate.

References

Ahl, Helene. 2006. "Why Research on Women Entrepreneurs Needs New Directions." *Entrepreneurship Theory and Practice* 30(5) (September): 595–621.

Bird, Barbara, and Candida Brush. 2002. "A Gendered Perspective on Organizational Creation." *Entrepreneurship: Theory and Practice* 26: 41–65.

Boserup, Ester. 1970. *Woman's Role in Economic Development*. London: Earthscan.

Browne, Katherine E. 2001. "Female Entrepreneurship in the Caribbean: A Multisite, Pilot Investigation of Gender and Work." *Human Organization* 60(4): 326–342.

Bruni, Attila. 2005. *Gender and Entrepreneurship: An Ethnographic Approach*. New York: Routledge.

Brush, Candida G. 1992. "Research on Women Business Owners: Past Trends, a New Perspective and Future Directions." *Entrepreneurship: Theory and Practice* 16: 5–26.

Brush, C. G., N. M. Carter, E. J. Gatewood, P. G. Greene, and M. M. Hart, eds. 2006a. *Growth-Oriented Women Entrepreneurs and their Businesses: A Global Research Perspective*. Cheltenham, U.K.: Edward Elgar.

———. 2006b. *Women and Entrepreneurship: Contemporary Classics*. Cheltenham, U.K.: Edward Elgar.

Brush, C. G., A. de Bruin, E. J. Gatewood, and C. Henry, eds. 2010. *Women Entrepreneurs and the Global Environment for Growth: A Research Perspective*. Cheltenham, U.K.: Edward Elgar.

Carter, N. M., C. Henry, B. Ó'Cinnéide, and K. Johnston, eds. 2007. *Female Entrepreneurship: Implications for Education, Training and Policy*. London: T&F Books.

Carter, Sara, Susan Anderson, and Eleanor Shaw. 2001. *Women's Business Ownership: A Review of the Academic, Popular and Internet Literature*. Glasgow: Department of Marketing, University of Strathclyde.

Carter, Sara, and Eleanor Shaw. 2006. *Women's Business Ownership: Recent Research and Policy Developments. Report to the Small Business Centre*. Stirling, U.K.: University of Stirling.

Eisenhardt, Kathleen M. 1989. "Building Theories from Case Study Research." *Academy of Management Review* 14: 532–550.

Esping-Andersen, Gøsta. 1999. *Social Foundations of Postindustrial Economies*. Oxford: Oxford University Press.

Fielden, S. L. and M. J. Davidson, eds. 2010a. *International Handbook of Women and Small Business Entrepreneurship*. London: Edward Elgar.

—— 2010b. *International Research Handbook on Successful Women Entrepreneurs*. Cheltenham, U.K.: Edward Elgar.

Flyvbjerg, Bent. 2006. "Five Misunderstandings about Case-Study Research." *Qualitative Inquiry* 12: 219–245.

GEM. 2009. *2007 Report on Women and Entrepreneurship*. Babson Park, MA: Global Entrepreneurship Monitor.

Gerring, John. 2007. *Case Study Research*. New York: Cambridge University Press.

Guillén, Mauro F. 2001. *The Limits of Convergence: Globalization and Organizational Change in Argentina, South Korea, and Spain*. Princeton, NJ: Princeton University Press.

Hamel, Jacques. 1993. *Case Study Methods*. Newbury Park, CA: Sage.

Harley, Sharon. 2007. *Women's Labor in the Global Economy: Speaking in Multiple Voices*. New Brunswick, NJ: Rutgers University Press.

International Labour Organization. 2009. *Global Employment Trends for Women*. Geneva: International Labour Office.

Jaquette, Jane S., and Kathleen Staudt. 2006. "Women, Gender, and Development." Pp. 17–52 in *Women and Gender Equity in Development Theory and Practice*, ed. Jane S. Jaquette and Gale Summerfield. Durham, NC: Duke University Press.

Klapper, Leora, Raphael S. Amit, and Mauro F. Guillén. 2010. "Entrepreneurship and Firm Formation across Countries." Pp. 129–158 in *International Differences in Entrepreneurship*, ed. Josh Lerner and Antoinette Schoar. Chicago: University of Chicago Press, and National Bureau of Economic Research.

La Porta, Rafael, Florencio Lopez-de-Silanes, Andrei Shleifer, and Robert W. Vishny. 1998. "Law and Finance." *Journal of Political Economy* 106: 113–155.

Lewis, Patricia. 2006. "The Quest for Invisibility: Female Entrepreneurs and the Masculine Norm of Entrepreneurship." *Gender, Work and Organization* 13(5) (September): 453–469.

Mirchandani, Kiran. 1999. "Feminist Insight on Gendered Work: New Directions in Research on Women and Entrepreneurship." *Gender, Work and Organization* 6(4) (October): 224–235.

Naudé, Wim. 2010. "Entrepreneurship Is Not a Binding Constraint on Growth and Development in the Poorest Countries." *World Development* 39(1): 33–44.

Nichter, Simeon, and Lara Goldmark. 2009. "Small Firm Growth in Developing Countries." *World Development* 37(9): 1453–1464.

OECD. 2004. *Women's Entrepreneurship: Issues and Policies*. Paris: Organization for Economic Cooperation and Development.

Rodrik, Dani. 2006. "Goodbye Washington Consensus, Hello Washington Confusion?" *Journal of Economic Literature* (December): 973–987.

Rothbard, Nancy P., and Jeanne M. Brett. 2000. "Promote Equal Opportunity by Recognizing Gender Differences in the Experience of Work and Family." Pp. 389–403 in *The Blackwell Handbook of Principles of Organizational Behavior*, ed. E. A. Locke. Oxford: Blackwell.

Schumpeter, Joseph Alois. 1934 [1911]. *The Theory of Economic Development*. Cambridge, MA: Harvard University Press.

—— 1975. *Capitalism, Socialism and Democracy*. New York: Harper.

Snyder, Margaret. 2000. *Women in African Economies: From Burning Sun to Boardroom.* Kampala, Uganda: Fountain Publishers.

UNIFEM. 2005. *Progress of the World's Women 2005.* New York: United Nations Development Fund for Women.

——2010. *Annual Report 2009–2010.* New York: United Nations Development Fund for Women.

Weber, Max. 1978. *Economy and Society.* Berkeley, CA: University of California Press.

World Bank. 2001. *Engendering Development through Gender Equality in Rights, Resources, and Voice.* Washington, DC: World Bank.

—— 2009. *Doing Business: Women in Africa.* Washington, DC: World Bank.

—— 2010a. "About Doing Business." www.doingbusiness.org/documents/DB10_About.pdf (accessed August 16, 2010).

—— 2010b. *Women, Business, and the Law.* Washington, DC: World Bank.

—— 2010c. *World Development Indicators.* Online Database. Washington, DC: World Bank.

—— 2011. *World Development Report 2012: Gender Equality and Development.* Washington, DC: World Bank.

World Economic Forum. 2011. *The Global Gender Gap Report.* Geneva: World Economic Forum.

Yin, Robert K. 2003. *Case Study Research: Design and Methods.* Third edition. Thousand Oaks, CA: Sage.

Contributors

Dalila Boclin graduated magna cum laude in 2010 from the University of Pennsylvania College of Arts and Sciences. She currently works as a strategist at a start-up in New York.

Claudia González Brambila is a professor at the School of Business at ITAM.

Felipe Burgos is Dean of the School of Business at the Universidad Popular Autonoma del Estado de Puebla (UPAEP), in Puebla, Mexico.

Christine Chang is a graduate of the Wharton School and the Lauder Institute of the University of Pennsylvania. She works in the financial services industry.

Swita Charanasomboon is a graduate of the Wharton School and the Lauder Institute of the University of Pennsylvania. A former management consultant, she now works in the consumer packaged goods industry.

Emily Di Capua is a graduate of the Wharton School and the Lauder Institute of the University of Pennsylvania, where she studied multinational management and Chinese language and history. She currently works as an emerging markets-focused management consultant.

Maha ElShinnawy is Professor of Leadership and Ethics at the American University in Cairo (AUC) and is the Director of the Goldman Sachs 10,000 Women's Entrepreneurship and Leadership Program for the Arab region.

Lilia Gamboa previously served as Director of Strategic Initiatives at the Instituto Tecnológico y de Estudios Superiores de Monterrey in Mexico. She now works as an educational consultant.

Gregory Gilbert is a graduate of Dartmouth College and the Wharton School and the Lauder Institute of the University of Pennsylvania. He is a real estate investment professional based in London and Spain.

Mauro F. Guillén is Director of the Lauder Institute of Management and International Studies, and the Dr Felix Zandman Professor of International Management at the Wharton School of the University of Pennsylvania.

Pablo Galindo Herrera is a professor at the EGADE Business School of the Instituto Tecnológico y de Estudios Superiores de Monterrey in Mexico and Professor of Entrepreneurship and Business Development at Universidad Iberoamericana. He is also an entrepreneur, serving as director of Netlan SA and Desarrollo Ejecutivo SA in Mexico City.

Victoria Johnson is Associate Professor of Organizational Studies at the University of Michigan.

Alison Jonas holds a B.A., summa cum laude, from Princeton University and an M.B.A. from the Wharton School of the University of Pennsylvania. Alison currently works in strategy at Li and Fung and has previously held positions at Goldman, Sachs and Co. and Analysis Group in New York.

Virginia Kalis is Professor of Accounting and Director of the Teaching Center at the Instituto Tecnológico Autónomo de México (ITAM).

Amanda Knauer received her bachelor's degree in international relations from Brown University and her M.B.A. from the Wharton School at the University of Pennsylvania.

Johanna Kuhn-Osius is a graduate of the Wharton School and the Lauder Institute of the University of Pennsylvania. Currently living in Korea, she works at Samsung Electronics.

Maya Perl-Kot is a graduate of the University of Pennsylvania and works in the management consulting industry.

Rajagopal is a professor of marketing in EGADE Business School of the Instituto Tecnológico y de Estudios Superiores de Monterrey in Mexico.

Leeatt Rothschild is a graduate of the Wharton School and Lauder Institute. She currently lives in Chicago and works in marketing strategy consulting.

Roberto Solano is Dean of the School of Business and Economics at the Universidad de las Américas Puebla in Mexico.

Roberto Tolosa holds a B.S. from the Wharton School of the University of Pennsylvania. Roberto currently works at Tenex Capital Management, a New York-based private equity firm.

María Fernanda Trigo is a graduate of the Wharton School and the Lauder Institute of the University of Pennsylvania. She works in consulting.

Adrian Tschoegl is a lecturer and senior fellow in the Management Department and of the Wharton Financial Institutions Center of the Wharton School of the University of Pennsylvania.

Humberto Valencia-Herrera is Professor of Finance at Instituto Tecnológico y de Estudios Superiores de Monterrey, Mexico City Campus, and, by courtesy, EGADE Business School.

Lilian Wouters is a graduate of the Wharton School and the Lauder Institute of the University of Pennsylvania, where she studied Japanese language and history.

Eduardo Zelaya is Professor of Management and Operations at the EGADE Business School of Tecnológico de Monterrey in Mexico.

Index

Page numbers in *italics* denotes an illustration/table.